Social Network Analysis

Social Network Analysis

A Handbook

Second Edition

JOHN SCOTT

SAGE Publications
London • Thousand Oaks • New Delhi

SAGE Publications Ltd
1 Oliver's Yard, 55 City Road
London EC1Y 1SP

SAGE Publications Inc
2455 Teller Road
Thousand Oaks, California 91320

SAGE Publications India Pvt Ltd
B-42 Panchsheel Enclave
Post Box 4109
New Delhi 100 017

British Library Cataloguing in Publication data

A catalogue record for this book is available
from the British Library

ISBN 0-7619-6338-3
ISBN 0-7619-6339-1 (pbk)

Typeset by Photoprint, Torquay, Devon
Printed and bound in Great Britain by
Athenaeum Press Ltd., Gateshead, Tyne & Wear

Contents

List of Figures

Preface to the Second Edition

This book was first published in 1991. For this second edition I have retained the basic structure of the book and have concentrated on updating the sources and improving the style. The principal changes have been made to Chapters 2, 3, 8 and the Appendix. As in the original edition, I have tried to simplify the techniques of social network analysis in order to make it accessible to newcomers. Those who have some competence with mathematics generally fail to appreciate the gulf that separates them from most practitioners, and this may lead them to believe that the book over-simplifies. I have never let my simplification result in distortion, and I hope that there is enough in it to satisfy both the newcomer and the more advanced researcher in need of information on current techniques.

Social network analysis gives itself easily to diagrammatic representation, and the book includes a large number of diagrams. I have emphasized the variety of diagrammatic forms, paying particular attention to the multidimensional displays which offer the greatest potential for the future development of social network analysis. One of the major changes in this edition is the inclusion of a new section on the new techniques of visualization and network representation made possible by advances in computing. Technical advances have been so great in information technology that the range of software available for social network analysis is radically different from that available at the time of the first edition. I have completely rewritten those parts of Chapter 3 that refer to computer techniques, and I have, throughout the book, tried to reflect current developments. The Appendix completely replaces that of the first edition and gives a review of the current range of social network packages. Those who wish to use these programs should, nevertheless, follow up the sources given, as new programs are bound to become available over the next few years.

In the first edition, I acknowledged the help of those who, consciously or inadvertently, helped in the preparation of the book since I first became involved in social network analysis in 1975. I would like to repeat their names here and add a few additional acknowledgements. They are, in alphabetical order: Steve Borgatti, Tony Coxon, Martin Everett, Sigmund Grønmo, Joel Levine, Beth Mintz,

Social network analysis

Clyde Mitchell, Rob Mokken, Mike Schwartz, John Stevens, Frans Stokman and Barry Wellman. I am also grateful to students at the Universities of Essex and Bergen who have participated in short courses on social network analysis.

All researchers in this area will get great intellectual support from *Connections*, the newsletter of the International Network for Social Network Analysis. A major development in the last few years has been the rapid advance in the use of the internet, and INSNA can now be contacted through its website. Details of this and of the SOCNET electronic mailing list can be found in the Appendix (notes 11 and 12).

John Scott

1
Networks and Relations

There has been a considerable growth of interest in the potential that is offered by the relatively new techniques of social network analysis. Unfortunately, this potential has been seen as unachievable for many researchers, who have found it difficult to come to grips with the highly technical and mathematical language in which much discussion of these techniques has been cast. Those who have wanted to take advantage of the techniques of social network analysis have been practical researchers with substantive interests, while texts and sources on these techniques have, by and large, been produced by highly numerate specialists with a mathematical background. There has even been great difficulty in finding out about the available computer programs for social network analysis; and when access to a program has been achieved, researchers often have little practical guidance on its uses and applications.

My aim in this book is to try to bridge this gap between theory and practice. I am not a specialist with a mathematical training, but a researcher who came to social network analysis because of the particular needs of data handling in a research project on corporate power. Over the years, I have struggled to achieve a degree of understanding of what the principal measures of network structure involve, and I have attempted to translate the mathematics into simpler language and to try to assess the relevance of particular models for specific research needs. The aim of the book, therefore, is to draw on this experience in order to present a systematic summary of these measures with some illustrations of their uses. I have not attempted to present a comprehensive treatise on structural analysis in sociology (see Berkowitz, 1982), nor have I aimed at reviewing the large number of applications of social network analysis which have been published (see Mizruchi and Schwartz, 1987; Wellman and Berkowitz, 1988). I have concentrated on identifying the key concepts used in assessing network structure – density, centrality, cliques and so on – and I have tried to translate the mathematical discussions of these ideas into more comprehensible terms.

It is of the utmost importance that researchers *understand* the concepts that they use. There are, for example, a large number of different definitions of the 'clique' and of related ideas, and a researcher cannot simply take a program 'off the shelf' and assume that its idea of the clique corresponds with that which the researcher has in mind. It is for this reason that I emphasize, at a number of points, that the choice of measures and of their application to particular topics are matters that require the *informed judgement* of the practising researcher. They are theoretical and empirical questions that cannot be avoided by a reliance on mathematical measures that are only partly, if at all, understood. Only if the researcher has a clear understanding of the logic of a particular measure can he or she make an informed *sociological* judgement about its relevance for a particular piece of research.

Relations and Attributes

The first task must be to define the kind of data for which social network analysis is most appropriate. Those who are interested in its applications will, undoubtedly, have some ideas about this already: it is useful for investigations of kinship patterns, community structure, interlocking directorships and so forth. But it is essential that the common features of these types of data are understood more clearly. It is my contention that social network analysis is appropriate for 'relational data', and that techniques developed for the analysis of other types of data are likely to be of limited value for research which generates data of this kind.

The most general characteristic of social science data is that they are rooted in cultural values and symbols. Unlike the physical data of the natural sciences, social science data are constituted through meanings, motives, definitions and typifications. As is well known, this means that the production of social science data involves a process of interpretation. On the basis of such processes of interpretation, social scientists have formulated distinct types of data, to each of which distinct methods of analysis are appropriate.

The principal types of data are 'attribute data' and 'relational data'.[1] **Attribute data** relate to the attitudes, opinions and behaviour of agents, in so far as these are regarded as the properties, qualities or characteristics that belong to them as individuals or groups. The items collected through surveys and interviews, for example, are often regarded simply as the attributes of particular individuals that can be quantified and analysed through the many available statistical procedures. The methods appropriate to attribute data are those of **variable analysis**, whereby attributes are measured as values of particular variables (income, occupation, education etc.).

Relational data, on the other hand, are the contacts, ties and connections, the group attachments and meetings, which relate one agent to another and so cannot be reduced to the properties of the individual agents themselves. Relations are not the properties of agents, but of systems of agents; these relations connect pairs of agents into larger relational systems. The methods appropriate to relational data are those of **network analysis,** whereby the relations are treated as expressing the linkages which run between agents. While it is, of course, possible to undertake quantitative and statistical counts of relations, network analysis consists of a body of qualitative measures of network structure.

Attribute and relational data are not the only types of social science data, although they are the most widely discussed in methods texts. A third type comprises **ideational data,** which describe the meanings, motives, definitions and typifications themselves. Techniques for the analysis of ideational data are less well developed than those for attribute and relational data, despite their centrality to the social sciences. **Typological analysis** of the kind outlined by Weber (1920–21) is the most fruitful approach here, but these methods are in need of further development (see Layder, 1992).[2]

Although there are distinct types of data (as set out in Figure 1.1) each with their own appropriate methods of analysis, there is nothing specific about the methods of data collection which can be used to produce them. There is, for example, nothing that distinguishes methods for the collection of attribute data from those for the collection of relational data. The three types of data are often collected alongside one another as integral aspects of the same investigation. A study of political attitudes, for example, may seek to link these to group memberships and community attachments; or an investigation of interlocking directorships may seek to link these to the size and profitability of the companies involved. In either case,

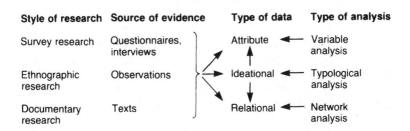

Style of research	Source of evidence	Type of data	Type of analysis
Survey research	Questionnaires, interviews	Attribute	Variable analysis
Ethnographic research	Observations	Ideational	Typological analysis
Documentary research	Texts	Relational	Network analysis

Figure 1.1 *Types of data and analysis*

questionnaires, interviews, participant observation or documentary sources can be consulted in order to generate the data.

Studies of friendship, for example, have tended to follow Moreno's (1934) lead in using questionnaires to investigate friendship choices. In such studies, researchers simply ask respondents to identify their friends, using such questions as 'Please name your four closest friends'. Methodological problems do, of course, arise with this kind of research. An unlimited choice question has sometimes been found to be difficult for respondents to answer. Some do not feel that they have four friends to name, and many find the open question both time-consuming and tedious.[3] An alternative approach is to use the roster choice method, in which respondents are asked 'Which of the following would you regard as a friend?' This requires considerable knowledge and preparation on the part of the researcher, who must compile the list – the roster – with which respondents are presented, but it has the advantage that it can be adapted by asking respondents to rank or to rate their affiliations, so indicating their 'intensity' or significance. In both cases, however, these methodological problems of knowledge and respondent co-operation are exactly the same as those that arise in collecting information on attitudes and opinions.

Relational data are central to the principal concerns of the sociological tradition, with its emphasis upon the investigation of the *structure* of social action. Structures are built from relations, and the structural concerns of sociology can be pursued through the collection and analysis of relational data. Paradoxically, most of the existing texts on research methods and methods of data collection give little attention to this type of data, concentrating instead on the use of variable analysis for the investigation of attribute data. The formal, mathematical techniques of social network analysis, the methods that are specifically geared to relational data, have developed and have been discussed outside the mainstream of research methods. Whilst they have made possible a number of spectacular breakthroughs in structural analysis, they have been largely inaccessible to many of those who would most wish to use them.

Social network analysis developed, initially, in a relatively non-technical form from the structural concerns of the great anthropologist Radcliffe-Brown. From the 1930s to the 1970s, an increasing number of social anthropologists and sociologists began to build on Radcliffe-Brown's concept of 'social structure' and, in doing so, began to take seriously the metaphors of the 'fabric' and 'web' of social life. From these textile metaphors, aimed at understanding the 'interweaving' and 'interlocking' relations through which social actions were organized, the metaphor of the social 'network' came to the fore, and researchers began to investigate the 'density' and 'texture' of the social networks which they studied. From the 1950s, however, a small group of specialists began to concern themselves with devising more formal translations of the metaphor and, from the early 1970s, an avalanche of technical work and specialist applications appeared. From these writings have emerged the key concepts of social network analysis, and it is time that the techniques returned to the mainstream of data analysis and a wider sphere of applications.

An Overview

This book is intended to be a guide or handbook to social network analysis, and not a text to be read through at one sitting. I have tried to confine subsidiary points and abstruse technicalities to footnotes, but a certain amount of complexity necessarily remains in the main text. I hope that this is at the absolute minimum. The newcomer to social network analysis is advised to read Chapters 2 and 3, and then to skim through the remainder of the book, coming back to points of difficulty later. Those readers with more familiarity with social network analysis may prefer to reverse this procedure, scanning Chapters 2 and 3 and then giving greater attention to a thorough review of Chapters 4–8. The chapters are best read in detail whenever a particular technique is to be used in a specific investigation. Although later chapters depend upon arguments raised in earlier chapters, each can be treated as a reference source to return to when attempting to use a particular technique.

Chapter 2 discusses the development of social network analysis, looking at its origins in the social psychology of groups and at its subsequent development in sociological and social anthropological studies of factories and communities. The chapter concentrates on the theoretical ideas that emerged in this work and shows how this was connected with the growing technical complexity of the work carried out from the 1970s. These late developments in social network analysis are illustrated through two of the benchmark studies of the early 1970s: Lee's work on the search for an abortionist (Lee, 1969) and Granovetter's work on the search for a job (Granovetter, 1974). In Chapter 3, I look at some of the issues that arise in defining the boundaries of social networks and in selecting relations for study. These discussions are used as a way of introducing some of the necessary paraphernalia of social network analysis. In particular, matrices and sociograms are introduced as easy and intuitive ways of modelling relational data.

Chapter 4 introduces the basic building blocks of social networks. The chapter starts from a consideration of the fundamental sociometric idea of representing a network as a 'graph' of 'points' and 'lines', and it shows how these can be used to develop concepts such as 'distance', 'direction' and 'density'. In Chapter 5, I look at the 'centrality' of points and the 'centralization' of whole networks, building on the argument of Chapter 4 to show how it is possible to move from local, 'ego-centric' measures to global, 'socio-centric' ones. Chapter 6 examines some of the principal concepts proposed for the investigation of sub-groups within social networks – the 'cliques' and 'circles' into which networks are divided. In Chapter 7 there is a shift of focus to the structure of the 'positions' that are defined by social relations and to the ways in which these articulate into more complex 'topological' structures. Chapter 8 looks at the formal approaches to the display of relational data, moving beyond the simple sociogram to the production of multidimensional 'maps' of social structures. Finally, an Appendix gives an introduction to and comparison of the main computer programs for social network analysis.

Chapters 4–8 each conclude with a consideration of the application of the measures discussed in particular empirical studies. The investigations that are reviewed cover such areas as kinship, community structure, corporate interlocks and elite power. The aim of these illustrations from leading researchers is to give a glimpse of the potential offered by social network analysis.

2

The Development of Social Network Analysis

A number of very diverse strands have shaped the development of present-day social network analysis. These strands have intersected with one another in a complex and fascinating history, sometimes fusing and other times diverging on to their separate paths. A clear lineage for the mainstream of social network analysis can, nevertheless, be constructed from this complex history. In this lineage there are three main traditions: the sociometric analysts, who worked on small groups and produced many technical advances with the methods of graph theory; the Harvard researchers of the 1930s, who explored patterns of interpersonal relations and the formation of 'cliques'; and the Manchester anthropologists, who built on both of these strands to investigate the structure of 'community' relations in tribal and village societies. These traditions were eventually brought together in the 1960s and 1970s, again at Harvard, when contemporary social network analysis was forged (Figure 2.1).

In the 1930s a group of German emigrés influenced by Wolfgang Köhler's 'gestalt' theory were working in the United States on cognitive and social psychology. This work led to a considerable amount of research on the problems of sociometry and 'group dynamics'. Using laboratory methods or laboratory-like case studies, they looked at group structure and at the flow of information and ideas through groups. At the same time, anthropologists and sociologists at Harvard University were developing some of the ideas of the British social anthropologist Radcliffe-Brown. Their work produced important factory and community studies that emphasized the importance of informal, interpersonal relations in social systems. In Britain, principally at Manchester University, a parallel line of development from the work of Radcliffe-Brown emphasized the analysis of conflict and contradiction and applied these ideas to the study of African tribal societies and, a little later, to rural and small town Britain. Building on the earlier traditions, they made considerable advances in allying mathematics with substantive social theory. Not until well into the 1960s, however, did the final breakthrough to a well-developed methodology of social network analysis occur. At Harvard, Harrison White began to extend his investigations of the mathematical basis of social structure, forging together some of

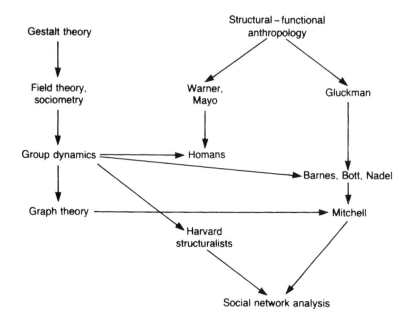

Figure 2.1   *The lineage of social network analysis*

the key insights of his North American predecessors and creating a unique synthesis which was developed and enlarged by the students that he trained. As these students moved through their careers to Departments across the world, the arguments of White and the work of the British researchers were united into a complex but increasingly coherent framework of social network analysis.

In this chapter, I give a brief outline of the three main traditions of social network analysis and the leading innovations of the Harrison White group at Harvard. This review will highlight the continuing topics of debate in social network analysis, and I show how these are rooted in the central substantive concerns of sociology.

Sociometric Analysis and Graph Theory

The 'gestalt' tradition in psychology, associated principally with the work of Köhler (see Köhler, 1925), stresses the organized patterns through which thoughts and perceptions are structured. These organized patterns are regarded as 'wholes' or systems that have properties distinct from those of their 'parts' and which, furthermore, *determine* the nature of those parts. The individual objects that people perceive, for example, are seen in the particular ways that they are because they are, literally, preconceived within the complex and organized conceptual schemes of the human mind. The objects of the world are not perceived independently of these mental schemes but are, in a fundamental sense, constituted by them. Social psychology in this research tradition has stressed the social determination of these conceptual schemes and has, therefore, emphasized the influence of group organization and its associated social climate on individual perceptions.

During the 1930s, many of the leading gestalt theorists fled from Nazi Germany and settled in the United States, where Kurt Lewin, Jacob Moreno (who had migrated in 1925) and Fritz Heider became prominent, though rather different, exponents of a gestalt-influenced social psychology. Lewin established a Research Centre at the Massachusetts Institute of Technology, later moving it to Michigan, and this centre became the focus of research on social perception and group structure. Moreno, on the other hand, explored the possibility of using psychotherapeutic methods to uncover the structure of friendship choices. Using experimentation, controlled observation and questionnaires, he and his colleagues aimed to explore the ways in which people's group relations served as both limitations and opportunities for their actions and, therefore, for their personal psychological development. Although the word 'sociometric' is particularly associated with Moreno, it is an apt description of the general style of research that arose from the gestalt tradition.

Moreno's work was firmly rooted in a therapeutic orientation towards interpersonal relations, reflecting his early medical training and psychiatric practice in Vienna. His aim, elaborated in a major book (Moreno, 1934) and in the founding of a journal (*Sociometry*, founded in 1937), was to investigate how psychological well-being is related to the structural features of what he termed 'social configurations'. These configurations are the result of the concrete patterns of interpersonal choice, attraction, repulsion, friendship, and other relations in which people are involved, and they are the basis upon which large-scale 'social aggregates', such as the economy and the state, are sustained and reproduced over time. Moreno's concern for the relationship between small-scale interpersonal configurations and large-scale social aggregates is a very clear expression of some of the leading ideas of classical German sociology, most notably those developed in the works of Weber, Tönnies and Simmel. Indeed, the latter's so-called formal sociology directly anticipated many sociometric concerns (Aron, 1964; Simmel, 1908).

Moreno's chief innovation was to devise the 'sociogram' as a way of representing the formal properties of social configurations.[1] These could be represented, he held, in diagrams analogous to those of spatial geometry, with individuals represented by 'points' and their social relationships to one another by 'lines'. This idea is now so well established and taken for granted that its novelty in the 1930s is difficult to appreciate. Before Moreno, people had spoken of 'webs' of connection, the 'social fabric' and, on occasion, of 'networks' of relations, but no one had attempted to systematize this metaphor into an analytical diagram.

For Moreno, social configurations had definite and discernible structures, and the mapping of these structures into a sociogram allowed a researcher to visualize the channels through which, for example, information could flow from one person to another and through which one individual could influence another. Moreno argued that the construction of sociograms allowed researchers to identify leaders and isolated individuals, to uncover asymmetry and reciprocity, and to map chains of connection. One of his principal sociometric concepts was that of the sociometric 'star': the recipient of numerous and frequent choices from others and who, therefore, held a position of great popularity and leadership. For Moreno, the concept of the star pointed to an easily visualized picture of the relations among group members. In Figure 2.2, for example, person A is the recipient of friendship choices from all the other members of a group, yet A gives reciprocal friendship choices only to persons B and C. A is, therefore, the star of attraction within the group.

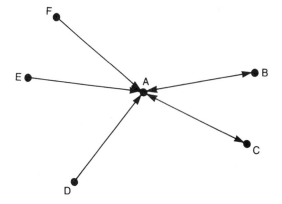

Figure 2.2   *A sociogram: the sociometric star*

Lewin's early work on group behaviour was published in a book that outlined his view that group behaviour was to be seen as determined by the *field* of social forces in which the group was located (Lewin, 1936). A social group, he argued, exists in a field: a social 'space' that comprises the group together with its surrounding environment. But the environment of the group is not seen as something purely external to and independent of the group. The environment that really matters to group members is the *perceived* environment. The perceived environment is what writers in the symbolic interactionist tradition called the 'definition of the situation', and its social meaning is actively constructed by group members on the basis of their perceptions and experiences of the contexts in which they act. The group and its environment are, therefore, elements within a single field of relations. The structural properties of this social space, Lewin argued, can be analysed through the mathematical techniques of topology and set theory (Lewin, 1951). The aim of 'field theory' is to explore, in mathematical terms, the interdependence between group and environment in a *system* of relations, a view that brought Lewin close to later developments in general systems theory. (See Buckley, 1967 for an application of this framework to sociology.)

In a topological approach, the social field is seen as comprising 'points' connected by 'paths'. The points, as in a sociogram, represent individual persons, their goals, or their actions, while the paths represent the interactional or causal sequences that connect them. The field model, therefore, describes causal and interactional interdependencies in social configurations. The paths that run between points tie them together, and the pattern of paths divides a field into a number of discrete 'regions'. Each region is separated from the others by the *absence* of paths between them: paths run within but not between the regions. The opportunities that individuals have to move about in their social world are determined by the boundaries between the different regions of the field in which they are located. The constraints imposed by these boundaries are the 'forces' that determine group behaviour. The total social field, therefore, is a field of forces acting on group members and shaping their actions and experiences.

A further strand of cognitive psychology that made a major contribution to the development of theories of group dynamics was the work of Heider. His initial work was on the social psychology of attitudes and perception, and he was especially concerned with how a person's various attitudes towards others are brought into a state of 'balance'. The different attitudes that an individual holds are balanced in his or her mind when they do not produce a state of psychological tension. Psychological balance, therefore, depends on the holding of attitudes that are not contradictory with one another. Heider's particular concern was with interpersonal balance, with the congruence (or lack of congruence) among attitudes to other people. He was concerned, for example, with how a person who is emotionally close to two other people might respond to any perceived conflict or hostility between them. In such a situation, there is an imbalance in the whole field of attitudes. Heider (1946) held that attitudes can be seen, at their simplest, as positive or negative. 'Balance' exists among a set of attitudes when they are similar to one another in their sign – all positive or all negative. If person A likes person B, and person B likes person C, a state of balance exists only if A also likes C. All the attitudes are 'positive'. It is important to note that, for Heider as for Lewin, this kind of analysis relates to the way in which the world is *perceived* from the standpoint of a focal individual: Heider was adopting an explicitly 'phenomenological' stance. From this point of view, the important thing is not the actual relation between B and C, but A's perception (accurate or otherwise) of this relationship. 'Balance' refers to a psychological, phenomenological state, and not to any actually existing relations in a social group.

While field theory, as a theoretical framework for social analysis, proved an intellectual dead-end, Lewin's advocacy of mathematical models of group relations proved to be a fruitful foundation for later work. Of particular importance in building on the insights of Lewin was Cartwright, who, together with the mathematician Harary, pioneered the application of graph theory to group behaviour (Cartwright and Zander, 1953; Harary and Norman, 1953. See also Bavelas, 1950). Graph theory had first been formulated by König (1936) but, like many works published in Germany in the 1930s, it had little immediate impact on the wider intellectual world. Its significance for the mainstream of intellectual effort was appreciated only in 1950, when his book was republished in the United States and its ideas were developed in the work of Harary and Norman (1953). These mathematical ideas made possible a crucial breakthrough in the theory of group dynamics. This breakthrough consisted of moving from the concept of *cognitive* balance in individual minds to that of *interpersonal* balance in social groups. Newcomb (1953) was one of the first researchers to move in this direction, arguing that there is a tendency for two people who are close to one another to each adopt similar attitudes towards third parties or events. Researchers could, therefore, build models of the systematic interdependence between the attitudes held by *different* individuals within a group. This claim was generalized in the theoretical framework outlined by Cartwright and Harary (1956). In the hands of these writers, the insights of Lewin, Moreno and Heider were brought together into a novel and more powerful synthesis. (See also

Harary et al., 1965, which was under preparation from the mid-1950s.) The attempt to apply mathematics to the structure of group relations was not, of course, a new idea – as well as the work of Lewin there were other early contributions, using different mathematical models, at the end of the 1940s (for example, Bavelas, 1948 and Festinger, 1949). Building on Lewin's work, however, Cartwright, Zander and Harary evolved powerful models of group cohesion, social pressure, cooperation, power and leadership.

Cartwright and Harary (1956) had outlined the basic idea of representing groups as collections of points connected by lines – the basic insight of Moreno. The resulting sociogram or 'graph' represented the network of actual interpersonal relations among group members and could be analysed, they argued, by using the mathematical ideas of graph theory. Graph theory has nothing to do with the graphs of variables familiar to many people from school mathematics. Instead, a graph is simply a set of lines connecting points, and graph theory consists of a body of mathematical axioms and formulae that describe the properties of the patterns formed by the lines. In the work of Cartwright and Harary, the points in a graph represented individuals and the lines showed their relations with one another. The lines in a graph can be given signs (+ or −) to indicate whether they refer to 'positive' or 'negative' relations, and they can be given arrow heads to indicate the 'direction' of the relationships. The direction attached to a line is a way of distinguishing, for example, person A's orientation to person B from B's orientation to A: person A may direct a positive relation to B (he likes B), while person B may direct a negative relation to A (she hates A). This construction of 'signed' and 'directed' graphs allowed Cartwright and Harary to analyse group structure from the standpoint of each of its members simultaneously, and not simply from the standpoint of a particular focal individual. It was, therefore, a major move forward in a strictly *sociological* direction.

The fundamental points that Cartwright and Harary were making can most easily be understood by considering undirected graphs. In an undirected graph, the relation of A to B is assumed to be identical with the relation of B to A. This can occur, for example, because their attitudes are perfectly reciprocated or because they have a common involvement in the same activity. For this reason, the line between any two points can be studied without considering its direction. In an undirected graph, 'balance' describes simply the particular pattern of signs attached to the lines that make up the graph. In Figure 2.3, for example, three different graphs of relations among three actors are shown. In graph (i), A and B have a positive relationship to one another and the whole graph is balanced because

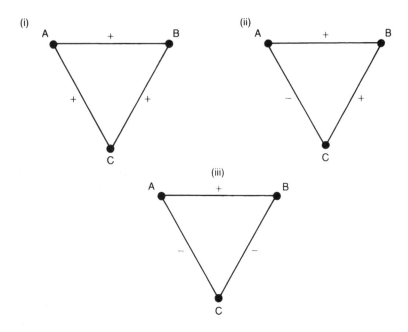

Figure 2.3   *Balanced and unbalanced structures*

of the existence of positive relations between A and C and between B and C. In graph (ii), however, a negative relation between A and C puts a strain on the positive relation between A and B, because of the positive relation that exists between B and C: the graph is unbalanced. Put simply, if my friend likes someone to whom I am antagonistic, there is likely to be a strain in the relation between us. I might be expected to respond to this by persuading my friend to give up his or her liking of the third party, by altering my own relation to that person, or by breaking the relationship with my friend. Each participant in an unbalanced network will be under a similar strain and so will be attempting to resolve the tensions that they experience.[2] Group relations are in a dynamic flux, with the final balanced outcome – if it is achieved – resulting from the actions and compromises of all the participants involved. Responses aimed at restoring balance to the group can be mapped in new graphs with different signs attached to the various lines. Graph (iii), for example, represents the situation where A successfully persuades B to dislike C, and so restores balance.

Cartwright and Harary argued that complex social structures can be seen as built from simple structures. More particularly, they are composed of overlapping 'triads' such as those depicted in Figure

2.3. Simple triadic structures are the building blocks of larger social structures, and the properties of complex networks of social relations can, they argue, be derived from an analysis of these building blocks. In the simplest case, for example, a whole network is balanced when all of its constituent triads are balanced.[3] While the idea of a balanced triad is, perhaps, fairly clear and comprehensible, the idea that a large and complex network is 'balanced' is less so. Indeed, the claim might seem to be neither an interesting nor a useful piece of information. This would, however, be an erroneous conclusion to draw. A very important finding, which has been derived from the work of Cartwright and Harary, is that any balanced graph, no matter how large or complex, can be divided into two sub-groups with rather interesting properties: the relations *within* each of these sub-groups will be positive, while those *between* the sub-groups will be negative. Thus, a balanced social network, defined, for example, by relations of solidarity, will consist of two cohesive sub-groupings between which there is conflict and antagonism.

In the simple case where all the relations in a network are positive, one of these sub-groups will be an empty or null set: all points will fall into a single group.[4] This will not be the case in more complex balanced structures, and a division into sub-groups might highlight important structural features of the network. So, the identification of a network as balanced or unbalanced is merely a first step in the move towards its 'decomposition' into its constituent sub-groups. Much of the mathematical work concerned with the analysis of balance has centred on the attempt to discover such decomposition techniques. The successful decomposition of a balanced network would allow researchers to derive an understanding of network structure simply from information about the relations between individuals. This discovery has enormous implications for the understanding of group structure, and James Davis (1967, 1968) has been a leading figure in the attempt to discover the conditions under which it might be possible to move towards more realistic decomposition techniques that would allow researchers to identify the existence of more than two sub-groups within a network.[5]

The concept of balance has been especially influential in experimental studies of group cooperation and leadership and has resulted in one classic study of small group behaviour in a natural setting (Festinger et al., 1959). Many of the ideas that emerged from the sociometric tradition of small group research were, however, taken up by researchers with an interest in general systems theory and in the mathematical aspects of cybernetics and rational action. Indeed, the first applications of sociometric ideas to large-scale social systems were initiated by just such researchers. Initial studies explored the spread of disease from one person to another through chains of contacts, aiming at the derivation of predictive epidemiological models of contagion. A leading figure in this work was Rapoport, who elaborated on the formal implications of the studies (Rapoport, 1952, 1958) and helped to stimulate an interest in applying similar ideas to the transmission of ideas and innovations. Although such work had been undertaken before, along with investigations of the spread of rumour and gossip, the 1960s saw the first major works of this kind to use network concepts (Coleman et al., 1966; Fararo and Sunshine, 1964).

Interpersonal Configurations and Cliques

Theoretical work in the sociometric tradition, I have argued, has involved a considerable effort to uncover ways of decomposing networks into their constituent sub-groups. This search for what have variously been termed 'cliques', 'clusters', or 'blocks' has also been a feature of the research tradition that developed at Harvard University during the 1930s and 1940s. In this line of work, the investigation of 'informal relations' in large-scale systems led to the empirical discovery that these systems did, in fact, contain cohesive sub-groupings. The task that the researchers then faced, and only partly solved, was to discover techniques that could disclose the sub-group structure of any social system for which relational data were available.

Radcliffe-Brown and, through him, Durkheim were the major influences on this tradition of research. Radcliffe-Brown's ideas had been especially influential among anthropologists in Australia, where he had taught for a number of years. His influence was particularly strong in the work of W. Lloyd Warner, who moved to Harvard in 1929 to join his fellow Australian, the psychologist Elton Mayo. The two men worked together in a series of closely related investigations of factory and community life in America, and they saw these investigations as applications of the structural concerns of Radcliffe-Brown.

Mayo had moved from Australia to Harvard in 1926 in order to take on a leading role in the newly developed research programme of its business school. His principal contact with sociological ideas was through the dominating influence of the biologist L.J. Henderson, who actively promoted the work of Pareto among his Harvard colleagues. Henderson held that this was the only appropriate basis for a truly scientific sociology and that it was, furthermore, the only viable political bulwark against revolutionary Marxism. Mayo's psychological concern for individual motivation was complemented by a growing awareness of what Pareto termed the 'non-rational' components of action. Economic action, for Mayo, was not a purely rational form of action, but was structured also by non-rational sentiments such as those of group solidarity. Pareto was also the great exponent of elite theory, and Mayo saw that a managerial elite that recognized this influence of group relations on economic motivation could most successfully control worker behaviour. Warner's contribution to the Harvard research programme, as befitted a trained field worker, showed a greater concern for detailed investigations of the actual patterns of group behaviour that could be found in particular social settings. To Mayo's theoretical and applied concerns, Warner brought an empirical dimension. Despite these differences – or, perhaps, because of them – the work that the two began at Harvard was crucially important in the development of social network analysis. Their careers overlapped there for only six years, but their research proved massively influential. The major projects that they and their colleagues undertook were investigations of the Hawthorne electrical factory in Chicago and a study of the New England community of 'Yankee City'.

The Hawthorne studies have become classics of social investigation, and they need little discussion here. (See the useful discussion in Rose, 1975.) Briefly, a series of studies of worker efficiency had been undertaken during the 1920s by managers in the Hawthorne works of the Western Electric Company in Chicago. These managers were attempting to discover how alterations in the physical conditions of work (heating, lighting, rest periods and so on) affected productivity, and they discovered, to their considerable surprise, that productivity increased almost regardless of the particular changes that were made. In an attempt to understand these paradoxical results, the managers called on Mayo and his Harvard team for some guidance in restructuring the research programme. Mayo concluded that the crucial factor responsible for increased productivity had been the very fact of participation in the research project: the workers were pleased that their managers were taking an interest in them, and their sense of involvement and integration into the life of the factory motivated them to greater efforts.

With the advice of Warner, the Hawthorne investigators began an 'anthropological' study, an observation of workgroup behaviour in a natural setting in the factory. The scene of their observations was the bank wiring room, and the team approached their research in the factory in the same way that a social anthropologist would carry out fieldwork in a village in an alien society. They recorded all that they could observe of group behaviour, aiming to construct a full

anthropological account. The particular importance of the Hawthorne studies in the development of social network analysis lies in
their use of sociograms to report on group structure. Just as the kinship structure of a village community might be illustrated by a
genealogical diagram, the Hawthorne team constructed sociograms
to illustrate the structure of informal relations within the workgroup.

The principal report on the Hawthorne studies (Roethlisberger and
Dickson, 1939: 500ff.)[6] includes various sociograms constructed
by the research team. They saw these as reflecting the 'informal
organization' of the bank wiring room, as opposed to the formal
organization that was depicted in the managerial organization chart.
Sociograms were constructed to show each of a number of aspects
of group behaviour: involvement in games, controversy over the
opening of windows, job trading, helping, and friendships and
antagonisms. The Hawthorne study was the first major investigation
to use sociograms to describe the actual relations observed in real
situations. In their diagrams, people are represented by circles and
their relationships by arrows. The similarity of these diagrams to
the sociograms subsequently developed by the group dynamics
researchers are obvious, but the researchers give no indication of
how they hit upon the idea of such diagrams. There is, for example,
no discussion of the evolving work of Moreno. It will be seen from
Figure 2.4, however, that the diagrams resemble not only the formal
organization charts which were used by managers, but also the
electrical wiring diagrams that would have been a very familiar
feature of the plant. It must be assumed that the influence of Warner
encouraged the researchers to adapt conventional anthropological
kinship diagrams by drawing on these other influences of the
organizational setting.

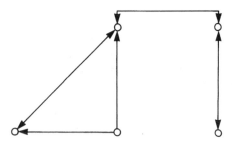

Figure 2.4   *A Hawthorne sociogram*

In drawing the sociograms of the bank wiring group, certain general conventions were followed, but these were artistic rather than sociological. The precise location of each circle on the page was decided by the artist, the principal constraint being simply that the members of any sub-group identified by the observers should be drawn as close to one another as possible. Apart from this, purely artistic principles of clarity and simplicity governed the design: the number of lines that cross one another, for example, should be as small as possible, and the lines should not vary too much in length. The sub-groups identified by the researchers – they called them 'cliques' – were those that the workers themselves recognized as important elements of their situation. Much as any anthropologist might use 'native' categories and concepts as pointers to the structural features of group life, the workers' own terms were taken as indicators of the existence of 'cliques'. 'The group in front' and 'the group in back' were identified from observations of group behaviour and from group vocabulary as the two sub-groups within the bank wiring group. There was no attempt to use the sociograms themselves to identify sociometrically defined 'cliques'; the socially perceived sub-groups were simply mapped onto the sociograms.[7] Having plotted group structure in this way, however, the researchers made little further use of the diagrams. They appear to lack any *theoretical* understanding of how social networks might shape the behaviour of individuals.

Warner, meanwhile, had begun a study of the small New England city of Newburyport, which he gave the pseudonym 'Yankee City'. His fieldwork was carried out between 1930 and 1935, and the research was conceived as a full-blown anthropological study of a modern, urban community. As such, it combined observation with the use of interviews and historical documents. The end of the main phase of fieldwork, however, coincided with a growing antagonism between Warner and Mayo, and Warner left Harvard for Chicago University, where his mentor, Radcliffe-Brown, was already a visiting professor. Warner and Radcliffe-Brown had two years together at Chicago, a period when the analysis of the fieldwork material from Yankee City would have been at its most intense. Warner spent the rest of his career at Chicago, and it was from there that he supervised and sponsored a number of related studies, most importantly that of 'Old City' in the Deep South.[8]

Warner's own early work had used the methods and ideas of Durkheim and Radcliffe-Brown in the traditional manner to study an Australian tribe, and it was through his contact with Mayo that he first formulated the idea of applying anthropological methods to the study of a modern urban community. Warner had originally intended to study the district of Chicago in which the Hawthorne works were located, but the work of the Chicago school of sociologists forced him to conclude that the district was 'disorganized' and so would not be amenable to anthropological investigation (Park et al., 1925). Warner felt that only in New England and in parts of the southern States would he find the kind of established and integrated communities that he wished to study.

Warner's work shows a rich variety of theoretical influences. While the influence of Radcliffe-Brown was uppermost, he allied this with an organismic, systems model of society which, undoubtedly, shows the influence of Henderson's interpretation of Pareto. This led Warner to emphasize such factors as stability, cohesion and integration in the structuring of communities. But he also drew on Simmel's ideas of reciprocal relations and of the influence of numbers on group life. It was, I have suggested, Simmel (1908) who pioneered the analysis of dyads and triads as the building blocks of social life. Following the terminology of Simmel and other German sociologists, also adopted by Moreno, Warner talked of social configurations, holding that the social organization of a community consists of a web of relations through which people interact with one another.

The social configuration that comprises a modern community, argued Warner, consists of various types of sub-group, such as the family, the church, classes and associations. Alongside these is also to be found the sub-group that he termed the 'clique': an informal association of people among whom there is a degree of group feeling and intimacy and in which certain group norms of behaviour have been established (Warner and Lunt, 1941: 32). A clique is 'an intimate non-kin group, membership in which may vary in numbers from two to thirty or more people' (Warner and Lunt, 1941: 110).[9] For Warner, therefore, the clique has the same social significance in community studies as the informal group had in the Hawthorne factory studies. The concept describes a particular configuration of *informal* interpersonal relations.

The Yankee City researchers claimed that a large number of these cliques could be identified in the city. The major cliques were the groups that many Yankee City respondents referred to by such terms as 'our crowd', 'our circle' and so on. Having discovered the existence of these cliques from the comments made by those they studied, Warner and his associates claimed that they were second in importance only to the family in placing people in society. People are integrated into communities through 'informal' and 'personal' relations of family and clique membership, not simply through the 'formal' relations of the economy and political system. Any person may be a member of several different cliques, and 'such overlapping in clique membership spreads out into a network of interrelations which integrate almost the entire population of a community in a single vast system of clique relations' (Warner and Lunt, 1941: 111). This is undoubtedly one of the earliest, if not *the* earliest use of network terminology to describe the structuring of whole societies into sub-groups.

The Yankee City reports used various diagrams to model such things as class structure and family organization, and it is hardly surprising that the researchers also constructed clique diagrams. To represent the social structure that they described, they drew cliques as a series of intersecting circles in a Venn diagram (Warner and Lunt, 1941: 113), but they did not advance to any formal, structural analyses of these diagrams. In the second volume of the Yankee City report, however, there was an attempt to undertake what would now be termed a 'positional analysis' (Warner and Lunt, 1942: 52, Figure X). They presented a series of matrices that show the numbers of people occupying each of a number of structurally defined positions. Figure 2.5 shows the format of one of these diagrams. Having identified six classes and 31 types of clique in Yankee City, Warner and Lunt cross-classified class and clique membership in a data matrix. Each type of clique was defined by the predominant class composition of its overall membership, and the cells of the matrix

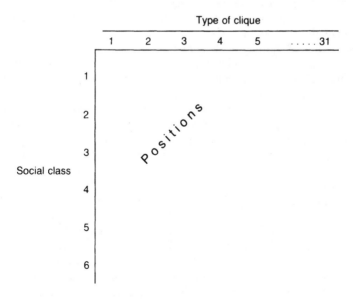

Figure 2.5   *A matrix of cliques*

show the numbers of people in each class who were members of each of the 31 types of clique.[10] From among the large number of possible combinations – 6 times 31, or 186 – they argue that only 73 positions actually occurred. All the remaining cells in the matrix were empty. By constructing similar matrices for class against each of a number of other social groupings (types of formal association, types of family etc.,) they were able to combine the matrices together, stacking them one on top of another, and they identified 89 structural positions in the overall, combined network.[11] The particular procedure that they employed was rather cumbersome, and it is unnecessary to go further into its outmoded operation, but the Yankee City work remains interesting for its attempt to pioneer such methods of formal structural analysis.

Colleagues of Warner began an investigation of 'Old City', in the southern States, during 1936, and in this research they further explored the idea of the 'clique' (Davis et al., 1941). In looking at 'colored society' in Old City, they followed Warner's method of seeing cliques as intersecting circles, mapping the overlapping memberships of the most active cliques in a space defined by class and age (Davis et al., 1941: 213, Figure 12). They referred to 'social space' and its 'two dimensions', but there is no explicit mention of any of the work of Lewin on topological field models. The major innovation of this study was its attempt to explore the internal structure of cliques. The researchers argued that a clique could be seen as comprising three layers: a 'core' of those who participate together most often and most intimately, a 'primary circle' of those who participate jointly with core members on some occasions but never as a group by themselves, and a 'secondary circle' of those who participate only infrequently and so are 'almost non-members'. On the basis of their investigation of 60 cliques, using similar techniques to those of the Yankee City researchers, they suggested a number of structural hypotheses about the connections *between* cliques. They argued, for example, that peripheral, lower-class members of a clique might be able to contact higher-class members of another clique only through the higher-class core members of their own clique.

The ideas that emerged in the Hawthorne, Yankee City and Old City research developed in parallel with those of the sociometric tradition of small group research, but there is no evidence that the leading figures in the two traditions were even aware of one another's work during the 1930s and 1940s. In the work of George Homans, however, there occurred the first important intersection of these two strands of research. Homans, a faculty member in the Harvard sociology department, was dissatisfied with the grand theory of Harvard colleagues such as Parsons, which he felt operated at a much too abstract level of analysis. Homans felt that social theory had to be built up from the foundations of a firm understanding of small-scale social interaction. To this end, he began, during the late 1940s, to try to synthesize the mass of small group research that had been undertaken in the United States. He aimed at nothing less than a theoretical synthesis of this work, drawing on the experimental work of the social psychologists and the observational work of sociologists and anthropologists. His theoretical synthesis centred around the idea that human activities bring people into interaction with one another, that these interactions vary in their 'frequency', 'duration' and 'direction',[12] and that interaction is the basis on which 'sentiments' develop among people. Homans saw Moreno's sociometry as providing a methodological framework for applying this theory to particular social situations. To illustrate his ideas, he re-examined a number of earlier studies.

One section of the Old City report has achieved considerable fame – among network analysts at least – because of its re-analysis by Homans. In this section, Davis and his colleagues had used matrix methods to look at the involvement of 18 women in 14 social events (Davis et al., 1941: ch. 7).[13] Homans took these data, presented them in matrix form, and set out one of the first published statements of the method of 'matrix re-arrangement' in social network analysis. (See also Festinger, 1949.) The Old City matrix shows 18 rows (women) and 14 columns (events), with an 'x' entry placed in a cell to represent the participation of a particular woman at a specific event. The raw matrix, argued Homans, was not necessarily arranged in any significant order – the columns, for example, were simply arranged in the date order of the events. For this reason, the crosses appear to be distributed at random across the matrix. A re-arrangement of the rows and columns of the matrix, bringing together the events in which particular women predominate, would, he believed, uncover important structural features of the clique. He described his method as follows:

> we put in the center the columns representing events . . . at which a large number of women were present, and we put toward the edges the columns representing the events . . . at which only a few women were present. As far as the lines [rows] are concerned, we put together toward the top or bottom the lines representing those women that participated most often together in social events. A great deal of reshuffling may have to be done before any pattern appears. (Homans, 1951: 83)

Homans argued that this 'reshuffling' must go on until the distribution of the crosses in the cells shows a clear pattern, and he produced a re-arranged matrix in which there were clear signs of a division into two 'cliques' among the women: there were two distinct clumps of crosses in the re-arranged matrix. Homans's method is analogous to what has subsequently come to be called 'block modelling', but he made no use of any formal mathematical methods. In fact, his re-arrangement seems to have been simply a trial-and-error process that continued until he was able to spot an apparently significant pattern.

Figure 2.6 shows a simplified version of the kind of re-analysis undertaken by Homans. The matrices show artificial data for the participation of eight people in eight events. In matrix (i), the 'x' entries are scattered evenly across the whole matrix, but a re-arrangement of the rows and columns into the order shown in matrix

(i) Original matrix

		Events							
		1	2	3	4	5	6	7	8
	Ann	X		X		X		X	
	Beth		X		X		X		X
	Chris	X		X		X		X	
People	Don		X		X		X		X
	Ed	X		X		X		X	
	Flo		X		X		X		X
	Gill	X		X		X		X	
	Hal		X		X		X		X

(ii) Re-arranged matrix

		Events							
		1	3	5	7	2	4	6	8
	Ann	X	X	X	X				
	Chris	X	X	X	X				
	Ed	X	X	X	X				
People	Gill	X	X	X	X				
	Beth					X	X	X	X
	Don					X	X	X	X
	Flo					X	X	X	X
	Hal					X	X	X	X

Figure 2.6 *Matrix re-arrangement*

(ii) brings out a structural opposition between two distinct sub-groups: Ann, Chris, Ed and Gill participate together in events 1, 3, 5 and 7, while Beth, Don, Flo and Hal participate jointly in events 2, 4, 6 and 8. There are two separate sets of people and two specific categories of events. It can be appreciated that re-arrangement by trial-and-error would not be such an easy task, even for such a small matrix, when the data are not so tightly structured as in this artificial example. The real data on 18 women and 14 events would have taken a considerable amount of time to analyse. There is, further-more, no certainty that the final results produced by Homans would be the same as those produced by any other researcher, as there are no criteria by which a 'correct' result can be identified. It is for these reasons that later attempts at this kind of analysis have involved a search for programmable algorithms, so that computers can reliably undertake the task of re-arrangement.

To illustrate his position further, Homans re-analysed the Hawthorne data on the bank wiring room. Using the sociograms constructed by the observers, he looked at the cliques that Roethlisberger and Dickson had identified (Homans, 1951: 66–70). But Homans retained these original clique identifications, and did not attempt a sociometric investigation of clique structure along the lines of his analysis of the Old City data. He did imply, however, albeit without elaboration, that the matrix re-arrangement method had been used by the original Hawthorne researchers (Homans, 1951: 84).[14]

The theoretical framework that Homans constructed to explain group behaviour was an elaboration of the model of the early small group researchers, in which the group is understood as a system within an environment. He divided the structure of any group into an 'internal system', which expresses the sentiments that arise through the interactions of its members, and an 'external system' through which group activities are related to the problem of environmental adaptation.[15] The environment itself consists of the physical, tech-nical and social contexts of group behaviour. Homans's main concern was with the internal system, which he saw as a more scientific concept than that of the 'informal organization' to which it referred. His interest, therefore, was in the scientific elaboration of the insights of research on informal organization by translating these insights into propositions about the structure of internal systems.

To this end, he set up a number of hypotheses about the internal system, starting from the assumption that people who interact frequently with one another will tend to like one another and that, as the frequency of their interaction increases, so the degree of their liking for one another will increase. If there are frequent interactions in the external system, because of such environmental constraints as the demands imposed by supervisors and managers, then the members of the workgroup will tend to develop sentiments of liking and will engage in further interactions with one another, unrelated to the needs of the external system. It is in this way, he argues, that the internal system gets elaborated into complex social configurations divisible into cliques.[16]

Despite the power of Homans's theoretical synthesis of sociometric and anthropological research, there were few major advances that were directly inspired by his work. Homans himself became increasingly concerned to explore the explanation of social behaviour using behaviourist and rational choice models, and he became identified with the framework of 'exchange theory' (Homans, 1961). Robert Bales, a colleague of Homans, carried out some interesting small group research (Bales, 1950), but he did not use a sociometric approach to his work and became increasingly linked with Parsonian structural functionalism (Parsons et al., 1953). The work of many who had contributed to the development of the idea of balance returned to exclusively psychologistic concerns, and the influential text of Festinger (1957) became an important charter statement in directing these researchers back into the social psychology of perception. The area of group dynamics all but stagnated, with most advances being in the purely mathematical problems of balance, cliques and clusters. While these mathematical explorations were to prove important and fertile sources for the advances later made by Harrison White, they had little impact on the shape of social research during the 1950s and 1960s.

Networks: Total and Partial

It was in the work of a small group of active fieldworkers associated with the Department of Social Anthropology at Manchester University – most notably, John Barnes, Clyde Mitchell and Elizabeth Bott[17] – that the framework of social network analysis took a novel turn. The 'Manchester' anthropologists were even more strongly influenced by Radcliffe-Brown than were their Harvard counterparts, and they sought to develop his ideas in a novel direction. Instead of emphasizing integration and cohesion, they emphasized conflict and change. A central figure at Manchester was Max Gluckman, who combined an interest in complex African societies with a concern to develop a structural approach that recognized the important part played by conflict and power in both the maintenance and the transformation of social structures. For Gluckman, conflict and power were integral elements of any social structure, and his analyses stressed the ever-present activities of negotiation, bargaining and coercion in the production of social integration. Gluckman actively encouraged his colleagues and students who were undertaking investigations of small scale interpersonal communities to pursue these themes.

The dominance of the Parsonian approach to sociology and of cultural approaches in anthropology during the 1950s was an important factor in directing the work of the Manchester school as a distinctly *critical* tradition. Where classical sociologists had emphasized that actions were to be understood in terms of their location in a structure of social relations, Parsons held that actions must be explained as expressions of internalized value orientations. The work of the Manchester anthropologists, with its emphasis on seeing structures as networks of relations, combined the formal techniques of network analysis with substantive sociological concepts. This proved an impressive and powerful mixture, which brought it close to the emerging framework of conflict theory in sociology, but their emphasis on interpersonal relations meant that it did not appear as a full-blown alternative to Parsonian theory. For this reason, social network analysis could not help but be seen as a specialized method of study rather than a critical alternative to conventional sociology.

The Manchester researchers, then, paid less attention to the formally institutionalized norms and institutions of a society and rather more to the actual configurations of relations that arise from the exercise of conflict and power. The theoretical ideas inherited from the past, geared to the understanding of simple, kinship-based societies, were unable to handle these phenomena. It was in recognition of this inadequacy that they began to try to systematize such metaphorical notions as the 'web' and 'network' of social relations to which such writers as Radcliffe-Brown had pointed.

Initially, these researchers began to employ the idea of a social network simply in its metaphorical sense, but Barnes, in the early 1950s, took a lead in applying this idea in a more rigorous and analytical way. His approach had a considerable influence on the work of Bott, and the two began to explore more closely the work that had been undertaken in the sociometric tradition. Their various papers (Barnes, 1954; Bott, 1955, 1956) received a broad welcome among social anthropologists, the concept of the social network seeming to meet a need for appropriate concepts to use in understanding complex societies. Siegfried Nadel espoused this approach in a set of lectures and an associated book (Nadel, 1957) that became a programmatic charter statement from a leading figure in the discipline. However, it was Clyde Mitchell who undertook the tasks outlined by Nadel and laid the basis for a systematic frame-work of social network analysis. Mitchell turned to the mathematics of graph theory that had emerged from the early sociometric concerns, and he reformulated these ideas as the basis of a distinctly *sociological* framework. Summarizing the ideas that had begun to crystallize during the 1950s in his own work and that of his colleagues (Mitchell, 1969), he set out a body of sociological concepts that, he believed, could adequately grasp the *structural* properties of social organization. Intriguingly, Mitchell's translation of graph theory and sociometry into a sociological framework led him to a concentration on exactly those features of informal and interpersonal organization that had been highlighted by Mayo, Warner and Homans.

Barnes began his academic career at the Rhodes–Livingstone Institute in Central Africa, a major research centre for many of the Manchester anthropologists. After joining the Manchester Depart-ment in 1949, he decided to undertake some fieldwork in a fishing village in south-west Norway. Although it was a small village community, Bremnes was an isolated locale structured almost exclusively through the kinship relations of its members. It was an integral part of a complex and socially differentiated national society, but it had its own economic, political, and other institutions, which were only imperfectly co-ordinated into an integrated system. Barnes was strongly drawn to the part played by kinship, friendship and neighbouring in the production of community integration. These primordial relations were not directly tied to territorial locales or to formal economic and political structures. Instead, they formed a distinct and relatively integrated sphere of informal, interpersonal relations. Barnes claimed that 'the whole of social life' could be seen as 'a set of points some of which are joined by lines' to form a 'total network' of relations. The informal sphere of interpersonal relations was to be seen as one part, a 'partial network', of this total network (Barnes, 1954: 43).

Bott, a Canadian psychologist, had studied anthropology under Lloyd Warner at Chicago, and it may be assumed that, like Barnes, she had some familiarity with the Yankee City studies. She joined the Tavistock Institute in 1950 and soon began some fieldwork on British families. Bott was principally concerned with their kinship relations, and she employed the concept of a 'network' as an analytical device for investigating the varying *forms* taken by these kinship relations. This work was published in two influential articles and a book (Bott, 1955, 1956, 1957), and it was the basis of the PhD that Bott received from the London School of Economics in 1956.

The evolving theoretical framework of her study was undoubtedly influenced by her colleagues at the Tavistock Institute, which had, in 1947, joined with the Research Centre for Group Dynamics at Ann Arbor to publish the journal *Human Relations*. As a psychologist with an interest in psychotherapy, Bott was aware of the work that had been undertaken by Moreno. Indeed, both she and Barnes cited Moreno in their own papers. The more immediate influence on Bott's work, however, was Lewin's field theory, and even Barnes wrote of the existence of distinct 'fields' of activity in Bremnes society. *Human Relations* published articles by Lewin, Festinger, Newcomb, Cartwright and other American leaders of small group research, and it was there that both Bott and Barnes published their work on social networks.

Barnes had presented his initial ideas in seminars at Manchester and Oxford during 1953. It was in 1954 that Bott learned of Barnes's work and adopted the term 'network' as the basis of her own theoretical interpretations. By the time that Barnes's article was published, he was working under Raymond Firth at the London School of Economics. Bott was already registered for her PhD, she presented drafts of her own paper that year at both the LSE and at Manchester. These biographical details are not given for purely antiquarian reasons, nor are they given simply as illustrations of the importance of academic networks. My concern is to show how a small number of key individuals were responsible, in a very short space of time, for constructing the basis of a major theoretical innovation in British social anthropology. Once Barnes and Bott had made their breakthrough, the way was open for further developments which would consolidate their advances with further lessons from the American researchers.

A key voice in legitimating this direction of theoretical advance was Siegfried Nadel. An Austrian psychologist, influenced by Köhler and Lewin, Nadel had transferred to anthropological studies in the early 1930s. In 1955 he presented a series of lectures on social structure at the LSE. Barnes and Bott had been important influences on the development of his work, and they were mentioned as both commentators and friends in the Preface to the published version of these lectures (Nadel, 1957). Nadel's starting point was a definition of structure as the articulation or arrangement of elements to form a whole. By separating the *forms* of relations from their *contents*, he argues, the general features of structures can be described and they can be investigated through a comparative method. To pursue the aim of the construction of formal models, he advocated a mathematical approach to structure.

Social structure, according to Nadel, is 'an overall system, network or pattern' of relations (1957: 12), which the analyst abstracts from the concretely observable actions of individuals. By 'network' he meant 'the interlocking of relationships whereby the interactions implicit in one determine those occurring in others' (Nadel, 1957: 16). A particular claim made by Nadel was the idea that 'role' should be seen as the central concept in sociological theory. Social structures are structures of roles, and roles, together with their role sets, are defined through networks of interdependent activities. Nadel argued that algebraic and matrix methods should be applied to role analysis, but apart from one or two brief illustrations, he gave little indication of how this was to be done. His early death, in 1956, prevented him from contributing further to the advances that he had signposted.

Mitchell and others associated with Manchester and the Rhodes–Livingstone Institute attempted to systematize this view during the 1950s and 1960s. Indeed, Mitchell can be seen as the true inheritor of Nadel's aspirations. Mitchell's codification of social network analysis in 1969 generalized Barnes's conception of the sphere of interpersonal relations into that of the 'personal order'.[18] The personal order is the pattern of 'personal links individuals have with a set of people and the links these people have in turn among themselves' (Mitchell, 1969: 10). These patterns of interaction are, for Mitchell, the sphere of network analysis. Such interpersonal networks, he added, are built from two different ideal types of action that combine in varying ways to form concrete interaction networks. There is, first of all, 'communication', which involves the transfer of information between individuals, the establishment of social norms, and the creation of a degree of consensus. On the other hand, there is the 'instrumental' or purposive type of action, which involves the transfer of material goods and services between people (1969: 36–9).[19] Any particular action will combine elements of both of these ideal types, and so particular social networks will embody both a flow of information and a transfer of resources and services.

Mitchell goes on to conceptualize the 'total network' of a society as 'the general ever-ramifying, ever-reticulating set of linkages that stretches within and beyond the confines of any community or organization' (Mitchell, 1969: 12). In actual research, he argues, it is always necessary to select particular aspects of the total network for attention, and these aspects he conceptualizes as 'partial networks'. There are two bases on which such abstraction can proceed, though Mitchell concentrates his own attention almost exclusively on one of these. First, there is abstraction that is anchored around a particular individual so as to generate 'ego-centred' networks of social relations of all kinds. Second, is abstraction of the overall, 'global' features of networks in relation to a particular aspect of social activity: political ties, kinship obligations, friendship or work relations etc. For Mitchell and for most of the Manchester researchers, it was individually anchored partial networks that were to be the focus of attention. In this kind of research, individuals are identified and their direct and indirect links to others are traced. Such research generates a collection of ego-centred networks, one for each of the individuals studied. A similar approach was taken in Bott's earlier investigation of the ego-centred networks of husbands and wives, where she measured the 'connectedness' of these networks and the degree of overlap between marital partners' networks.

Mitchell recognizes the importance of the second mode of abstraction identified above – that which defines partial networks by the 'content' or meaning of the relations involved – but he sees this also as needing to be anchored around particular individuals. The 'partial networks' studied by sociologists and social anthropologists are always ego-centred networks focused around particular types of social relationship. Most such networks, Mitchell argues, are 'multi-stranded' or 'multiplex': they involve the combination of a number of meaningfully distinct relations. Thus, Barnes's original notion of the network, and that taken up by Bott, was a partial network in which kinship, friendship and neighbourliness were combined into a single, multi-stranded relationship that it was inappropriate to break down into its constituent elements.

Interpersonal networks, Mitchell claimed, can be analysed through a number of concepts that describe the quality of the relations involved. These are the 'reciprocity', the 'intensity' and the 'durability' of the relations (Mitchell, 1969: 24–9), concepts that echo Homans's distinctions between direction, frequency and intensity. Some, but not all, relationships involve a transaction or exchange, and so can be considered as 'directed' from one person to another. An important measure of such relations, therefore, is the degree to which the transaction or orientation is reciprocated. One person may, for example, choose another as a friend, but this choice may not be returned: the chooser may be ignored or spurned. Multi-stranded relationships can involve a complex balance of compensating relations, reciprocated and unreciprocated. Through these relations, financial aid, for example, might flow in one direction and political support in the other.[20] 'Durability' is a measure of how enduring are the underlying relations and obligations that are activated in particular transactions (Mitchell refers to Katz, 1966). Those that are constantly being activated in interaction are highly durable, while those that persist only for one or two activities are highly transient. While kinship obligations, for example, are very durable – they generally last for the whole of one's life – those that arise for a particularly limited purpose are more likely to be transient. 'Intensity' refers to the strength of the obligations involved in a relation. This reflects either the strength of the commitment to these obligations or the multiplexity of the relationship: multi-stranded relationships tend to be more intense because they are more diffuse in character.[21]

Mitchell adds a further set of concepts, derived from a translation of graph theory into sociological language, which can be used to describe the texture of social networks. 'Density', for example, he sees as the completeness of the network: the extent to which all possible relations are actually present. This is what Barnes and Bott had tried to describe with their notions of the 'mesh' and 'connectedness' of networks. 'Reachability' refers to how easy it is for all people to contact one another through a limited number of steps: how easy is it, for example, for gossip, ideas, or resources to be diffused through the network. To these concepts, Barnes (1969) has added 'cliques' and 'clusters' as terms for identifying social groupings within networks, but these were not taken up in the empirical studies collected together by Mitchell (1969).

Institutionalized roles and statuses are the framework within which interpersonal networks are constructed, but they exist only in and through the reproduction of interpersonal networks. But Mitchell and the Manchester tradition equivocated about whether the institutional structure of roles is itself a part of network analysis or is separate from it. While some of the Manchester school saw the institutional role structure as a network of relations that exists alongside the interpersonal network, Mitchell often distinguished *networks* of interpersonal relations from *structures* of institutional relations. Mitchell's discussion, therefore, tended towards a 'residual' definition of the social network: network analysis concerns only the interpersonal sphere that is left behind after formal economic, political and other roles are extracted (Whitten and Wolfe, 1973). This proved to be highly significant for the subsequent development of social network analysis in Britain. To the extent that he sees social network analysis as a *special* method for the analysis of interpersonal relations, Mitchell departs from Nadel's aspiration for a general framework of structural sociology rooted in formal network analysis. This proved fateful for the development of social network analysis in Britain, which largely failed to attract adherents from outside the area of community studies.

The Harvard Breakthrough

The arguments of Mitchell, Barnes and Bott were extremely influential in Britain (see Frankenberg, 1966), but their very success meant that social network analysis came to be identified with the specific ideas of the Manchester anthropologists. That is to say, network analysis was seen to be concerned specifically with informal, interpersonal relations of a 'communal' type, and the method was seen as specifically concerned with the investigation of ego-centric networks. As a result, the crucial breakthrough to the study of the global properties of social networks in all fields of social life was not made in Britain.

It was, in fact, at Harvard that the crucial breakthrough occurred. A decade after Homans's initial explorations, a trickle of papers began to appear from Harrison White and his associates. These pushed the analysis much further. Soon, the work of students and colleagues of the authors of these papers produced a torrent of papers that firmly established social network analysis as a method of structural analysis.

The key elements in this breakthrough were two parallel mathematical innovations (see the discussion in Berkowitz, 1982). The first of these was the development of algebraic models of groups using set theory to model kinship and other relations in the spirit of Lévi-Strauss. This led to a re-consideration of the early work in graph theory and in other branches of mathematics and to the attempt to use algebraic methods to conceptualize the concept of 'role' in social structure (Boyd, 1969; Lorrain and White, 1971; White, 1963). White's continued explorations of 'block modelling' (see Chapter 7 below) can be seen as carrying forward the very emphasis on role structure to which Nadel had pointed. The second innovation was the development of multidimensional scaling, a 'scaling' technique for translating relationships into social 'distances' and for mapping them in a social space. Very much in the tradition of Lewin's work on field theory, these developments proved extremely powerful methods of analysis. (For applications in sociology see Laumann, 1966 and Levine, 1972.)

The confluence of these two strands led to the important and influential work of the new Harvard group centred around White (see Mullins, 1973). White had moved to Harvard from Chicago, and his work retained important links with that of Davis and others, who had elaborated on the basic sociometric views through the 1960s. The Harvard group developed as mathematically orientated structural analysts, concerned with the modelling of social structures of all kinds. There was no single theoretical focus to their work, the unifying idea being simply that of using algebraic ideas to model deep and surface structure relations. It was network analysis as a method that united them. The public reception of Granovetter's article (1973) popularized this viewpoint in American sociology and helped to stimulate many other studies. Although it was not a highly technical piece of mathematics – or, perhaps, because of this – Granovetter's work was of central importance as a charter statement for popularizing and legitimating the position (see also Granovetter, 1982). Although many researchers continued to work in such areas as the analysis of community structure, others were interested in such phenomena as corporate interlocks and so helped to move network analysis away from its focus on purely interpersonal relations. In doing so, they stimulated numerous substantive applications of the techniques. Much of the effort of the Harvard group – no longer based solely at Harvard – was focused in the International Network for Social Network Analysis (INSNA), founded at Toronto, which acted as a focus for the development of social network analysis under the leadership of Wellman and Berkowitz, both former students of White.[22]

Two classic studies by Granovetter and by Lee grew out of the earliest discussions of the Harvard school. While they were not explicitly algebraic in their approach, they became important exemplars for others. This was not least because they offered substantive and analytical continuity with earlier sociometric work.

Granovetter's work in *Getting a Job* (1974) started out from a critical consideration of attempts by labour economists to explain how people find work. In particular, he wanted to explore the ways in which people acquire *information* about job opportunities through the informal social contacts that they have. His interest was in the kinds of links involved in the transmission of information, whether these were 'strong' or 'weak', and how they were maintained over time. To this end, he selected a sample of male professional, technical and managerial workers in a suburb of Boston who had changed their jobs during the previous five years. Granovetter found that informal, personal contacts were the primary channels through which individuals found out about job opportunities: 56 per cent of his respondents relied on this means, and this was particularly true for information about the higher-paying jobs. These results were not especially striking, being broadly in line with earlier research, and Granovetter set himself the task of identifying those who provided information and the circumstances under which they passed it.

Granovetter showed that 'rational' choice was of little importance in deciding methods for acquiring job information. Individuals did not really compare the rewards and costs attached to different sources of information, and there was little active 'search' for jobs. Instead, information was acquired accidentally, whenever contacts volunteered it. The most important people in providing information were work or work-related contacts. They were rarely family or friends, and they tended to be people who were in different occupations from the respondent. The probability that a person would make a job change was dependent on the proportion of work contacts who were in different occupations from him or herself.

To explain these findings, Granovetter drew on an information diffusion model. Those people with job information were assumed to pass this on to a certain proportion of their immediate contacts, who passed it on, in turn, to a certain proportion of their contacts, and so on. Assuming that the information attenuates over time as it passes through subsequent links in the chain,[23] it is possible to track its passage through a social network and to discover the number of people who will acquire the information and their various locations in the network. The acquisition of information, therefore, depends upon, first, the motivation of those with information to pass it on, and, second, the strategic location of a person's contacts in the overall flow of information (Granovetter, 1974: 52).

It was at this point in his argument that Granovetter introduced his now-famous argument on 'the strength of weak ties'. The importance of strong ties is well understood. Those to whom a person is closest (family and close friends, workmates etc.) have many overlapping contacts. They all tend to know and to interact with one another in numerous situations and so there is a tendency for them to possess the *same* knowledge about job opportunities. Information that reaches any one of them is more than likely to reach them all. Conversely, they are less likely to be the sources of new information from more distant parts of the network. The information received is likely to be 'stale' information, already received from someone else. It is through the relatively weak ties of less frequent contacts and of people in different work situations that new and different information is likely to become available. What this means is that 'acquaintances are more likely to pass job information than close friends' (Granovetter, 1974: 54). In almost all cases studied by Granovetter, information came directly from an employer or one of the employer's direct contacts – there was, typically, a maximum of one intermediary. Links through more than two intermediaries were very rare. It was the short, weak chains of connection that were of greatest significance in the receipt of useful job information.

A comparable, and slightly earlier study was Lee's work in *The Search for an Abortionist* (1969). Lee wanted to discover how women acquired information about the opportunities for terminations in a situation where abortion is illegal. Doctors who undertake illegal terminations cannot advertise and must often operate from hotel rooms rather than from clinics. Those who seek an abortion must, therefore, try to obtain information from those of their friends and acquaintances who may have had some experience with abortion in the past, as these people are likely to have that information or to be able to put them in contact with others who can help.

To study this process, Lee contacted abortionists and women who had had recent experience of an abortion. In constructing her sample she was, interestingly, having to use information search techniques that were similar to those used by the women themselves. Like Granovetter, she used a mixture of interviews and questionnaires to gather her data. Having explored various aspects of their life and social background and their attitudes towards conception and abortion, Lee turned to an examination of their search for an abortionist. The search for an abortionist involved the making of informed guesses about who might be able to help, either by providing the name of an abortionist or mentioning a further contact who might help. Lee found that women approached an average of 5.8 people before successfully contacting an abortionist, the actual numbers of contacts ranging from 1 to 31. A number of the contacts, of course, were 'dead ends', and the 'successful chains' varied in length from 1 to 7 steps, the average length being 2.8. Over three-quarters of the successful chains involved two or fewer intermediaries (Lee, 1969: ch. 5). Contacts tended not to be relatives or those in authority (employers, teachers, etc.), and the most important channels were female friends of the same age.

Both Granovetter and Lee explored network processes through the use of simple frequency tabulations, making only qualitative comments on the *structure* of the network relations that they discovered. Indeed, Lee argued that it is extremely difficult to trace the structure of overlapping personal networks in large-scale systems. Their studies were, however, important as outgrowths of and contributions to the systematic and analytical development of social network analysis. Their studies showed the power of even the most basic of social network methods, and they suggested an immense power for the more rigorous techniques being developed by their Harvard colleagues.

The power of social network analysis has become apparent in its use as an orientating idea and specific body of methods. But the application of formal mathematical ideas to the study of social networks has encouraged some writers to suggest that social network analysis offers the basis for a new theory of social structure. Barnes and Harary (1983), for example, have argued that it is possible to advance from the use of formal *concepts* to the use of formal *theory*. They argue that the promise of social network analysis can be realized only if researchers move beyond the use of formal concepts for purely descriptive purposes (see also Granovetter, 1979). Mathematics consists of theorems that specify the determinate logical links between formal concepts. Barnes and Harary argue that if the formal concepts prove to be useful ways of organizing relational data, then the theorems too should be applicable to those data. The application of theorems drawn from formal mathematics, then, 'reveals real world implications of the model that might otherwise have not been noticed or utilized by the designer of the model' (Barnes and Harary, 1983: 239).

Some have gone further, and have suggested that developments in social network analysis already point the way to novel frameworks of sociological theory, or to the re-assertion of earlier theories. Particularly influential, for example, have been advocates of an exchange theoretical perspective on social networks (Cook, 1977, 1982; Emerson, 1962, 1964; Cook and Whitmeyer, 1992), which is associated with wider 'transactionalist' approaches (Bailey, 1969; Boissevain, 1974) and rational choice theories (Lin, 1982). (See also the discussions in Banck, 1973 and van Poucke, 1979.) Most recently, Emirbayer (1997; Emirbayer and Goodwin, 1994) has set out an argument for network analysis as the basis of a 'relational sociology' that can replace approaches that have stressed culture and meaning, but is not linked to exchange or rational choice theories.[24]

Whether social network analysis will, in the long run, point to the predominance of a particular theoretical framework is not a matter that will detain me in this book. It is undoubtedly the case that social network analysis embodies a particular theoretical orientation towards the *structure* of the social world and that it is, therefore, linked with structural theories of action. But it seems unlikely that any one substantive theory should be regarded as embodying the essence of social network analysis. The point of view that I will elaborate in this book is that social network analysis is an orientation towards the social world that inheres in a particular set of *methods*. It is not a specific body of formal or substantive social theory.

3

Handling Relational Data

Social network analysis emerged as a set of methods for the analysis of social structures, methods that specifically allow an investigation of the *relational* aspects of these structures. The use of these methods, therefore, depends on the availability of relational rather than attribute data. In this Chapter I will show how these relational data can be collected, stored and prepared for social network analysis. Many of the general considerations that arise in handling relational data are not specific to this type of research. They are those that arise with all social science data: gaining access, designing questionnaires, drawing samples, dealing with non-response, storing data on computers and so on. These issues are adequately covered in the many general and specialist texts on research methods, and it is not necessary to cover the same ground here. However, a number of specific problems do arise when research concerns relational data. As these problems are not, in general, covered in the existing texts on research methods, it is important to review them here before going on to consider the techniques of social network analysis themselves.

The Organization of Relational Data

All social research data, once collected, must be held in some kind of **data matrix** (Galtung, 1967), a framework in which the raw or coded data can be organized in a more or less efficient way. At its simplest, a data matrix is a table of figures, a pattern of rows and columns drawn on paper. When the data set is large or complex, the data matrix may need to be stored on record cards or in a computer file. Whatever the physical form taken, the logical structure of the data matrix is always that of a table. In variable analysis, attribute data can be organized in a case-by-variable matrix. Each case studied (for example, each respondent) is represented by a row in the matrix, while the columns refer to the variables on which their attributes are measured. Figure 3.1 shows a simple form of such a data matrix, with illustrative variables. This is the way in which data are organized, on paper or in a computer, for most standard statistical procedures.

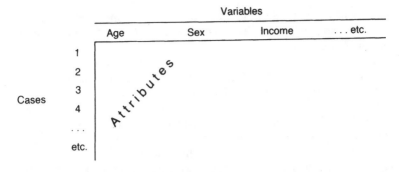

Figure 3.1   *A data matrix for variable analysis*

The case-by-variable data matrix cannot be used for relational data. These data must, instead, be seen in terms of a case-by-affiliation matrix. The cases are still the particular agents that form the units of analysis, but the affiliations are the organizations, events, or activities in which these agents are involved. The columns of the matrix, then, refer to the affiliations in terms of which the involvements, memberships, or participations of the agents can be identified. From this case-by-affiliation matrix can be derived information on the direct and indirect connections among the agents. In Figure 3.2, for example, a simple case-by-affiliation matrix is shown for the involvement of three people (labelled 1, 2 and 3) in three events (labelled A, B and C). Where a specific individual participates in a particular event, there is a '1' in the corresponding cell of the matrix; non-participation is shown by a '0' entry. It can be seen that all three people participate in event A, but none of them is involved in events B or C. Thus, the sociogram that can be drawn from this

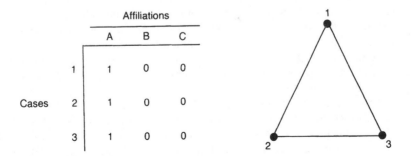

Figure 3.2   *A simple matrix and sociogram*

matrix shows a simple triad of mutual contacts among the individuals. The sociogram can be read as saying that each person meets the other two at a particular event.

It can be quite difficult to construct sociograms for even moderate-sized data sets. Lines will criss-cross one another at all sorts of angles to form a thicket of connections, and any visual appreciation of the structure is lost. Indeed, it may be quite impossible, using conventional manual methods of drawing, to construct a sociogram for a large network. For this reason, social network analysts have attempted to find alternative ways of recording the connections. Following the principle of the data matrix, the solution that has been most widely adopted has been to construct a case-by-case matrix in which each agent is listed twice – once in the rows and once in the columns. The presence or absence of connections between pairs of agents is represented by '1' or '0' entries in the appropriate cells of the matrix. This idea is not, perhaps, as immediately comprehensible as the sociogram, and so it is worthwhile spelling it out at greater length.

Figure 3.3 shows the general form of data matrices for social networks. The most general form for raw or coded data is what I have called the case-by-affiliation matrix, in which agents are shown in the rows and their affiliations in the columns. Such a matrix is described as being two-mode or 'rectangular', because the rows and columns refer to different sets of data. For this reason, the numbers of rows and of columns in the matrix are generally different.[1] From this basic rectangular data matrix can be derived *two* square, or one-mode matrices. In the case-by-case matrix both the rows and the columns will represent the cases, and the individual cells will show whether or not particular pairs of individuals are related through a common affiliation. This matrix, therefore, shows the actual relations or ties among the agents. It is exactly equivalent to the sociogram in the information that it contains. The second square matrix shows affiliations in both its rows and its columns, with the individual cells showing whether particular pairs of affiliations are linked through common agents. This matrix, the affiliation-by-affiliation matrix, is extremely important in network analysis and can often throw light on important aspects of the social structure that are not apparent from the case-by-case matrix.

Thus, a single rectangular matrix of two-mode data can be transformed into two square matrices of one-mode data.[2] One of the square matrices describes the rows of the original matrix and the other describes its columns. Nothing is added to the original data, the production of the two square matrices is a simple transformation of it. The rectangular matrix and the two square matrices are

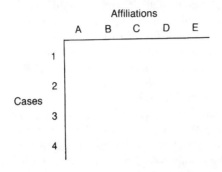

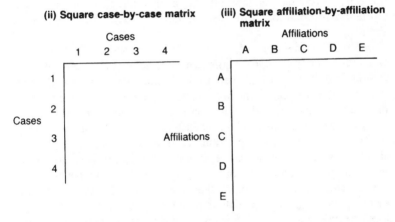

Figure 3.3 *Matrices for social networks*

equivalent ways of representing the same relational data. In social network analysis the rectangular matrix is generally termed an 'incidence' matrix, while the square matrices are termed 'adjacency' matrices. These terms derive from graph theory, and they will be explained more fully in the following chapter. For the moment, it is sufficient merely to know the names, as they are the most generally used terms for relational data matrices. Most techniques of network analysis involve the direct manipulation of adjacency matrices, and so involve a prior conversion of the original incidence matrix into its two constituent adjacency matrices. It is critically important, therefore, that researchers understand the form of their data (whether it is incidence or adjacency data) and the assumptions that underpin particular procedures of network analysis.

In those situations where a researcher collects two-mode data on cases and their affiliations, then, it will generally be most appropriate to organize this information into an incidence matrix from which the adjacency matrices used in network analysis can later be derived. In some situations, however, it will be possible for a researcher to collect relational data in a direct case-by-case form. This would be the situation with, for example, friendship choices made within a small group. In this situation of what is called direct sociometric choice data, the information can be immediately organized in an adjacency matrix. Without entering into all the complications, there is, in this situation, no corresponding incidence matrix and no complementary adjacency matrix of affiliations. The reason for this, of course, is that all the agents have merely a single affiliation in common – the fact of having chosen one another as friends.[3]

For many social network purposes, the distinction between cases and affiliations may appear somewhat artificial. In a study of, say, the involvement of 18 women in 14 social events, it would seem only sensible to regard the women as the cases and the events as their affiliations. Indeed, this would be in line with the normal survey practice of treating the agents as the cases. But with such phenomena as overlapping group memberships, for example, the situation is far less clear-cut. This kind of research is interested in the extent to which a group of organizations overlap in their membership, with how similar they are in their patterns of recruitment. Both the groups and their members are agents in the sociological sense, and so both have an equal right to be considered as the 'cases'. The members may be treated as the cases, in which case the organizations of which they are members will be treated as their affiliations; or the organizations may be treated as cases and the members that they share will be seen as their affiliations. The choice of which set of agents to treat as the cases for the purpose of network analysis will depend simply on which is seen as being the most significant in terms of the research design.

This decision will normally have been reflected in prior sampling decisions. If the organizations are assumed to be of the greatest importance, then a sample of organizations will be selected for study and the only people who will figure in the subsequent analysis will be those who happen to be members of these organizations. In such a research design, the organizations have a theoretical priority and it would seem sensible to treat the members as indicating affiliations between organizations. As far as the techniques of network analysis are concerned, however, it makes no difference which of the two are regarded as the cases. The same procedures may be applied whichever choice is made, and it is the task of the researcher to decide which of them may have a meaningful sociological interpretation.[4]

The distinction between cases and affiliations, therefore, may generally be regarded as a purely conventional feature of research designs for network analysis. A further aspect of this convention is to place the cases on the rows of the incidence matrix and the affiliations on its columns. This is based on the conventions employed in attribute analysis, where the cases are treated as rows and the variables are treated as columns.

If the data matrix is to be used as a basic organizational framework for relational data, certain other conventions must also be understood. These other conventions can be recommended as the basis of best practice in network analysis, as they help to ensure maximum clarity in research discussions. Most readers will be familiar with the importance of conventions in basic mathematics. It is conventional when drawing ordinary graphs of variables, for example, to use the vertical axis for the dependent variable and to label this as the 'y' axis. The horizontal axis is used for the independent variable and is labelled as the 'x' axis. This convention prevents any confusion about how the graph is to be read and it ensures that any statements made about the graph will be unambiguous. The conventions surrounding the relational data matrix have the same purpose.

In the discussion of matrices, it is conventional to designate the number of rows in a matrix as 'm' and the number of columns as 'n'. It is also customary to list the rows first when describing its size. The overall size of a matrix can, therefore, be summarized by referring to it as an $m \times n$ matrix. The incidence matrix of Figure 3.3, for example, is a 4×5 matrix. It is also conventional to refer to the rows before the columns when describing the contents of any particular cell, and to use the letter 'a' to refer to the actual value contained in the cell. Thus, the value contained in the cell corresponding to the intersection of row 3 with column 2 would be designated as $a(3,2)$. This can be generalized by using the convention of referring to the individual rows by 'i' and the columns by 'j'. Thus, the general form for the content of a cell is $a(i,j)$, where the researcher may then go on to specify the relevant values for i and j. These conventions are summarized in Figure 3.4.

The usefulness of the matrix approach to relational data can best be illustrated through a concrete example. Figure 3.5 contains some artificial data on interlocking directorships among companies. An interlocking directorship, or interlock, exists where a particular person sits as a director on the boards of two or more companies.

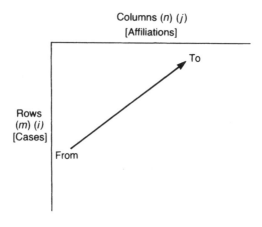

Figure 3.4   *Matrix conventions: best practice*

His or her presence on the two boards establishes a relation between the companies. In many investigations of interlocking directorships, it is the companies that are of central interest. For this reason, they are generally treated as the cases and so they are shown as the rows of the incidence matrix of Figure 3.5. The affiliations, shown in the columns of this matrix, are the directors that the companies have, or do not have, in common with one another. Each cell of the matrix contains a binary digit, '1' or '0', which indicates the presence or absence of each director on each company. Thus, company 1 has four directors (A, B, C and D), and director A sits on the board of company 2 as well as company 1. This means that there is an interlock between company A and company B. Adjacency matrix (ii) in the diagram shows the interlocks that exist among all companies. In this matrix, each cell shows more than the mere presence or absence of an interlock, it shows the number of directors in common between a pair of companies. The cells contain actual values, rather than simply binary digits, because companies may have more than one director in common. Thus, company 1 and company 4 have just one director in common (director C), while companies 2 and 3 have two directors in common (directors B and C). This can be confirmed by examining the columns of the original incidence matrix, which show that director C sits on companies 1 and 4, and that directors B and C each sit on companies 2 and 3.

The simplest kind of analysis of this adjacency matrix might suggest that the strength of a relation can be measured by the *number* of interlocks that it involves. The strongest relations, then, exist between companies 1 and 2 and between companies 1 and 3,

(i) Incidence matrix

Directors

	A	B	C	D	E
Companies 1	1	1	1	1	0
2	1	1	1	0	1
3	0	1	1	1	0
4	0	0	1	0	1

(ii) Adjacency matrix: companies-by-companies

	1	2	3	4
1	–	3	3	1
2	3	–	2	2
3	3	2	–	1
4	1	2	1	–

(iii) Adjacency matrix: directors-by-directors

	A	B	C	D	E
A	–	2	2	1	1
B	2	–	3	2	1
C	2	3	–	2	2
D	1	2	2	–	0
E	1	1	2	0	–

(iv) Sociogram: companies

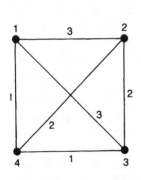

(v) Sociogram: directors

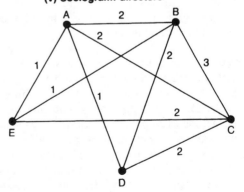

Figure 3.5 *Matrices for interlocking directorships*

each of these relations involving three directors. The weakest links would be those that involve just one director. The sociogram of companies indicates the structure of the matrix quite clearly, with the numbers attached to the lines indicating the strength or 'value' of the lines. This sociogram could equally well have been drawn in other ways: for example, with the thickness of the lines representing their value, or with the points connected by one, two, or three parallel lines. Each method would convey the same information about the structure of the matrix.

It will be recalled that it is possible to derive two adjacency matrices from a single incidence matrix. In this example, it is possible to derive not only the company-by-company adjacency matrix but also a director-by-director adjacency matrix. This matrix and its associated sociogram of directors, in Figure 3.5, show the relations among the directors that exist when they sit on the same company board. There is, for example, a strong relation between B and C, who meet one another on three separate corporate boards (the boards of companies 1, 2 and 3), and rather weaker, single board relations between A and D, between A and E, and between B and E. The sociogram of directors also illustrates such sociometric ideas as that D and E are relatively more 'peripheral' to the network than are the other directors: they have fewer connections, their connections are generally weaker, and they are not connected to one another.

The adjacency matrices shown in Figure 3.5 also illustrate some further general considerations in social network analysis. First, it is important to note something about the diagonal cells running from the top left to the bottom right. In matrix analysis this particular diagonal is referred to simply as 'the diagonal', because the cells are different from all others in the matrix. In a square matrix the diagonal cells show the relation between any particular case and itself. In some situations this is a trivial relation that exists simply by definition, while in others it may be an important feature of the network. The cells on the diagonal of matrix (ii) of Figure 3.5, for example, refer to the relation of each company to itself. In this example, these data would not have any particular meaning. The fact that a company is connected to itself through all its directors is true but trivial, as our concern is with *inter*-company relations. For this reason, the diagonal cells contain no values and should be ignored in the analysis. Many technical procedures in network analysis require the researcher to specify whether diagonal values are to be included or excluded, if this is at all ambiguous. For this reason, researchers must always be aware of the status of the diagonals in their matrices and will need to understand how particular procedures handle the diagonal values.

Figure 3.5 also shows that the adjacency matrices are *symmetrical* around their diagonals: the top half of each matrix is an identical, mirror image of its bottom half. The reason for this is that the data describe an 'undirected' network, a network in which the relation of company 1 to company 2, for example, is the same as the relation of company 2 to company 1. The existence of a relation between the two is considered independently of any question of whether the relation involves the exercise of power and influence in one direction but not in the other. For this reason, all the relational information in an adjacency matrix for an undirected network is contained in the bottom half of the matrix alone; the top half is, strictly speaking, redundant. Many analytical procedures in network analysis, therefore, require only the bottom half of the adjacency matrix and not the full matrix. For undirected networks, no information is lost in this method of analysis.

Undirected data are the simplest and easiest type of relational data to handle, and it is, perhaps, necessary to spend a little time in discussing some of the more complex types of data. One of the most important considerations in variable analysis is the level of measurement that is appropriate for a variable. This is the question of whether attribute data should be measured in nominal, ordinal, ratio, or interval terms. From this decision flow many other decisions about which particular analytical procedures can appropriately be used for the data. Similar measurement problems arise with relational data, according to whether the data are 'directed' and/or 'numbered'. Figure 3.6 uses these two dimensions to classify the four main levels of measurement in relational data.

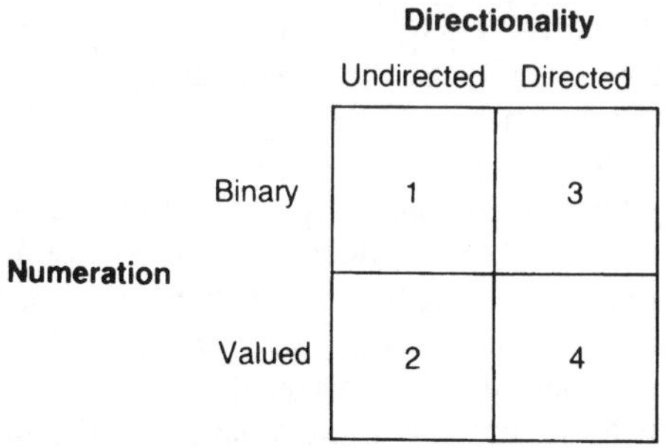

Figure 3.6   *Levels of measurement in relational data*

The simplest type of relational data (type 1) is that which is both undirected and binary. This is the form taken by the data in the incidence matrix of Figure 3.5. The adjacency matrices in that Figure contain relational data of type two: the relations are undirected but valued.[5] I have already shown that the 'valued' data (type 2) in the adjacency matrices of Figure 3.5 are derived from the binary data of the original incidence matrix. Values typically indicate the strength of a relation rather than its mere presence. The signed data that were discussed in the previous chapter in connection with theories of balance, are relational data where a '+' or '−' is attached to each line. These relations can be regarded as intermediate between the binary and valued types. Such data show more than simply the presence or absence of a relation, as the presence is qualified by the addition of a positive or negative sign; but the nature of the relation is indicated simply by the polarity and not by an actual value. It is, of course, possible to combine a sign with a value and to code relational data as varying from, say, −9 to +9. In such a procedure, the value could not represent simply the number of common affiliations between cases, as they cannot have a negative number of affiliations in common. The values must, therefore, be some other measure of the strength or closeness of the relation. Such a procedure would, of course, rest upon a *sociological* argument that produced solid theoretical or empirical reasons for treating the data in this way.

Valued data can always be converted into binary data, albeit with some loss of information, by using a cut-off value for 'slicing' or dichotomizing the matrix. In a slicing procedure, the researcher chooses to consider only those relations with a value above a particular level as being significant. Values above this level are sliced off and used to construct a new matrix in which values at or below this level are replaced by '0' entries and values above it are replaced by '1' entries. This procedure of slicing the data matrix is a very important technique in network analysis, and will be discussed more fully in Chapter 5. Directed data can also take binary or valued forms, and similar slicing procedures can be applied to reduce valued and directed data (type 4) to binary and directed data (type 3). It is also possible to reduce directed data to undirected data, by the simple expedient of ignoring the direction. Thus, a researcher may decide that the important thing to consider is the mere presence or absence of a relation, and not its direction. In this case, then, it makes sense to ignore the directionality of the data. A further matrix convention may appropriately be mentioned at this point. In adjacency matrices that contain directed data, the usual convention is to present the direction of a relation as running 'from' a row element 'to' a column element. Thus, the entry in cell (3,6) of a directed matrix would show the presence or strength of the relation directed *from* person 3 *to* person 6. The relation directed from person 6 to person 3 would be found in cell (6,3). This convention is shown in

Figure 3.4. It is for this reason that a directed matrix is asymmetrical around its diagonal, and that, therefore, the whole matrix must be considered, and not simply its bottom half.

Complex types of relational data can always be reduced to more simple types and, in the last instance, *any* type of relational data may be treated as if it were undirected and binary (type 1). Techniques appropriate to this type of data, therefore, have the widest application of all the techniques of social network analysis. It is not, of course, possible to undertake the reverse operation, converting simple to complex data, unless additional information is available over and above that contained in the original data matrix.[6]

Researchers must always take great care over the nature of their relational data. They must, in particular, be sure that the level of measurement used is sociologically appropriate. The attempt to use valued data in studies of interlocks, for example, rests upon assumptions about the significance of multiple directorships that may or may not be appropriate. It might be assumed, for example, that the *number* of directors in common between two companies is an indicator of the strength or closeness of a relation. Having four directors in common, on this basis, would mean that two companies are 'closer' than those that have only two directors in common. But is this a valid sociological assumption? If it is not, the mathematical procedure should not be used. Mathematics itself cannot provide an answer for the researcher. The relevance of particular mathematical concepts and models is always a matter for the informed sociological judgement of the researcher. Even if it is decided that it is reasonable to use valued data, the researcher must be alive to other assumptions that might be contained in the mathematical procedures. Does a procedure, for example, treat the values as ordinal or as ratio variables? In the former case, a value of four would be regarded simply as being stronger than a value of two; in the latter case the relationship would be regarded as being *twice* as strong. The choice of a level of measurement is, again, a sociological question and not a mathematical one.

The Storage of Relational Data

The analysis of very small data sets is often quite straightforward. An adjacency matrix and sociogram for a four- or five-person group, for example, can easily be constructed by hand. However, this becomes more difficult when the size of the network is any greater than this. When dealing with data sets that have more than about ten cases and five affiliations, it is all but essential to use a computer. Not only does computer processing save a considerable amount of time – the matrix re-arrangement undertaken by Homans in his investigation of the involvement of 18 women in 14 social events, for example, can be undertaken on a computer in a few seconds at most – it also allows analyses to be undertaken that are simply not possible by hand.

If relational data are properly stored, they can be managed and manipulated more efficiently. The need to use computers for network analysis, then, means that it is important to consider how the logical structure of the data matrix can be translated into a computer file. The first step is often to sort names of agents or events in order to generate listings that can be analysed for their connections. Research on interlocking directorships, for example, involves generating a list of directors in the target companies, sorting this into alphabetical order, and then identifying those names that appear two or more times. The most straightforward method for doing this is to use a text editor or word processor to create a data file, as the names can be typed in as text and then sorted and edited. Many word processors will allow data to be sorted into alphabetical or numerical order as an aid to its analysis and manipulation.[7]

The most usual result of this processing is data in 'linked list' format. In a linked list, each line of text in the file shows a case followed by its affiliations. It might show, for example, the name of a director followed by the names of all the companies of which he or she is a director. However, this cannot usually be transformed into an incidence matrix (as shown in Figure 3.3) simply with a word processor. Unless the user wishes to undertake some difficult – and error-prone – manual processing, it is useful to move the data directly into a social network analysis program such as UCINET. In this program, linked list data can be imported and can be invisibly converted to an incidence matrix. The program also allows the new data files to be directly edited in their original linked list format.

The linked list format of UCINET is presented on the screen as a spreadsheet, and a number of data processing tasks can, in fact, be carried out with a spreadsheet program such as EXCEL. Indeed, a spreadsheet can import linked lists directly from a word processor if no social network program is available. While the spreadsheet is, still, widely seen as a financial tool for accountants and stock market analysts, it is essentially an electronic matrix manipulator. Even the simplest of spreadsheets can be used to store and to organize relational data, and they can be used to prepare these data in files readable by many other specialist packages. Suitable spreadsheet programs are so widely available that it is worth considering them as a basic data storage and manipulation system for social network data. If the data have been converted from linked lists to matrices in binary or valued form, the spreadsheet can be used to calculate basic statistical measures, such as row and column sums, frequency distributions, correlations, and so on. Many of these measures can be converted into screen graphics and then printed out. Frequency distributions, for example, can be instantly plotted on a histogram or bar chart. While the major mathematical functions built into spreadsheets are the kind of financial and statistical procedures most appropriate for variable analysis, a number of spreadsheet programs include facilities for matrix mathematics that allow the calculation of various structural properties of networks.[8]

Data stored on a spreadsheet can be manipulated very easily, providing a solution to the practical problems of data preparation that have often plagued network analysis. Virtually all spreadsheets, for example, will allow rows and columns to be sorted into alphabetical or numerical order, automatically re-arranging the corresponding data. The spreadsheet's 'range' options can be used to specify particular parts of a matrix for copying to a new file. If, for example, a matrix of friendship relations among people is stored in a file, it is possible to select the male or the female data alone for separate analysis. It is even possible to transform an incidence matrix into its corresponding adjacency matrices. This kind of use of a spreadsheet, however, is probably best attempted only if other programs specifically designed for social network analysis are not available. The principal use of the spreadsheet should be to store the data and to carry out the straightforward data management functions of re-arrangement and manipulation.[9]

The two most widely used social network packages – UCINET and STRUCTURE – both store their data in simple matrix form, and it is easy to transfer an appropriate file directly from a spreadsheet to either of these packages.[10] For most purposes, it is best to import data into one of the specialist packages as early as possible, reading it back into a spreadsheet only when attribute data have to be added and used in statistical analyses. In these circumstances, in fact, it may be preferable to export the data files to a specialist statistical package such as SPSS.

One of the most powerful network analysis packages is GRADAP, but this program uses data files in a format that is different from the matrix structure discussed so far. GRADAP can exchange data files with SPSS, but it cannot handle direct input of the incidence and adjacency matrices. GRADAP data files can be produced in a spreadsheet or a word processor, or in the SPSS text editor, but the format is less intuitive than the data matrix. GRADAP aims at a complete translation of relational data into the terminology of graph theory, and so requires that there be an explicit identification of the points and lines that comprise the data. Instead of an incidence matrix, GRADAP requires that the adjacency matrices themselves be specified in two separate files: a 'point file' that lists the cases, and a 'line file' that lists each relation. A line is defined by the points at either end of it. Where the researcher has direct sociometric choice data, or where actual patterns of relations are observable in some way, this poses few problems. But where the data exist in linked lists or incidence matrices, it can be quite difficult to produce the necessary files. Even with the help of spreadsheet or database programs, a considerable amount of manual processing is required to produce the GRADAP files.

Line number	Tail	Head	Line info
1	1	2	A
2	1	2	B
3	1	2	C
4	2	3	B
5	2	3	C
6	1	3	B
7	1	3	C
8	1	3	D
9	1	4	C
10	3	4	C
11	2	4	C
12	2	4	E

Figure 3.7   *A GRADAP line file*

Figure 3.7 shows the form of a GRADAP line file for the data contained in the incidence matrix of Figure 3.5. There are 12 interlocking directorships in this network – the total can be confirmed by adding the values in the bottom half of the corresponding adjacency matrix (ii) of Figure 3.5. Each interlock is counted as a separate 'line' for data input to GRADAP, and so the line file contains 12 entries.[11] Each of the 12 lines is identified by the points that lie at its 'tail' and its 'head', and further information about the line (such as the name of the director responsible for it) can be added to the file.[12] A comparison of Figures 3.7 and 3.5 will confirm that the GRADAP line file contains all the information that is contained in the incidence matrix, and this is the reason why GRADAP can, from its line files, invisibly construct the two adjacency matrices.

Once a GRADAP file structure has been created, the program offers powerful data management facilities, acting almost like a specialist database management system for relational data. However, the program requires a thorough knowledge of graph theory if it is to be used for even the simplest of analyses. For the newcomer and the occasional network analyst, therefore, UCINET, together with a word processor, offers the best facilities. For the advanced user who is able to use other programs to generate the line file, GRADAP has many advantages. These programs are discussed more fully in the Appendix.

The Selection of Relational Data

In the first two sections of this chapter I have looked at the nature of relational data and at how it can be organized and managed for network analysis. Having clarified the ways in which the collected data can be organized and stored, it is possible to examine some remaining issues concerning the data collection process. I have argued that few distinct problems arise in this area, but the question of the *selection* of data is one that does pose considerable problems for social network analysis. These selection problems concern the boundedness of social relations and the possibility of drawing relational data from samples.

A common strategy in the study of small scale social networks has been to identify all the members of a particular group and to trace their various connections with one another. But this is a far from straightforward matter. Social relations are social constructs, produced on the basis of the definitions of the situation made by group members. A relation of 'close friendship', for example, may mean different things to different people, according to their conceptions of what it means to be 'close'. The researcher who simply asks respondents to identify their 'close friends' cannot be sure that all respondents will have the same understanding of 'closeness'. Respondents with a restrictive definition of closeness will draw narrow boundaries around themselves, while those with a more inclusive conception of friendship will recognize more extensive boundaries. The very boundaries of the group of close friends, therefore, will vary from one person to another. Any boundaries identified by the researcher through an aggregation of these individual perceptions may be wholly artificial – simple artefacts of question wording. If, on the other hand, the researcher explicitly defines 'close' – by, for example, frequency of interaction – he or she will be imposing a definition of closeness on the respondents and the boundaries of friendship may, again, be artificial.

This issue is important, as researchers often have unrealistic views about the boundaries of relational systems (Laumann et al., 1989). It is often assumed that the social relations of individuals will be confined to the particular group or locale under investigation. To the extent that connections outside this locale are ignored, the social network studied will be an imperfect representation of the full network. This is especially clear in the case of informal groups, such as street gangs, where the boundaries of the group are loosely drawn and where gang members' activities stretch well beyond its core membership (Yablonsky, 1962). But the same is also true for more formal groups. Kerr and Fisher (1957), for example, discussed the 'plant sociology' that focuses its attention on the physical boundaries of particular workshops and offices in isolation from the wider economy. Such investigations isolate their research locale from the larger regional, national and international systems in which they are embedded. Research that is confined to the local work situation may fail to identify those relations that extend beyond the plant.

In a similar vein, Stacey (1969) has criticized locality studies for their assumption that bonds of 'communal' solidarity are confined within the local social system. She holds that they must be seen as stretching out to entwine with the larger economic and political systems. Similarly, Laumann et al. (1983: 31) have argued that a locality study of the flow of money through a network ought not to limit its attention to that geographical locality. Many of the most important agencies in the circulation of money will lie outside the locality: federal government agencies, regional and national banks, multinational companies, and so on. If, as is likely, these are more important to the flow of money than are the local organizations and agencies, a locality-based research project faces the possibility of a totally inadequate view of the structure of the relevant network of transactions.

What these problems point to is the fact that the determination of network boundaries is not simply a matter of identifying the apparently natural or obvious boundaries of the situation under investigation. Although 'natural' boundaries may, indeed, exist, the determination of boundaries in a research project is the outcome of a theoretically informed decision about what is *significant* in the situation under investigation. A study of political relations, for example, must recognize that what counts as 'political', how this is to be distinguished from 'economic', 'religious' and other social relations, and the choice of boundaries for the relevant political unit, are all theoretically informed decisions. Researchers are involved in a process of conceptual elaboration and model building, not a simple process of collecting pre-formed data.

Assuming that relevant boundaries can be identified, the research may proceed to define the target population for study. Two general approaches to this task have been identified: the 'positional' and the 'reputational' approaches.[13] In the **positional approach**, the researcher samples from among the occupants of particular formally defined positions or group memberships. First, the positions or groups that are of interest are identified, and then their occupants or members are sampled. Unless the population under investigation is very small, this is likely to require some kind of enumerated list that covers the whole of the target population. Examples of this kind of strategy would be samples drawn from a school class, a village, a workgroup, or from institutions such as a political elite or corporate directorate. A familiar problem with positional studies is that of determining which positions to include. Studies of elites, for example, have often been criticized for their identification of top positions in institutional hierarchies, especially when the researcher offers no real justification for the cut-off threshold used to distinguish the 'top' from other positions in the institutional hierarchy. This problem is, of course, a reflection of the general boundary problem that has already been discussed, and it is important that researchers have theoretically and empirically justifiable reasons for the inclusion or exclusion of particular positions.

This sometimes involves an assumption that there are 'natural' sub-groups within the population. Research on business interlocks, for example, has often focused attention on the 'top 250' companies in an economy.[14] This research strategy involves the assumption that the division between the 250th and the 251st company forms a natural boundary between large-scale and medium-scale business. However, such boundaries can rarely be drawn with precision. There is a continuous gradation in size from large to small, and, while it may be possible to identify the points in the size distribution at which the gradient alters, it will not generally be possible to draw sharp boundaries. Indeed, most such research does not examine the overall size distribution for shifts of gradient, but simply uses an arbitrary and *a priori* cut-off threshold: while some researchers investigate the top 250, others investigate the top 50, top 100, or top 500 slices of the distribution.[15]

In the positional approach the selection of cases for investigation may sometimes follow from an earlier decision about the selection of affiliations. A directorship, for example, can be regarded as a person's affiliation with a company, and a researcher may already have decided to limit attention to a particular group of companies. In such a situation, the selection of directors for study is determined by the selection criteria used for the companies.[16]

The **reputational approach** can be used where there are no relevant positions, where there is no comprehensive listing available, or where the knowledge of the agents themselves is crucial in determining the boundaries of the population. In the reputational approach, the researcher studies all or some of those named on a list of nominees produced by knowledgeable informants. Those included on the list are those who are reputed to be the members of the target population. The informants are asked to nominate, for example, 'powerful members of the community', 'people of high standing in business', and so on, depending on the purposes of the research, and these nominations are combined into a target population. The choice of informants is, obviously, of crucial importance in the reputational approach. The researcher must have good reasons to believe that the informants will have a good knowledge of the target population and are able to report this accurately. Whether or not this is the case will often be known only when the research has been completed, and so there is an element of circularity in the strategy. For this reason, researchers ought to endeavour to come up with theoretical and empirical reasons for the choice of informant which are, so far as is possible, independent of the particular social relations under investigation.

This will not always be possible, and one particular variant of this reputational strategy, using the so-called 'snowballing' technique, follows exactly the opposite procedure. In this approach, a small number of informants are studied and each is asked to nominate others for study. These nominees are, in turn, interviewed and are asked for further nominations. As this procedure continues, the group of interviewees builds up like a snowball. Eventually, few additional nominees are identified in each round of interviews. In the snowballing method, the social relation itself is used as a chain of connection for building the group. By its very nature, however, a snowball sample is likely to be organized around the connections of the particular individuals who formed its starting point. For this reason, the method of selection tends to determine many of the relational features of the resulting social network. This network is built from the relations of a group of connected agents and, as Laumann et al. remark, 'it is scarcely informative to learn that a network constituted by a snowball sampling procedure is well-connected' (1983: 22).

A final strategy of selection, neither positional nor reputational, occurs when the columns of the incidence matrix are true affiliations and the researcher aims to select these separately from the cases. Such research would be concerned with choosing, say, the activities and events in which people are involved, independently of any positions or organizations that may have been used to identify the people themselves. In his study of New Haven, for example, Dahl (1961) used participation in the making of key decisions as the basis of selection. Involvement in decision-making, therefore, was seen as an 'affiliation' for which people could be given a binary or numeric value independently of whatever organizational positions they held. This allowed Dahl, or so he believed, to assess the relative power of different categories of agents, instead of assuming that power was an automatic correlate of position. A similar strategy was that of Davis (1941) and his colleagues in *Deep South*, where social events were studied, resulting in a matrix showing the participation of 18 women in 14 events. The problem in this kind of strategy, of course, is that of how to justify the choice of affiliations: have the most important events been chosen, and what is a 'key issue'? Selection of true affiliations, therefore, involves precisely the same problems as the direct selection of cases. Activities and events can be chosen because they are regarded as objectively significant (a variant of the positional approach) or because knowledgeable informants believe them to be important (a variant of the reputational approach).

I have written so far mainly of the selection of whole populations through complete or quasi-enumeration. But it may often be necessary to use sample data, and these matters become more complicated. Few sampling problems arise in small group studies, where it is generally possible to undertake a complete enumeration of all group members and of their relations with one another. When research on large-scale social systems is being undertaken, however, a complete enumeration may not be a viable aim, and there will be particularly intractable sampling problems. The sheer scale of the resources needed will often preclude the complete enumeration of large populations, but, even if such research proved possible – for example, in a census of population – the scale of the resulting data matrix would make any analysis impossible. As square adjacency matrices must be constructed before most network analyses can be undertaken, the data matrices can be quite enormous. Attribute data for, say, 1000 cases and 50 variables would involve 50,000 entries in a data matrix. Advances in computing have made such matrices relatively easy to handle for most statistical purposes. In the case of relational data, however, the case-by-case adjacency matrix for 1000 cases would contain 1,000,000 cells. In the case of a fairly small village with a population of 5,000 people, the adjacency matrix would contain 25,000,000 cells, which is beyond the capacity of most available computers and software.[17] For a national population running into the millions, the sheer quantity of data can hardly be imagined, and the computing power required to handle this simply does not exist outside the realms of science fiction.

It was, of course, similar problems that, in the pre-computer age, led to the development of sampling techniques that would allow, say, a sample of 1000 to be used instead of a complete enumeration of a population of many thousands. The statistical theory of sampling sets out the conditions under which attribute data collected from a sample of cases can be generalized into estimates for larger populations. It might be assumed, therefore, that sampling from large populations would provide a similar workable solution for social network analysis. Figure 3.8 gives a schematic account of the ideal sampling process in social network analysis. A particular population of agents will be involved in a complex system of social relations of all types that make up the total network. Within this relational system, sociologists may identify such 'partial' networks as those comprising economic relations, political relations, religious relations, and so on. When a strategy of complete enumeration is followed, the researcher can attempt to ensure that full information is obtained on all the relevant relations, and so can construct adequate models of the partial networks.

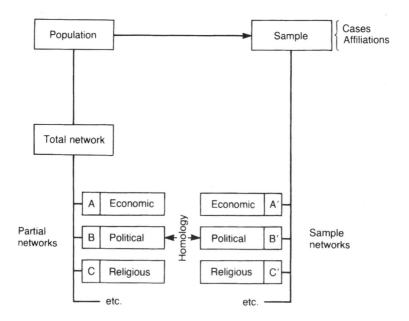

Figure 3.8 *Networks and sampling: the ideal*

The task of sampling would appear to be obvious and straight-forward, involving nothing more than the general principles of sampling in survey research: a representative sample of cases is drawn from the population in question, their relations are investigated, and sample networks are constructed that will be homologous to the partial systems that occur in the population as a whole. But things are not, in fact, as simple as this. The general principles of sampling are based on the application of the theory of probability to large numbers of observations, and there are well-established mathematical rules for judging the reliability of sample data. There are no such rules for judging the quality of relational data derived from a sample; and there are good reasons for assuming that sampling may result in unreliable data. Although it is possible to draw a sample of 1000 cases for analysis and it might be possible to find a computer and program capable of handling a 1000 × 1000 adjacency matrix, there is no guarantee that the structure of this sample network would bear any relationship to the structure of the corresponding partial network. A representative sample of *agents*, does not, in itself, give a useful sample of *relations* (Alba, 1982: 44).

It might seem, at first sight, that this is not a real problem. The overall distribution of relations among agents and their 'density',[18] for example, might seem an easy matter to estimate from sample data: the sample provides data on the network attributes of the individual cases, and these can be used to calculate overall network parameters. The density of the friendship ties in a country, for example, could be assessed by asking a random sample of people how many friends they have. If the sample is large enough, these estimates ought to be reliable. But it is almost impossible to go beyond such basic parameters to measure the more qualitative aspects of network structure.

The reasons for this relate to the sparsity of the relational data that can be obtained from a sample survey of agents. Even if there was a perfect response rate and all respondents answered all the questions in full, many of the contacts named by respondents will not themselves be members of the sample. This means that the number of relations among members of the sample will be a very small sub-set of all their relations, and there is no reason to believe that the relations identified among the agents in the sample would themselves be a random sample of *all* the relations of these same agents. With a very large population, such as that of a national study, it is very unlikely that *any* member of a random sample will have any kind of social relation with others in the same sample. The probability of a connection existing between two individuals drawn at random from a population of many millions is so low as to be negligible. It is, therefore, unlikely that a researcher could say anything at all about the relational structure of the national population from a random sample. Burt (1983a) has made a rough estimate that the amount of relational data lost through sampling is equal to $(100 - k)$ per cent, where k is the sample size as a percentage of the population. Thus, he argues that a 10 per cent sample involves the loss of 90 per cent of the relational data – even a massive 50 per cent sample would involve the loss of half of the data. Such a loss of data makes the identification of cliques, clusters and a whole range of other structural features virtually impossible in conventional sample research.

Sample data can also lead to difficulties in arriving at basic measures of the relational attributes of the particular individuals studied, especially if there is any amount of non-response in the survey. Imagine, for example, an attempt to estimate the sociometric popularity of agents in a network in which there is a very small number of very popular agents and a much larger number of less popular ones.[19] Because they exist in very small numbers, a sample is unlikely to include sufficient of the very popular agents to allow any generalizations to be made about the overall patterns of popularity in the network. This is akin to the problem of studying a small elite or dominant class through a national random sample survey. Unless the sample is very large indeed, they will not appear in adequate numbers, and a very large sample defeats much of the point of sampling. One way around this, of course, might be to use a stratified sample, in which popular agents have a higher probability of selection. The obvious difficulty with this, however, is that such a sampling strategy could be implemented only if the researcher already knew something about the distribution of popularity in the population.

There seem, at present, to be three different responses to these sampling problems. The first is to abandon any attempt to measure the global properties of social networks and to restrict attention to personal, ego-centric networks. This research strategy involves looking at the unrestricted choices that people make, including those to others not included in the sample, and calculating, for example, the density and certain other ego-centric features of their contacts. As no attempt is made to generalize about, for example, the density or 'close knit' texture of the overall network, sampling poses few difficulties other than those that arise in any kind of social research. This is the strategy used in studies of friendship and community undertaken by Wellman (1979), Fischer (1982) and Willmott (1986, 1987).

The second response is to use a form of snowballing. Frank (1978a, 1979) argues that researchers should draw an initial sample of cases and then collect information on all the contacts of the sample members, regardless of whether these are members of the original sample. These contacts are added to the sample and their contacts are discovered in the same way. By extending this process through a number of stages, more and more of the indirect contacts of the members of the initial sample will be discovered. The researcher must decide how far to continue this snowballing. This will generally be to the point at which the number of additional members added to the sample drops substantially, because names that have already been included are being mentioned for the second or third time. Frank has shown that such a snowballing method allows a reasonable estimate to be made of such things as the distribution of contacts and the numbers of dyads and triads. A snowball sample, of course, is not a random sample: the structure that is discovered is, in fact, 'built in' to a snowball sampling method itself. But this is precisely what is necessary in order to avoid the sparsity of connections found in a random sample. The assumption of the snowball sampling method is that the connected segment of the network that forms the sample network is representative of all other segments of the network. The researcher, then, must have some knowledge about the population and their relations in order to make this assessment of representativeness. But snowballing does, at the very least, make it possible to try to estimate which features of the structure may be an artefact of the sampling method itself and so to control for these in the analysis.[20]

The third response to the sampling problem is that of Burt (1983a), who has suggested a way of moving on to some of the more qualitative features of social networks. In particular, Burt is concerned with the identification of 'positions' or structural locations, such as roles. If it is assumed that agents in a similar structural location in a network will have various social attributes in common, then it is possible to use survey data on the typical relations between agents with particular attributes as a way of estimating what structural locations might exist in the network. From each respondent it is necessary to obtain information about their social attributes and the attributes of those to whom they are connected (including people outside the sample). Agents can then be grouped into sets of agents with commonly occurring combinations of attributes, and these sets can be arranged into a sets-by-sets square matrix that shows the frequency of relations between members of the various categories. It might be discovered, for example, that 70 per cent of white men have black male friends, while only 20 per cent of white women have black male friends. Such measures, argues Burt, provide estimates of the valued relations between social 'roles' that could be expected to occur if the researcher had undertaken a complete enumeration of all men and women in the population.

There are glimmers of what can be achieved in the study of large scale social systems using sampling methods. Though it might seem, at present, impossible to discover anything about such things as cliques and clusters from sample data, it is to be hoped that further advances in the techniques of network sampling will make this possible (Alba, 1982: 46; Frank, 1988).

4
Points, Lines and Density

In the previous chapter I looked at the ways in which relational data can be handled and managed in matrix form. Many fundamental features of social networks can be analysed through the direct manipulation of matrices – the transposing, adding and multiplying of matrices all yield information on their structure. Matrix algebra, however, is rather complex for most researchers (but see Meek and Bradley, 1986). Although matrices are useful for the organization and storage of relational data, specialist computer programs allow an easier and more direct approach to network analysis. The available packages implement a variety of analytical procedures, and any user of the programs must have some understanding of how they work.

A common framework for social network analysis programs is the mathematical approach of graph theory, which provides a formal language for describing networks and their features. Graph theory offers a translation of matrix data into formal concepts and theorems that can be directly related to the substantive features of social networks. If the sociogram is one way of representing relational matrix data, the language of graph theory is another, and more general, way of doing this. While it is not the only mathematical theory that has been used for modelling social networks, it is a starting point for many of the most fundamental ideas of social network analysis.

It is the concepts of graph theory which figure as the principal procedures in the UCINET and GRADAP programs, though the readily accessible computer programs endeavour to keep as much of the mathematics as possible hidden from the user. Data in matrix form can be read by the programs, and suitable graph theoretical concepts can be explored without the researcher needing to know anything at all about the mechanics of the theory or of matrix algebra. Nevertheless, an understanding of graph theory will significantly help to improve the sophistication of a researcher's analyses, by ensuring that he or she chooses *appropriate* procedures. Indeed, GRADAP's data structure and management procedures require an understanding of basic graph theoretical ideas.

Graph theory concerns sets of elements and the relations among these, the elements being termed **points** and the relations **lines**.[1] Thus, a matrix describing the relations among a group of people can be converted into a graph of points connected by lines. A sociogram, therefore, is a 'graph'. So far, this should be very familiar from what has already been discussed in Chapters 2 and 3. It is important to be clear about the difference between this idea of a 'graph' and the graphs of variables used in statistics and other branches of quantitative mathematics. These more familiar graphs – we might term them 'graphs of variables' – plot, for example, frequency data on axes that represent the variables. The graphs of graph theory – 'graphs of networks' – express the qualitative patterns of connection among points. Indeed, graph diagrams themselves are of secondary importance in graph theory. As has already been suggested, it is often very difficult to draw a clear and comprehensible diagram for large sets of points with complex patterns of connection. By expressing the properties of the graph in a more abstract mathematical form, it is possible to dispense with the need to draw a sociogram and so make it easier to manipulate very large graphs.

Nevertheless, the drawing of graph diagrams has always been of great illustrative importance in graph theory, and many others will be used in this book. Because of the visual simplicity of small sociograms, I will begin with an introduction to the principles involved in drawing graph diagrams before going on to introduce the basic concepts of graph theory.

Sociograms and Graph Theory

A graph diagram[2] aims to represent each row or column in an incidence matrix – each of the cases or affiliations under investigation – by a point on the paper. Once the appropriate adjacency matrix has been derived, the '1' and '0' entries in the cells of the matrix, representing the presence or absence of a relation, can be indicated by the presence or absence of lines between the points. In Figure 3.5, for example, the symmetrical 4×4 adjacency matrix of companies can be drawn as a four-point graph containing six lines, which correspond to the non-zero entries in the matrix.

In a graph, it is the *pattern* of connections that is important, and not the actual positioning of the points on the page. The graph theorist has no interest in the relative position of two points on the page, the lengths of the lines that are drawn between them, or the size of character used to indicate the points. Graph theory does involve concepts of length and location, for example, but these do not correspond to those concepts of physical length and location with which we are most familiar. It is usual in a graph diagram to draw all the lines with the same physical length, wherever this is possible, but this is a purely aesthetic convention and a matter of practical convenience. Indeed, it is not always possible to maintain this convention if the graph is to be drawn with any clarity. For this reason, there is no one correct way to draw a graph. The graph diagrams in Figure 4.1, for example, are equally valid ways of drawing the same graph – all convey exactly the same graph theoretical information.

The concepts of graph theory, then, are used to describe the pattern of connections among points. The simplest of graph theoretical concepts refer to the properties of the individual points and lines from which a graph is constructed, and these are the building blocks for more complex structural ideas. In this chapter I will review these basic concepts and show how they can be used to give an overview of both the ego-centric and the global features of networks. Subsequent chapters will explore some of the more complex concepts.

It is necessary first to consider the types of lines that can be used in the construction of graphs. Lines can correspond to any of the types of relational data distinguished in Figure 3.6: undirected, directed, valued, or both directed and valued. The graphs in Figure 4.1 consist of undirected lines. These graphs derive from a sym-metrical data matrix where it is simply the presence or absence of a relation that is of importance. If the relations are directed from one agent to another, then they can be represented in a **directed graph**, sometimes termed a 'digraph'. A directed graph is represented in drawn form by attaching an arrow head to each line, the direction of the arrow indicating the direction of the relation. Figure 4.2 shows a simple directed graph.

If, on the other hand, the intensity of the relation is an important consideration and can be represented by a numerical value, the researcher can construct a **valued graph** in which numerical values are attached to each of the lines. I have already shown that a matrix for a directed graph will not usually be symmetrical, as relations will not normally be reciprocated. A matrix for a valued graph may or may not be symmetrical, but it will contain values instead of simple binary entries.[3] An example of a valued graph is that in Figure 3.5. One of the simplest and most widely used measures of intensity is the **multiplicity** of a line. This is simply the number of separate contacts which make up the relationship. If, for example, two companies have two directors in common, the relation between the companies can be represented by a line of multiplicity 2. If they

(i) Adjacency matrix

	A	B	C	D	E	Row sum
A	–	1	0	0	1	2
B	1	–	1	1	1	4
C	0	1	–	1	0	2
D	0	1	1	–	0	2
E	1	1	0	0	–	2
Column sum	2	4	2	2	2	

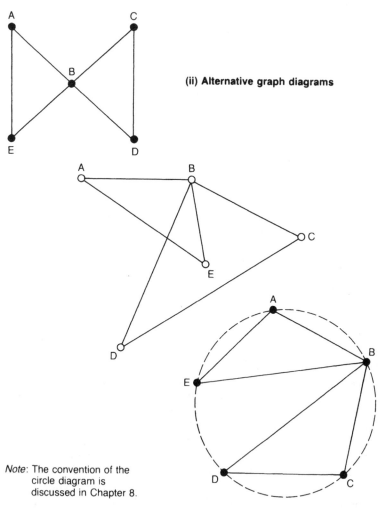

(ii) Alternative graph diagrams

Note: The convention of the circle diagram is discussed in Chapter 8.

Figure 4.1   *Alternative drawings of a graph*

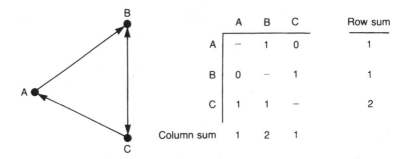

Figure 4.2 *A directed graph and its matrix*

have three directors in common, the interlocking directorship can be seen as a line of multiplicity 3. The values in a graph can, of course, relate to any other suitable measure of intensity, such as, for example, the frequency of the relation.

The fundamental ideas of graph theory can most easily be understood in relation to simple undirected and un-valued graphs. A number of apparently straightforward words are used to refer to graph theoretical terms, and it may appear pedantic to define these at great length. But these definitional matters are important, as the apparently simple words are used in highly specific and technical ways. It is essential that their meanings are clarified if the power of graph theory is to be understood.

Two points that are connected by a line are said to be **adjacent** to one another. Adjacency is the graph theoretical expression of the fact that two agents represented by points are directly related or connected with one another. Those points to which a particular point is adjacent are termed its **neighbourhood**, and the total number of other points in its neighbourhood is termed its **degree** (strictly, its 'degree of connection'). Thus, the degree of a point is a numerical measure of the size of its neighbourhood. The degree of a point is shown by the number of non-zero entries for that point in its row or column entry in the adjacency matrix. Where the data are binary, as in Figure 4.1, the degree is simply the row or column sum for that point.[4] Because each line in a graph connects two points – it is 'incident' to two points – the total sum of the degrees of all the points in a graph must equal twice the total number of lines in the graph. The reason for this is that each line is counted twice when calculating the degrees of the separate points. This can be confirmed by examining Figure 4.1. In this graph, point B has a degree of 4 and all the other points have a degree of 2. Thus, the sum of the degrees is 12, which is equal to twice the number of lines (six).

Points may be directly connected by a line, or they may be indirectly connected through a sequence of lines. A sequence of lines in a graph is a 'walk', and a walk in which each point and each line are distinct is called a **path**. The concept of the path is, after those of the point and the line, one of the most basic of all graph theoretical concepts. The **length** of a path is measured by the number of lines that make it up. In Figure 4.1, for example, points A and D are not directly connected by a line, but they are connected through the path ABD, which has a length of 2. A particularly important concept in graph theory is that of 'distance', but neither distance nor length correspond to their everyday physical meanings. The length of a path, I have said, is simply the number of lines it contains – the number of 'steps' necessary to get from one point to another. The **distance** between two points is the length of the shortest path (the 'geodesic') that connects them.

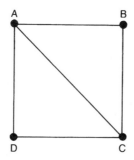

Figure 4.3   *Lines and paths*

Consider the simple graph in Figure 4.3. In this graph, AD is a path of length 1 (it is a line), while ABCD is a path of length 3. The walk ABCAD is not a path, as it passes twice through point A. It can be seen that points A and D are connected by three distinct paths: AD at length 1, ACD at length 2, and ABCD at length 3.[5] The distance between A and D, however, is the length of the shortest path between them, which, in this case, is 1. The distance between points B and D, on the other hand, is 2. Many of the more complex graph theoretical measures take account only of geodesics – shortest paths – while others consider all the paths in a graph.

These same concepts can be used with directed graphs, though some modifications must be made to them. In a directed graph, lines are directed to or from the various points. Each line must be considered along with its direction, and there will not be the symmetry that exists in simple, undirected relational data. The fact that, for example, A chooses B as a friend does not mean that there will be a matching friendship choice from B to A. For this reason, the 'degree' of a point in a directed graph comprises two distinct elements, called the 'indegree' and the 'outdegree'. These are defined by the direction of the lines that represent the social relations. The **indegree** of a point is the total number of other points that have lines directed towards it; and its **outdegree** is the total number of other points to which it directs lines. The indegree of a point, therefore, is shown by its column sum in the matrix of the directed graph, while its outdegree is shown by its row sum. The column sum of point B in Figure 4.2, for example, is 2, as it 'receives' two lines (from A and from C). The corresponding sociogram shows clearly that its indegree is 2. The row sum for B, on the other hand, is 1, reflecting the fact that it directs just one line, to point C.

A path in a directed graph is a sequence of lines in which all the arrows point in the same direction. The sequence CAB in Figure 4.2, for example, is a path, but CBA is not: the changing direction of the arrows means that it is not possible to 'reach' A from C by passing through B.[6] It can be seen that the criteria for connection are much stricter in a directed graph, as the researcher must take account of the direction of the lines rather than simply the presence or absence of a line. The distance between two points in a directed graph, for example, must be measured only along the paths that can be identified when direction is taken into account. When agents are regarded as either 'sources' or 'sinks' for the 'flow' of resources or information through a network, for example, it is sensible to take serious account of this directional information in analysing the graph of the network. Sometimes, however, the direction of the lines can legitimately be ignored. If it *is* the mere presence or absence of a line that is important, its direction being a relatively unimportant factor, it is possible to relax the usual strict criteria of connection and to regard any two points as connected if there is a sequence of lines between them, regardless of the directions of the arrows. In such an analysis it is usual to speak of the presence of a 'semi-path' rather than a path. CBA in Figure 4.2 is a semi-path. Treating directed data as if they were undirected, therefore, means that all the usual measures for undirected data may then be used.

Density: Ego-centric and Socio-centric

One of the most widely used, and perhaps over-used, concepts in graph theory is that of 'density'. This describes the general level of linkage among the points in a graph. A 'complete' graph is one in which all the points are adjacent to one another: each point is connected directly to every other point. Such completion is very rare, even in very small networks, and the concept of density is an attempt to summarize the overall distribution of lines in order to measure how far from this state of completion the graph is. The more points that are connected to one another, the more dense will the graph be.

Density, then, depends upon two other parameters of network structure: these are the 'inclusiveness' of the graph and the sum of the degrees of its points. **Inclusiveness** refers to the number of points that are included within the various connected parts of the graph. Put in another way, the inclusiveness of a graph is the total number of points minus the number of isolated points. The most useful measure of inclusiveness for comparing various graphs is the number of connected points expressed as a proportion of the total number of points. Thus, a 20-point graph with five isolated points would have an inclusiveness of 0.75. An isolated point is incident with no lines and so can contribute nothing to the density of the graph. Thus, the more inclusive is the graph, the more dense will it be. Those points that are connected to one another, however, will vary in their degree of connection. Some points will be connected to many other points, while others will be less well connected. The higher the degrees of the points in a graph, the more dense will it be. In order to measure density, then, it is necessary to use a formula that incorporates these two parameters. This involves comparing the actual number of lines present in a graph with the total number of lines that would be present if the graph were complete.

The actual number of lines in a graph is a direct reflection of its inclusiveness and the degrees of its points. This may be calculated directly in small graphs, but in larger graphs it must be calculated from the adjacency matrix. The number of lines in any graph is equal to half the sum of the degrees. In Figure 4.1, as I have already shown, half the sum of the row or column totals is six. The maximum number of lines that could be present in this graph can be easily calculated from the number of points that it contains. Each point may be connected to all except one other point (itself), and so an undirected graph with n points can contain a maximum of $n(n-1)/2$ distinct lines. Calculating $n(n-1)$ would give the total number of pairs of points in the graph, but the number of lines that could connect these points is half this total, as the line connecting the pair A and B is the same as that connecting the pair B and A. Thus, a graph with three points can have a maximum of three lines connecting its points; one with four points can have a maximum of six lines; one with five points can have a maximum of ten lines; and so on. It can be seen that the number of lines increases at a much faster rate than the number of points. Indeed, this is one of the biggest obstacles to computing measures for large networks. A graph with 250 points, for example, can contain up to 31,125 lines.

The **density** of a graph is defined as the number of lines in a graph, expressed as a proportion of the maximum possible number of lines. The formula for the density is

$$\frac{l}{n(n-1)/2}$$

where l is the number of lines present.[7] This measure can vary from 0 to 1, the density of a complete graph being 1. The densities of various graphs can be seen in Figure 4.4: each graph contains four points and so could contain a maximum of six lines. It can be seen how the density varies with the inclusiveness and the sum of the degrees.[8]

No. of connected points	4	4	4	3	2	0
Inclusiveness	1.0	1.0	1.0	0.7	0.5	0
Sum of degrees	12	8	6	4	2	0
No. of lines	6	4	3	2	1	0
Density	1.0	0.7	0.5	0.3	0.1	0

Figure 4.4 *Density comparisons*

In directed graphs the calculation of the density must be slightly different. The matrix for directed data is asymmetrical, as a directed line from A to B will not necessarily involve a reciprocated line directed from B to A. For this reason, the maximum number of lines that could be present in a directed graph is equal to the total number of pairs that it contains. This is simply calculated as $n(n-1)$. The density formula for a directed graph, therefore, is $l/n(n-1)$.

Barnes (1974) has contrasted two approaches to social network analysis. On the one hand is the approach of those who seek to anchor social networks around particular points of reference (e.g., Mitchell, 1969) and which, therefore, advocates the investigation of 'ego-centric' networks. From such a standpoint, the analysis of density would be concerned with the density of links surrounding particular agents. On the other hand, Barnes sees the 'socio-centric' approach, which focuses on the pattern of connections in the network as a whole, as being the distinctive contribution of social network analysis. From this standpoint, the density is that of the overall network, and not simply the 'personal networks' of focal agents. Barnes holds that the socio-centric approach is of central importance, as the constraining power of a network on its members is not mediated only through their direct links. It is the concatenation of indirect linkages, through a configuration of relations with properties that exist independently of particular agents, that should be at the centre of attention.

In the case of an ego-centric approach, an important qualification must be made to the way in which density is measured. In an ego-centric network it is usual to disregard the focal agent and his or her direct contacts, concentrating only on the links that exist among these contacts. Figure 4.5 shows the consequences of this. Sociogram (i) shows a network of five individuals anchored around 'ego'. The sociogram shows ego's direct contacts and the relations that exist among these contacts. There is a total of six lines, and the

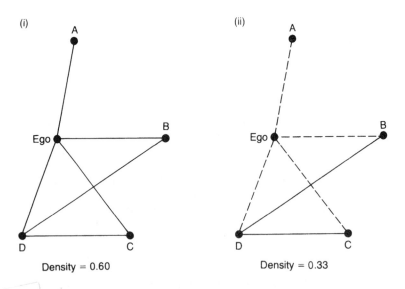

(i)   A   (ii)   A

B   B

Ego   Ego

D   C   D   C

Density = 0.60   Density = 0.33

e 4.5   Ego-centric measures of density

density of the sociogram is 0.60. But the density is at this relatively high level principally because of the four lines that connect ego to A, B, C and D. These relations will exist almost by definition, and should usually be ignored. If these data had, for example, been obtained through a questionnaire that asked respondents to name their four best friends, the high density would be an artifact of the question wording. The relations to the four nominated contacts of each respondent will swamp any information about the relations among those who are named by each respondent. The significant fact about sociogram (i) is that there are relatively *few* connections among ego's own contacts. In sociogram (ii), where ego's direct contacts are shown as dotted lines, there are two relations among A, B, C and D (shown as solid lines), and the four person network has a density of 0.33. It should be clear that this is a more useful measure of the density of the ego-centric network.[9]

It is also possible to use the density measure with valued graphs, though there is very little agreement about how this should be done. The simplest solution, of course, would be to disregard the values of the lines and to treat the graph as a simple directed or undirected graph. This involves a considerable loss of information. It might be reasonable, for example, to see lines with a high multiplicity as contributing more to the density of the graph than lines with a low multiplicity. This would suggest that the number of lines in a valued graph might be weighted by their multiplicities: a line with multiplicity 3 might be counted as being the equivalent of three lines. Simple multiplication, then, would give a weighted total for the actual number of lines in a graph. But the denominator of the density formula is not so easy to calculate for valued graphs. The denominator, it will be recalled, is the maximum possible number of lines that a graph could contain. This figure would need to be based on some assumption about the maximum possible value that could be taken by the multiplicity in the network in question. If the maximum multiplicity is assumed to be 4, then the weighted maximum number of lines would be equal to four times the figure that would apply for a similar unvalued graph. But how might a researcher decide on an estimate of what the maximum multiplicity for a particular relation might be? One solution would be to take the highest multiplicity actually found in the network and to use this as the weighting (Barnes, 1969). There is, however, no particular reason why the highest multiplicity actually found should correspond to the theoretically possible maximum. In fact, a maximum value for the multiplicity can be estimated only when the researcher has some independent information about the nature of the relationships under investigation. In the case of company interlocks, for example, average board size and the number of directorships might be taken as weightings. If the mean board size was five, for example, and it is assumed that no person can hold more than two director- ships, then the mean multiplicity would be 5 in a complete and fully connected graph.

In the case of the company sociogram in Figure 3.5, for example, the weighted total of lines measured on this basis would be 5 times 6, or 30. The actual total of weighted lines in the same sociogram, produced by adding the values of all the lines, is 12, and so the multiplicity-based density would be 12/30, or 0.4. This compares with a density of 1.0 which would be calculated if the data were treated as if they were unvalued. It must be remembered, however, that the multiplicity-based calculation is based on an argument about the assumed maximum number of directorships that a person can hold. If it were assumed that a person could hold a maximum of three directorships, for example, then the density of the company sociogram would fall from 0.4 to 0.2. For other measures of intensity, there is no obvious way of weighting lines.[10]

The density measure for valued graphs, therefore, is highly sensitive to those assumptions that a researcher makes about the data. A measure of density calculated in this way, however, is totally incommensurable with a measure of density for unvalued data. For this reason, it is important that a researcher does not simply use a measure because it is available in a standard program. A researcher must always be perfectly clear about the assumptions that are involved in any particular procedure, and must report these along with the density measures calculated. The problem in handling valued data may be even more complex if the values do not refer to multiplicities.

A far more fundamental problem that affects all measures of density must now be considered. This is the problem of the dependence of the density on the size of a graph, which prevents density measures being compared across networks of different sizes (see Friedkin, 1981; Niemeijer, 1973; Snijders, 1981). Density, it will be recalled, varies with the number of lines that are present in a graph, this being compared with the number of lines that would be present in a complete graph. There are very good reasons to believe that the maximum number of lines achievable in any real graph may be well below the theoretically possible maximum. If there is an upper limit to the number of relations that each agent can sustain, the total number of lines in the graph will be limited by the number of agents. This limit on the total number of lines means that larger graphs will, other things being equal, have lower densities than small graphs. This is linked, in particular, to the time constraints under which agents operate. Mayhew and Levinger (1976) argue that there are limits on the amount of time that people can invest in making and maintaining relations. The time that can be allocated to any particular relation, they argue, is limited, and it will decline as the number of contacts increases. Agents will, therefore, decide to stop making new relations – new investments of time – when the rewards decline and it becomes too costly. The number of contacts that they can sustain, therefore, declines as the size of the network increases. Time constraints, therefore, produce a limit to the number of contacts and, therefore, to the density of the network. Mayhew and Levinger have used models of random choice to suggest that the maximum value for density that is likely to be found in actual graphs is 0.5.[11]

The ability of agents to sustain relations is also limited by the particular kind of relation that is involved. A 'loving' relation, for example, generally involves more emotional commitment than an 'awareness' relation, and it is likely that people can be aware of many more people than they could love. This means that any network of loving relations is likely to have a lower density than any network of awareness relations.

I suggested in Chapter 3 that density was one of the network measures that might reasonably be estimated from sample data. Now that the measurement of density has been more fully discussed, it is possible to look at this suggestion in greater detail. The simplest and most straightforward way to measure the density of a large network from sample data would be to estimate it from the mean degree of the cases included in the sample. With a representative sample of a sufficient size, a measure of the mean degree would be as reliable as any measure of population attributes derived from sample data, though I have suggested in the previous chapter some of the reasons why sample data may fail to reflect the full range of relations. If the estimate was, indeed, felt to be reliable, it can be used to calculate the number of lines in the network. The degree sum – the sum of the degrees of all the points in the graph – is equal to the estimated mean degree multiplied by the total number of cases in the population. Once this sum is calculated, the number of lines is easily calculated as half this figure. As the maximum possible number of lines can always be calculated directly from the total number of points (it is always equal to $n(n-1)/2$ in an undirected graph), the density of the graph can be estimated by calculating

$$\frac{(n \times \text{mean degree})/2}{n(n-1)/2}$$

which reduces to $(n \times \text{mean degree})/n(n-1)$.

Granovetter (1976) has gone further than this and has attempted to provide a method of density estimation that can be used when the researcher is uncertain about the reliability of the initial estimate of the mean degree. In some situations there will be a high reliability to this estimate. With company interlock data, for example, the available directories of company information allow researchers to obtain complete information on the connections of the sample companies to all companies in the population, within the limits of accuracy achieved by the directories. In such circumstances, an estimate of mean degree would be reliable. In studies of acquaintance, on the other hand, such reliability is not normally the case, especially when the population is very large. Granovetter's solution is to reject a single large sample in favour of a number of smaller samples. The graphs of acquaintance in each of the sub-samples (the 'random sub-graphs') can be examined for their densities, and Granovetter shows that an average of the random sub-graph densities results in a reliable estimate of the population network density. Using standard statistical theory, Granovetter has shown that, for a population of 100,000, samples of between 100 and 200 cases will allow reliable estimates to be made. With a sample size of 100, five such samples would be needed; with a sample size of 200, only two samples would be needed.[12] These points have been further explored in field research, which has confirmed the general strategy (Erickson and Nosanchuck, 1983; Erickson et al., 1981).

Density is, then, an easily calculated measure for both undirected and directed graphs, it can be used in both ego-centric and socio-centric studies, and it can reliably be estimated from sample data. It is hardly surprising that it has become one of the commonest measures in social network analysis. I hope that I have suggested, however, some of the limits on its usefulness. It is a problematic measure to use with valued data, it varies with the type of relation and with the size of the graph, and, for this reason, it cannot be used for comparisons across networks that vary significantly in size. Despite these limitations, the measurement of density will, rightly, retain its importance in social network analysis. If it is reported along with such other measures as the inclusiveness and the network size, it can continue to play a powerful role in the comparative study of social networks.

Community Structure and Density

The power and utility of density analysis can be illustrated through some concrete studies. Barry Wellman (1979, 1982), a member of Harrison White's original cohort of network analysts at Harvard, has supervised a large study of community structure, in which density plays a key role. He took as his starting point the long-standing tradition of community studies, in which writers on 'community' were generally concerned to investigate whether the communal solidarities associated with small-scale, rural villages had been able to withstand the modernizing forces of industrialization and urbanization. Wellman wanted to use social network analysis to see whether the development of modern society had resulted in the disappearance of community and the emergence of urban anomie. It had been pointed out by some critics of community studies that social relations of all kinds had become detached from specific localities, with relations having an increasingly national or international scope (see the discussion in Bulmer, 1985). Wellman's research aimed to investigate this issue for a particular urban area in Toronto – East York – and, like Fischer (1977, 1982), he focused on the question of whether 'personal communities' had stretched beyond the bounds of the local neighbourhood itself.

East York is an inner city suburb of private houses and apartment blocks and was, at the time of the research in 1968, occupied mainly by skilled manual workers and routine white collar workers. The fieldwork involved interviews with a random sample of 845 adults, and a central question in the interview asked people to name their six closest associates. They were then asked to say whether those named were themselves close to one another (see also McCallister and Fischer, 1978). The responses to these questions could be used to construct ego-centric networks of intimate association for each respondent. By asking about the connections among the persons who were named by each respondent, Wellman was able to measure the density of each personal network. The calculation of density followed the strategy outlined earlier, and ignored links between respondents and their intimates. That is, data were collected on ego and his or her six intimate associates, but the densities of the ego-centric networks were calculated for the links among the six associates only.

Wellman discovered that many of the intimate associates (about a half) were relatives of the respondents, but kin and non-kin associates were all to be found across a wide geographical area. The majority of all links were with people who lived in the city itself, though very few of these links were based in the immediate locality of East York. A quarter of all the intimate associates who were named lived outside the city, some living overseas. Having made a number of these summary statements about the broad framework of people's social networks, Wellman turned to the densities of these networks. The mean density of the ego-centric personal networks of the respondents was 0.33,[13] only one-fifth of networks having a density greater than 0.50 (Wellman, 1979: 1215). A density of 0.33 meant that five out of the 15 possible links among intimate associates were actually present.[14] Wellman discovered that the densest networks tended to be those that were composed mainly of kin, owing to the fact that it was more likely that the kin of the respondents would maintain mutual contacts. Where kinship obligations were absent, such contacts were less likely to be maintained.

Density	% of networks	% of network members who are kin
0–0.25	47.1	36.4
0.26–0.50	31.7	56.9
0.51–0.75	7.9	56.9
0.76–1.00	13.3	73.7
	100.0	
	(n = 824)	

Figure 4.6   *Density of personal networks*

Wellman's principal findings on personal networks are summarized in Figure 4.6. He interprets these data as indicating that people were involved in networks that were 'sparsely knit' – i.e., networks of low density. 'Communal' links were neither solidaristic nor localized. People had others that they could rely on, but the low density of their personal networks, their lack of mutual cross-linkages, meant that such help was limited. These personal networks were, nevertheless, important sources of help and support, on both an everyday basis and in emergencies: 'East Yorkers can almost always count on help from at least one of their intimates, but they cannot count on such help from most of them' (Wellman, 1979: 1217). Those intimate associates who were less likely to give help and support were more likely to be significant for sociability. Helpers were more likely to be kin, while those who were most important for sociability were more likely to be co-residents or co-workers.

To pursue some further issues, a follow-up study was undertaken in which in-depth interviews were carried out, during 1977–8, with 34 of the original respondents. The aim was to get more 'qualitative' contextual data for the structural data of the earlier study. Although the detailed results of this stage of the inquiry go beyond the immediate concerns of this chapter, some of the directions pursued can usefully be outlined. Wellman discovered that the interpersonal networks of households were differentiated by gender divisions and by the involvement of household members in paid work. The research discovered, for example, a number of differences between households where women were involved in paid employment and those where they were involved only in domestic work. He discovered that the social relations of a household and their access to interpersonal support from their kin, friends, neighbours and co-workers were most likely to be maintained by women rather than by men. This was, in particular, true of households where women were engaged solely in domestic work. Households where women were involved in both domestic work and in paid employment had far less dense networks of relations and were, therefore, able to obtain less support and fewer services from their contacts (Wellman, 1985).[15]

Wellman's investigations used survey analysis to generate the relational data that he used in the study, but similar ideas can be used on other forms of relational data. Smith (1979), for example, used historical data derived from documentary sources to investigate communal patterns in an English village in the thirteenth century. Smith's data came from the records of the manor court of Redgrave in Suffolk, these records showing such things as patterns of landholding, property transactions and financial disputes among the villagers. In total, he considered 13,592 relations among 575 individuals over the period 1259 to 1293. Initially, he analysed the different types of relations and their frequency, which showed that about two-thirds of the relations were 'pledging' relations. These were relations in which one person gave a specific legal commitment in support of another person in relation to debt re-payments and other financial arrangements.

Smith's concern was with the role of kinship and other local ties in organizing these relations and in structuring communal relations. Homans (1941) had previously undertaken a similar historical study of communal solidarity, but had not applied any social network concepts in his study. By contrast, Smith used the idea of the ego-centric network as his principal orientating concept. The 425 Redgrave landholders of the year 1289 were divided into four categories according to the size of their landholdings, and equal-sized random samples were drawn from each category. This gave 112 individuals for analysis, and their documented relations with all other people over the ten-year period from 1283 to 1292 were extracted from the database. The personal, ego-centric networks of the 112 people, taking account of the distance 1 relations, were then analysed in terms of their social bases and geographical spread. The distribution of the densities of the personal networks showed a curvilinear relation to landholding. Density increased steadily with size of landholding among those with four acres of land or less, and it decreased steadily with the size of holding for those with more than four acres. Those with three or four acres, therefore, had the densest personal networks, median density among these households being between 0.2 and 0.4. They were also the most involved in multiplex relations. It was, therefore, the middling landholders who were best integrated into their village community. In the light of the earlier discussion of the relation between network size and density, it is interesting to note that Smith discovered a correlation of just 0.012 between the two measures. He concluded, therefore, that the variations in network density which were observed were not a mere artefact of network size, but reflected real variations in the quality of interpersonal relations.

Taking account of all his network data, Smith rejects the idea of a tightly knit organic community organized around kin and neighbours. The network structure of the medieval village, at least so far as Redgrave was concerned, was much looser than this image. Neither were distant kin an especially important source of social support:

> those individuals who interacted most frequently with near neighbours also interacted most frequently with kin, although probably on most occasions residing apart from them. These kin, however, tended to be close: siblings, uncles, nephews, nieces, fathers and mothers, sons and daughters. (Smith, 1979: 244)

Wellman recognized that the ego-centric networks that he studied in East York were linked into chains of connection through overlapping associations: there was, he held, a 'concatenation of networks' with personal networks being 'strands in the larger metropolitan web' (Wellman, 1979: 1227). But he did not directly investigate these global features of the socio-centric networks of East York. Some pointers to this 'concatenation' are provided in Grieco's (1987) extension of the work of White (1970) and Granovetter (1974). Grieco's research concerned the giving and receiving of information about job opportunities, and she showed that the flow of help from particular individuals to their network contacts produces an alteration in the global structure of the network. Where information is received indirectly, from contacts at a distance of 2 or more, there is a tendency for a new direct link, albeit a weak one, to be established between the originator of the information and those who received it (Grieco, 1987: 108ff.). The overall density of the network, therefore, increases, and some of these links may be solidified and strengthened through feelings of solidarity and obligation. Thus, some of the initial increase in density will persist. When others in the network acquire the ability to reciprocate for the help that they have received they will, in turn, tend to create new direct links and a further alteration in the density of the network. In this way, changes at the individual level of ego-centric contacts result in a continual transformation of the density and the other socio-centric, global features of the network.

5

Centrality and Centralization

The idea of the centrality of individuals and organizations in their social networks was one of the earliest to be pursued by social network analysts. The immediate origins of this idea are to be found in the sociometric concept of the 'star' – that person who is the most 'popular' in his or her group or who stands at the centre of attention. The formal properties of centrality were initially investigated by Bavelas (1950), and, since his pioneering work, a number of competing concepts of centrality have been proposed. As a result of this proliferation of formal measures of centrality, there is considerable confusion in the area. What unites the majority of the approaches to centrality is a concern for the relative centrality of the various points in the graph – the question of so-called 'point centrality'. But from this common concern they diverge sharply. In this chapter I will review a number of measures of point centrality, focusing on the important distinction between 'local' and 'global' point centrality. A point is locally central if it has a large number of connections with the other points in its immediate environment – if, for example, it has a large neighbourhood of direct contacts. A point is globally central, on the other hand, when it has a position of strategic significance in the overall structure of the network. Local centrality is concerned with the relative prominence of a focal point in its neighbourhood, while global centrality concerns prominence within the whole network.

Related to the measurement of point centrality is the idea of the overall 'centralization' of a graph, and these two ideas have sometimes been confused by the use of the same term to describe them both. Freeman's important and influential study (1979), for example, talks of both 'point centrality' and 'graph centrality'. Confusion is most likely to be avoided if the term 'centrality' is restricted to the idea of point centrality, while the term 'centralization' is used to refer to particular properties of the graph structure as a whole. Centralization, therefore, refers not to the relative prominence of points, but to the overall cohesion or integration of the graph. Graphs may, for example, be more or less centralized around particular points or sets of points. A number of different procedures have been suggested for the measurement of centralization, contributing further to the confusion that besets this area. Implicit in the idea of centralization is that of the structural 'centre' of the graph, the point or set of points around which a centralized graph is organized. There have been relatively few attempts to define the idea of the structural centre of a graph, and it will be necessary to give some consideration to this.

Centrality: Local and Global

The concept of point centrality, I have argued, originated in the sociometric concept of the 'star'. A central point was one which was 'at the centre' of a number of connections, a point with a great many direct contacts with other points. The simplest and most straightforward way to measure point centrality, therefore, is by the degrees of the various points in the graph. The degree, it will be recalled, is simply the number of other points to which a point is adjacent. A point is central, then, if it has a high degree; the corresponding agent is central in the sense of being 'well-connected' or 'in the thick of things'. A degree-based measure of point centrality, therefore, corresponds to the intuitive notion of how well connected a point is within its local environment. Because this is calculated simply in terms of the number of points to which a particular point is adjacent, ignoring any indirect connections it may have, the degree can be regarded as a measure of **local centrality**. The most systematic elaboration of this concept is to be found in Nieminen (1974). Degree-based measures of local centrality can also be computed for points in directed graphs, though in these situations each point will have two measures of its local centrality, one corresponding to its indegree and the other to its outdegree. In directed graphs, then, it makes sense to distinguish between the 'in-centrality' and the 'out-centrality' of the various points (Knoke and Burt, 1983).

A degree-based measure of point centrality can be extended beyond direct connections to those at various path distances. In this case, the relevant neighbourhood is widened to include the more distant connections of the points. A point may, then, be assessed for its local centrality in terms of both direct (distance 1) and distance 2 connections – or, indeed, whatever cut-off path distance is chosen. The principal problem with extending this measure of point centrality beyond distance 2 connections is that, in graphs with even a very modest density, the majority of the points tend to be linked through indirect connections at relatively short path distances. Thus, comparisons of local centrality scores at distance 4, for example, are unlikely to be informative if most of the points are connected to most other points at this distance. Clearly, the cut-off threshold which is to be used is a matter for the informed judgement of the researcher who is undertaking the investigation, but distance 1 and distance 2 connections are likely to be the most informative in the majority of studies.

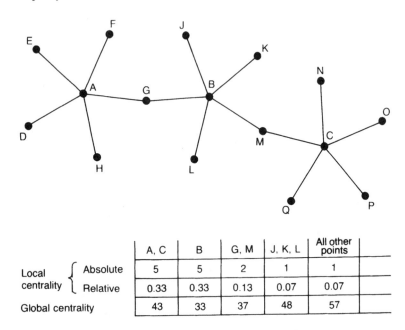

	A, C	B	G, M	J, K, L	All other points	
Local centrality { Absolute	5	5	2	1	1	
Relative	0.33	0.33	0.13	0.07	0.07	
Global centrality	43	33	37	48	57	

Figure 5.1   *Local and global centrality*

It is important to recognize that the measurement of local centrality does not involve the idea that there will be any unique 'central' point in the network. In Figure 5.1, for example, points A, B and C can each be seen as local centres: they each have a degree of 5, compared with degrees of 1 or 2 for all other points. Even if point A had many more direct connections than points B and C it would not be 'the' centre of the network: it lies physically towards one 'side' of the chain of points, and its centrality is a purely 'local' phenomenon. The degree, therefore, is a measure of local centrality, and a comparison of the degrees of the various points in a graph can show how well connected the points are with their local environments.

This measure of local centrality has, however, one major limitation. This is that comparisons of centrality scores can only meaningfully be made among the members of the same graph or between graphs that are the same size. The degree of a point depends on, among other things, the size of the graph, and so measures of local centrality cannot be compared when graphs differ significantly in size. The use of the raw degree score may, therefore, be misleading. A central point with a degree of 25 in a graph of 100 points, for example, is not as central as one with a degree of 25 in a graph of 30 points, and neither can be easily compared with a central point with a degree of 6 in a graph of 10 points. In an attempt to overcome this problem, Freeman (1979) has proposed a *relative* measure of local centrality in which the actual number of connections is related to the maximum number that it could sustain. A degree of 25 in a graph of 100 points, therefore, indicates a relative local centrality of 0.25, while a degree of 25 in a graph of 30 points indicates a relative centrality of 0.86, and a degree of 6 in a graph of 10 points indicates a relative centrality of 0.66.[1] Figure 5.1 shows that relative centrality can also be used to compare points within the same network. It should also be clear that this idea can be extended to directed graphs. A relative measure, therefore, gives a far more standardized approach to the measurement of local centrality.

The problem of comparison that arises with raw degree measures of centrality is related to the problem of comparing densities between different graphs, which was discussed in the previous chapter. Both are limited by the question of the size of the graphs. It will be recalled, however, that the density level also depends on the type of relation that is being analysed. The density of an 'awareness' network, I suggested, would tend to be higher than that of a 'loving' network. Because both density and point centrality are computed from degree measures, exactly the same considerations apply to measures of point centrality. Centrality measured in a loving network, for example, is likely to be lower, other things being equal, than centrality in an awareness network. Relative measures of point centrality do nothing to help with this problem. Even if local centrality scores are calculated in Freeman's relative terms, they should be compared only for networks which involve similar types of relations.

Local centrality is, however, only one conceptualization of point centrality, and Freeman (1979, 1980) has proposed a measure of **global centrality** based around what he terms the 'closeness' of the points. Local centrality measures, whatever path distance is used, are expressed in terms of the number or proportion of *points* to which a point is connected. Freeman's measure of global centrality is expressed in terms of the *distances* among the various points. It will be recalled that two points are connected by a path if there is a sequence of distinct lines connecting them, and the length of a path is measured by the number of lines that make it up. In graph theory, the length of the shortest path between two points is a measure of the distance between them. The shortest distance between two points on the surface of the earth lies along the geodesic that connects them, and, by analogy, the shortest path between any particular pair of points in a graph is termed a 'geodesic'. A point is globally central if it lies at short distances from many other points. Such a point is 'close' to many of the other points in the graph.

The simplest notion of closeness is, perhaps, that calculated from the 'sum distance', the sum of the geodesic distances to all other points in the graph (Sabidussi, 1966). If the matrix of distances between points in an undirected graph is calculated, the sum distance of a point is its column or row sum in this matrix (the two values are the same). A point with a low sum distance is 'close' to a large number of other points, and so closeness can be seen as the reciprocal of the sum distance. In a directed graph, of course, paths must be measured through lines that run in the same direction, and, for this reason, calculations based on row and column sums will differ. Global centrality in a directed graph, then, can be seen in terms of what might be termed 'in-closeness' and 'out-closeness'.

The table in Figure 5.1 compares a sum distance measure of global centrality with degree-based measures of absolute and relative local centrality. It can be seen that A, B and C are equally central in local terms, but that B is more globally central than either A or C. In global terms, G and M are less central than B, but more central than the locally central points A and C. These distinctions made on the basis of the sum distances measure, therefore, confirm the impression gained from a visual inspection of the graph. This is also apparent in the measures for the less central points. All the remaining points have a degree of 1, indicating low local centrality, yet the sum distance measure clearly brings out the fact that J, K and L are more central in global terms than are the other points with degree 1.

Freeman (1979) adds yet a further concept of point centrality, which he terms the **betweenness**. This concept measures the extent to which a particular point lies 'between' the various other points in the graph: a point of relatively low degree may play an important 'intermediary' role and so be very central to the network. Points G and M in Figure 5.1, for example, lie between a great many pairs of points. The betweenness of a point measures the extent to which an agent can play the part of a 'broker' or 'gatekeeper' with a potential for control over others.[2] G could, therefore, be interpreted as an intermediary between the set of agents centred around B and that centred around A, while M might play the same role for the sets of B and C.

Freeman's approach to betweenness is built around the concept of 'local dependency'. A point is dependent upon another if the paths which connect it to the other points pass through this point. Burt (1992) has described this in terms of 'structural holes'. A structural hole exists where two points are connected at distance 2, but not at distance 1. The existence of a structural hole allows the third point to act as a broker or intermediary. In Figure 5.1, for example, point E is dependent on point A for access to all other parts of the graph, and it is also dependent, though to a lesser extent, on points G, B, M and C.

Betweenness is, perhaps, the most complex of the measures of point centrality to calculate. The 'betweenness proportion' of a point Y for a particular pair of points X and Z is defined as the proportion of geodesics connecting that pair which passes through Y – it measures the extent to which Y is 'between' X and Z.[3] The 'pair dependency' of point X on point Y is then defined as the sum of the betweenness proportions of Y for all pairs that involve X. The 'local dependency matrix' contains these pair dependency scores, the entries in the matrix showing the dependence of each row element on each column element. The overall 'betweenness' of a point is calculated as half the sum of the values in the columns of this matrix, i.e., half the sum of all pair dependency scores for the points represented by the columns. Despite this rather complex calculation, the measure is intuitively meaningful, and it is easily computed with the UCINET and GRADAP programs.

In Freeman's work, then, can be found the basis for a whole family of point centrality measures: local centrality (degree), betweenness, and global centrality (closeness). I have shown how comparability between different social networks can be furthered by calculating local centrality in relative rather than absolute terms, and Freeman has made similar proposals for his other measures of centrality. He has produced his own relative measure of betweenness, and he has used a formula of Beauchamp (1965) for a relative closeness measure. All these measures, however, are based on raw scores of degree and distance, and it is necessary to turn to Bonacich (1972, 1987) for an alternative approach which uses weighted scores.

Bonacich holds that the centrality of a particular point cannot be assessed in isolation from the centrality of all the other points to which it is connected. A point that is connected to central points has its own centrality boosted, and this, in turn, boosts the centrality of the other points to which it is connected (Bonacich, 1972). There is, therefore, an inherent circularity involved in the calculation of centrality. According to Bonacich, the local centrality of point i in a graph, c_i, is calculated by the formula $\Sigma_j r_{ij} c_j$, where r_{ij} is the value of the line connecting point i and point j and c_j is the centrality of point j. That is to say, the centrality of i equals the sum of its connections to other points, weighted by the centrality of each of these other points.[4]

Bonacich (1987) has subsequently generalized his initial approach, as did Freeman, to a whole family of local and global measures. The most general formula for centrality, he argued, is $c_i = \Sigma_j r_{ij} (\alpha + \beta c_j)$. In this formula, the centrality weighting is itself modified by the two parameters α and β. α is introduced simply as an arbitrary standardizing constant which ensures that the final centrality measures will vary around a mean value of 1. β, on the other hand, is of more substantive significance. It is a positive or negative value which allows the researcher to set the path distances that are to be used in the calculation of centrality.[5] Where β is set as equal to zero, no indirect links are taken into account, and the measure of centrality is a simple degree-based measure of local centrality. Higher levels of β increase the path length, so allowing the calculation to take account of progressively more distant connections. Bonacich claims that measures based on positive values of β correlate highly with Freeman's measure of closeness.

A major difficulty with Bonacich's argument, however, is that the values given to β are the results of arbitrary choices made by researchers. It is difficult to know what theoretical reasons there might be for using one β level rather than another. While the original Bonacich measure may be intuitively comprehensible, the generalized model is more difficult to interpret for values of β that are greater than zero. On the other hand, the suggestion that the value of β can be either positive or negative does provide a way forward for the analysis of signed graphs. Bonacich himself suggests that negative values correspond to 'zero-sum' relations, such as those involved in the holding of money and other financial resources. Positive values, on the other hand, correspond to 'non-zero-sum' relations, such as those involving access to information.

I have discussed centrality principally in terms of the most central points in a graph, but it should be clear that centrality scores also allow the least central points to be identified. Those points with the lowest centrality, however this is measured, can be regarded as the **peripheral** points of the graph. This is true, for example, for all the points in Figure 5.1 that have degree 1. They are locally peripheral in so far as they are loosely connected into the network. The global centrality scores in Figure 5.1, however, show that points J, K and L are not as globally peripheral as the other points with degree 1.

Centralization and Graph Centres

I have concentrated, so far, on the question of the centrality of particular points. But it is also possible to examine the extent to which a whole graph has a centralized structure. The concepts of density and centralization refer to differing aspects of the overall 'compactness' of a graph. Density describes the general level of cohesion in a graph; centralization describes the extent to which this cohesion is organized around particular focal points. Centralization and density, therefore, are important complementary measures.

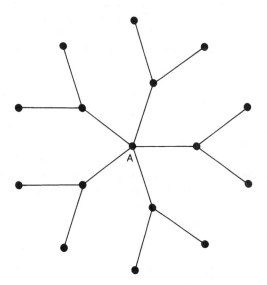

Figure 5.2 *A highly centralized graph*

Figure 5.2 shows a simplified model of a highly centralized graph: the whole graph is organized, in important respects, around point A as its focal point. How is this level of centralization to be measured? Freeman (1979) has shown how measures of point centrality can be converted into measures of the overall level of centralization that is found in different graphs. A graph centralization measure is an expression of how tightly the graph is organized around its most central point. Freeman's measures of centralization are attempts to isolate the various aspects of the simplified notion of centralization. On this basis, he identifies three types of graph centralization, rooted in the varying conceptions of point centrality that he has defined. The general procedure involved in any measure of graph centralization is to look at the differences between the centrality scores of the most central point and those of all other points. **Centralization**, then, is the ratio of the actual sum of differences to the maximum possible sum of differences. The three different ways of operationalizing this general measure that Freeman discusses follow from the use of one or other of the three concepts of point centrality. Freeman (1979) shows that all three measures vary from 0 to 1 and that a value of 1 is achieved on all three measures for graphs structured in the form of a 'star' or 'wheel'. He further shows that a value of 0 is obtained on all three measures for a 'complete' graph. Between these two extremes lie the majority of graphs for real social networks, and it is in these cases that the choice of one or other of the measures will be important in illuminating specific structural features of the graphs. A degree-based measure of graph centralization, for example, seems to be particularly sensitive to the local dominance of points, while a betweenness-based measure is rather more sensitive to the 'chaining' of points.

Assessing the centralization of a graph around a particular focal point is the starting point for a broader understanding of centralization. Measures of centralization can tell us whether a graph is organized around its most central points, but they do not tell us whether these central points comprise a distinct set of points that cluster together in a particular part of the graph. The points in the graph that are individually most central, for example, may be spread widely through the graph, and in such cases a measure of centralization might not be especially informative. It is necessary, therefore, to investigate whether there is an identifiable 'structural centre' to a graph. The **structural centre** of a graph is a single point or a cluster of points that, like the centre of a circle or a sphere, is the pivot of its organization.

This approach to what might be called 'nuclear centralization' has been outlined in an unpublished work of Stokman and Snijders.[6] Their approach is to define the set of points with the highest point centrality scores as the 'centre' of the graph. Having identified this set, researchers can then examine the structure of the relations between this set of points and all other points in the graph. A schematic outline of the Stokman and Snijders approach is shown in Figure 5.3.

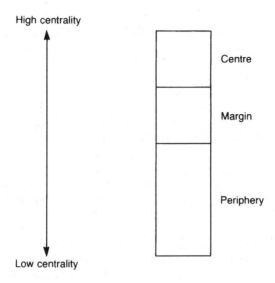

Figure 5.3   *The structural centre of a graph*

If all the points in a graph are listed in order of their point centrality – Stokman and Snijders use local centrality – then the set of points with the highest centrality is the centre. The boundary between the centre and the rest of the graph is drawn wherever there appears to be a 'natural break' in the distribution of centrality scores. The decrease in the centrality score of each successive point may, for example, show a sharp jump at a particular point in the distribution, and this is regarded as the boundary between the centre and its 'margin'. The margin is the set of points that clusters close to the centre and that is, in turn, divided from the 'peripheral' points by a further break in the distribution of centrality scores.

The Stokman and Snijders concept applies only to highly centralized graphs. In a graph such as that in Figure 5.2, which is centralized around a particular set of central points, as measured by one of Freeman's indicators, it may be very informative to try to identify the sets defined by Stokman and Snijders. There will be an inevitable arbitrariness in identifying the boundaries between centre, margin and periphery. A solution to both of these problems, though not one pursued by Stokman and Snijders, is to use some kind of clique or cluster analysis to identify the boundaries of the structural centre: if the most central points, for example, constitute a clearly defined and well-bounded 'clique', then it may make sense to regard them as forming the nuclear centre of the graph.[7] But not all graphs will have such a hierarchical structure of concentric sets. Where the central points do not cluster together as the nucleus of a centralized graph, the Stokman and Snijders 'centre' will constitute simply a set of locally central, though dispersed, points. In such circumstances, it is not helpful to use the term 'centre'.

It is possible to extend the analysis of centralization a little further by considering the possibility that there might be an 'absolute centre' to a graph. The **absolute centre** of a graph corresponds closely to the idea of the centre of a circle or a sphere; it is the focal point around which the graph is structured. The structural centre, as a *set* of points, does not meet this criterion. The absolute centre must be a *single* point. The centre of a circle, for example, is that unique place which is equidistant from all points on its circumference. By strict analogy, the absolute centre of a graph ought to be equidistant from all points in the graph. This idea is difficult to operationalize for a graph, and a more sensible idea would be to relax the criterion of equidistance and to use, instead, the idea of minimum distance. That is to say, the absolute centre is that point which is 'closest' to all the other points in terms of path distance.

Christofides (1975: ch. 5) has suggested using the distance matrix to conceptualize and compute the absolute centre of a graph. The first step in his argument follows a similar strategy to that used by Freeman to measure 'closeness'. Having constructed the distance matrix, which shows the shortest path distances between each pair of points, he defines the **eccentricity**, or 'separation', of a point as its maximum column (or row) entry in the matrix.[8] The eccentricity of a point, therefore, is the length of the longest geodesic incident to it. Christofides's first approximation to the idea of absolute centrality is to call the point with the lowest eccentricity the absolute centre. Point B in sociogram (i) of Figure 5.4 has an eccentricity of 1, and all the other points in the graph have eccentricity 2. In this sociogram, then, point B, with the lowest eccentricity, is the absolute centre.[9] In other graphs, however, there may be no single point with minimum eccentricity. There may be a number of points with equally low eccentricity, and in these circumstances a second step is needed.

This second step in the identification of the absolute centre involves searching for an *imaginary point* that has the lowest possible eccentricity for the particular graph. The crucial claim here is that, while the absolute centre of a graph will be found on one of its constituent paths, this place may not correspond to any *actual* point in the graph. Any graph will have an absolute centre, but in some graphs this centre will be an imaginary rather than an actual point.

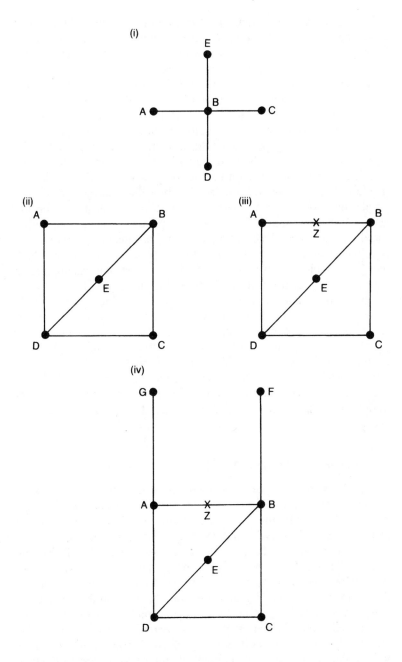

Figure 5.4   *The absolute centre of a graph*

This claim is not so strange as it might at first seem. All the points in sociogram (ii) in Figure 5.4 have eccentricity 2, and so all are equally 'central'. It is possible, however, to conceive of an imaginary point, Z, which is mid-way between points A and B, as in sociogram (iii). 'Point' Z is distance 0.5 from both A and B, and it is distance 1.5 from points C, D and E. The artificial point Z is more central than any of the actual points, as its eccentricity is 1.5. But it is still not possible to find a single absolute centre for this sociogram. The imaginary point Z could, in fact, have been placed at the mid-point of any of the lines in the sociogram with the same results, and there is no other location for the imaginary point that would not increase its minimum eccentricity. The best that can be said for this graph, therefore, is that there are six possible locations for the absolute centre, none of which corresponds to an actual point. Moving to the second step of searching for an imaginary point as the absolute centre, then, will reduce the number of graphs for which there is no unique absolute centre, but it does not ensure that a single absolute centre can be identified for all graphs.[10]

Thus, some graphs will have a unique absolute centre, while others will have a number of absolute centres. Christofides provides an algorithm that would identify, through iteration, whether a graph contains a mid-point or actual point that is its unique absolute centre.[11] In sociogram (iv) of Figure 5.4, for example, there is a unique absolute centre. Its 'point' Z has an eccentricity of 1.5, compared with eccentricity scores of 2.5 for any other imaginary mid-point, 2 for points A and B, and 3 for points C, D, E, F and G.

A Digression on Absolute Density[12]

The problem with the existing measures of density, as I showed in the previous chapter, is that they are size-dependent. Density is a measure that is difficult to use in comparisons of graphs of radically different sizes. Density is relative to size. This raises the question of whether it might not be possible to devise a measure of absolute density that would be of more use in comparative studies. I cannot give a comprehensive answer to that question here, but the idea of the absolute centre of a graph does raise the possibility that other concepts required for a measure of absolute density might be formulated along similar lines. A concept of density modelled on that used in physics for the study of solid bodies, for example, would require measures of 'radius', 'diameter' and 'circumference', all of which depend on the idea of the absolute centre.

The radius of a circular or spherical object is the distance from its centre to its circumference, on which are found its most distant reachable points. Translating this into graph theoretical terms, the eccentricity of the absolute centre of a graph can be regarded as the 'radius' of the graph. The 'diameter' of a graph, as will be shown in the following chapter, is defined as the greatest distance between any pair of its points. In sociogram (iv) of Figure 5.4, for example, the radius is 1.5 and the diameter is 3. In this case, then, the diameter is equal to twice the radius, as would be the case in the conventional geometry of a circle or a sphere. This will not, however, be true for all graphs.

In geometry there is a definite relationship between the area and the volume of a body, these relationships being generalizable to objects located in more than three dimensions. The area of a circle is πr^2 and the volume of a sphere is $4\pi r^3/3$, where π is the ratio of the circumference to the diameter. The general formula for the area of a circle, therefore, is cr^2/d, and that for the volume of a sphere is $4cr^3/3d$, where c is the circumference, r is the radius and d is the diameter. Applying this to the simple sociogram (iv) of Figure 5.4 would show that it has a volume of $4c(1.5)^3/9$, or $1.5c$.[13] But what value is to be given to c in this formula? If the diameter of a graph is taken to be the length of the geodesic between its most distant points (the longest geodesic), the circumference might most naturally be seen as the longest possible path in the graph. In sociogram (iv), this is the path of length 5 that connects point G to point F. Thus, the 'volume' of the example sociogram is 7.5.

Relatively simple geometry has, therefore, enabled us to move a part of the way towards a measure of the absolute density of a graph in three dimensions. Density in physics is defined as mass divided by volume, and so to complete the calculation a measure of the 'mass' of a graph is required. Mass in physics is simply the amount of matter that a body contains, and the most straightforward graph theoretical concept of mass is simply the number of lines that a graph contains. In sociogram (iv) there are eight lines, and so its absolute density would be 8/7.5, or 1.06.

Generalizing from this case, it can be suggested that the **absolute density** of a graph is given by the formula $l/(4cr^3/3d)$, where l is the number of lines. Unlike the relative density measure discussed in the previous chapter, this formula gives an absolute value that can be compared for any and all graphs, regardless of their size. But one important reservation must be entered: the value of the absolute density measure is dependent on the number of dimensions in which it is measured. The absolute density measure given here has been calculated for graphs in three dimensions. The concept could be generalized to higher dimensions, by using established formulae for 'hyper-volumes', but such an approach would require some agreement about how to determine the dimensionality of a graph. This issue will be approached again in Chapter 8, drawing on the arguments of Freeman (1983).[14]

Bank Centrality in Corporate Networks

Studies of interlocking directorships among corporate enterprises are far from new, but most of the studies that had been carried out prior to the 1970s had made little use of the formal techniques of social network analysis. Despite some limited use of density measures and cluster analysis, most of these studies took a strictly quantitative approach, simply counting the numbers of directorships and interlocks among the companies. Levine's influential paper (1972) marked a shift in the direction of this research while, at about the same time, Mokken and his associates in the Netherlands began a pioneering study in the systematic use of graph theory to explore corporate interlocks (Helmers et al., 1975). The major turning point, however, occurred in 1975, when Michael Schwartz and his students presented their major conference paper that applied the concept of centrality to corporate networks (Bearden et al., 1975). This long paper circulated widely in cyclostyled form and, despite the fact that it remains unpublished, it has been enormously influential. The work of Schwartz's group, and that which it has stimulated, provides a compelling illustration of the conceptual power of the idea of point centrality.

Michael Schwartz and Peter Mariolis had begun to build a database of top American companies during the early 1970s, and their efforts provided a pool of data for many subsequent studies (see, for example, Mariolis, 1975; Sonquist and Koenig, 1975). They gradually extended the database to include the top 500 industrial and the top 250 commercial and financial companies operating in the United States in 1962, together with all new entrants to this 'top 750' for each successive year from 1963 to 1973. The final database included the names of all the directors of the 1131 largest American companies in business during the period 1962–73: a total of 13,574 directors. This database is, by any standard, that for a large social network. As such, it lends itself to the selection of substantial sub-sets of data for particular years. One such sub-set is the group of the 797 top enterprises of 1969 that were studied by Mariolis (1975).

The path-breaking paper of Schwartz and his colleagues (Bearden et al., 1975) drew on the Schwartz-Mariolis database, and it analysed the data using Granovetter's (1973) conceptual distinction between strong and weak ties. The basis of their argument was that those interlocks that involved the full-time executive officers of the enterprises could be regarded as the 'strong' ties of the corporate network, while those that involved only the part-time non-executive directors were its 'weak' ties. The basis of this theoretical claim was that the interlocks that were carried by full-time executive officers were the most likely board-level links to have a strategic salience for the enterprises concerned. For this reason, they tended to be associated with intercorporate shareholdings and trading relations between the companies.[15] Interlocks created by non-executive directors, on the other hand, involved less of a time commitment and so had less strategic significance for the enterprises concerned.

The top enterprises were examined for their centrality, using Bonacich's (1972) measure. This, it will be recalled, is a measure in which the centrality of a particular point could be measured by a combination of its degree, the value of each line incident to it, and the centrality of the other points to which it is connected. This is a 'recursive', circular measure that, therefore, requires a considerable amount of computation. A network containing 750 enterprises, for example, will require the solution of 750 simultaneous equations. The first step in Bearden et al.'s analysis was to decide on an appropriate measure for the value of the lines that connected the enterprises. For the weak, undirected lines, Bearden et al. held that the value of each should be simply the number of separate interlocks, weighted by the sizes of the two boards. This weighting rested on the supposition that having a large number of interlocks was less significant for those enterprises with large boards than it was for those with small boards. The formula used in the calculation was $b_{ij}/\sqrt{d_i d_j}$, where b_{ij} is the number of interlocks between the two companies i and j, and d_i and d_j are the sizes of their respective boards. This formula allows Bonacich's centrality measure to be calculated on the basis of all the 'weak ties' in the graph.

A more complex formula was required to measure centrality in terms of the strong ties. In this case, the measure of the value of each line needed to take some account of the direction that was attached to the lines in the graph. For those companies that were the 'senders' of lines (the 'tails', in the terminology of the GRADAP program) the value of the lines was calculated by the number of directors 'sent', weighted by the board size of the 'receiving' company. The attempt in this procedure was to weight the line by the salience of the interlock for the receiving board. Conversely, for those companies that were the 'receivers' of interlocks (the 'heads'), the number of directors received was weighted by the sender's board size.[16] For the final calculation of centrality scores, Bearden et al. introduced a further weighting. Instead of taking simply the raw weighted scores for the tails and the heads, they took 90 per cent of the score for the senders and 10 per cent of the score for the recipients. The reasoning behind this weighting of the scores was the theoretical judgement that, in the world of corporate interlocking, it is 'more important to give than to receive': the sending of a director was more likely to be a sign of corporate power than was the receiving of a directorship. Thus, the arbitrary adjustment to the centrality scores was introduced as a way of embodying this judgement in the final results. It should be noted, however, that centrality will not always be a sign of power. In some situations, the prominent and most visible actors may be among the weakest (Mizruchi, 1994: 331–2).

The Bonacich measure of centrality which was calculated for the companies in the study correlated very highly, at 0.91, with the degrees of the companies. Bearden et al. held, however, that the more complex Bonacich measure was preferable because it had the potential to highlight those enterprises that had a low degree but which were, nevertheless, connected to highly central companies. Such a position, they argued, may be of great importance in determining the structural significance of the companies in the economy.

Schwartz and his colleagues also used a further approach to centrality, which they termed 'peak analysis'. This was later elaborated by Mizruchi (1982) as the basis for an interpretation of the development of the American corporate network during the twentieth century. A point is a **peak**, it was argued, if it is more central than any other point to which it is connected. Mintz and Schwartz (1985) extend this idea by defining a **bridge** as a central point that connects two or more peaks (see Figure 5.5). They further see a

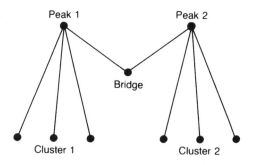

Figure 5.5   *Peaks and bridges*

'cluster' as comprising all the direct contacts of a peak, except for those that have a similar distance 1 connection to another peak. Thus, peaks lie at the hearts of their clusters.[17]

The results that were arrived at through the use of these techniques for the measurement of point centrality have become widely accepted as indicating some of the most fundamental features of intercorporate networks. In summary, Bearden et al. argued that the American intercorporate network showed an overall pattern of 'bank centrality': banks were the most central enterprises in the network, whether measured by the strong or the weak ties. Bank centrality was manifest in the co-existence of an extensive national interlock network (structured predominantly by weak ties) and intensive regional groupings (structured by the strong ties). Strong ties had a definite regional base to them. The intensive regional clusters were created by the strong ties of both the financial and the non-financial enterprises, but the strong ties of the banks were the focal centres of the network of strong ties. The intercorporate network of 1962, for example, consisted of one very large connected component,[18] two small groupings each of four or five enterprises, and a large number of pairs and isolated enterprises. Within the large connected component, there were five peaks and their associated clusters. The dominant element in the network of strong ties was a regional cluster around the Continental Illinois peak, which, with two other Chicago banks, was connected with a group of 11 mid-Western enterprises with extensive connections to a larger grouping of 132 enterprises. The remaining four peaks in the network of strong ties were Mellon National Bank, J.P. Morgan, Bankers Trust and United California Bank, their clusters varying in size from four to ten enterprises.

Overlying this highly clustered network of strong, regional ties was an extensive national network created by the weak ties that linked the separate clusters together. This national network, Bearden et al. argued, reflected the common orientation to business affairs and a similarity of interests that all large companies shared. Interlocks among the non-executive directors expressed this commonality and produced integration, unity and interdependence at the national level (see also Useem, 1984). The great majority of the enterprises were tied into a single large component in this network, most of the remainder being isolates. Banks were, once more, the most central enterprises, especially those New York banks that played a 'national' rather than a 'regional' role. It was the non-executive directors of the banks who cemented together the overall national network.[19]

6
Components, Cores and Cliques

One of the most enduring concerns of those who have turned to social network analysis has been the attempt to discover the various 'cliques' and cohesive sub-groups into which a network can be divided. The early researchers of the Hawthorne and Yankee City studies, I have shown, saw the idea of the 'clique' as being their central theoretical discovery. The argument was that people's informal social relations tied them into cohesive sub-groupings that had their own norms, values, orientations and sub-cultures, and that may run counter to the 'official' or formal social structure. The cliques were, they held, among the most important sources of a person's identity and sense of belonging, and their existence was widely recognized in the everyday terms – such as 'our set' and 'the group in the back' – that people used to describe their social world.

Once analysts began to try to formalize the idea of the clique and to devise mathematical measures of the number and cohesion of cliques, it was appreciated that the idea was not limited to informal relations. There were also political cliques and factions, economic cliques and interest groups, and so on. It was also recognized that there were a number of different ways of operationalizing the apparently simple idea of the 'clique': for example, cliques could be seen as groups of mutually connected individuals or as pockets of high density. Thus, a number of different theoretical models of sub-groups emerged, variously described as 'cliques', 'clusters', 'components', 'cores' and 'circles'. Apart from beginning with the letter 'c', these concepts have very little in common with one another. In this chapter I shall discuss their varying theoretical bases, though I will leave the issue of 'cluster analysis' until the following chapter.

The starting point for all of these measures of group structure is the idea of a 'sub-graph'. A sub-graph is any collection of points selected from the whole graph of a network, together with the lines connecting those points. Any aspect of the graph can be chosen for identifying its sub-graphs, though not all of these criteria will be substantively useful in research. A random sample of points, for example, could be treated as a sub-graph and its structural properties could be examined. But a random sub-graph is not, in general, likely to correspond to a meaningful social group. A more useful approach to the identification of sub-graphs might be to divide the members of a network by, say, gender and to investigate the separate sub-graphs of men and women. Any such choice will depend on the theoretical and empirical concerns of the researcher. The general aim would simply be to define a meaningful category of agents and to explore their distinct patterns of network formation. From this point of view, therefore, the identification of sub-graphs is no different from the initial identification of the graphs themselves. All the considerations of boundaries and sampling that have been considered in earlier chapters will be equally relevant here and no new issues are involved (see, for example, Frank, 1978b).

Clique and similar analyses normally adopt an alternative approach to the study of sub-graphs. Their aim has been to investigate the structural properties of the whole graph itself in order to discover the 'naturally existing' sub-graphs into which it can be divided. From this point of view, a sub-graph must have some defining characteristic drawn from the mathematical principles of graph theory: the connectedness of its points, the intensity of their connection, and so on. It is a sub-graph that is *maximal* in relation to a particular defining characteristic: it is the largest sub-graph that can be formed in the graph without this defining quality disappearing. The choice of a particular characteristic depends on the researcher's decision that a particular mathematical criterion can be given a meaningful and useful sociological interpretation. Unfortunately, this is rarely made explicit, and far too many researchers assume that whatever mathematical procedures are available in social network analysis programs *must*, almost by definition, be useful sociological measures. My aim in this chapter is to uncover the mathematical assumptions of the various available procedures so that researchers can make an informed decision about those that might be relevant to their particular investigations.

Components, Cycles and Knots

The simplest of the various sub-graph concepts is that of the **component**, which is formally defined as a 'maximal connected sub-graph'. A sub-graph, like a graph, is 'connected' when all of its points are linked to one another through paths: all points in a connected sub-graph can 'reach' one another through one or more paths, but they have no connections outside the sub-graph. Within a component, all points are connected through paths, but no paths run to points outside the component. When the connected sub-graph is maximal, it is impossible to add any new members without destroying the quality of connectedness. Isolated points, for example, cannot be joined with an existing component, as they have no connections to any of its members. The boundary of a component, therefore, is identified by tracing through the paths from its potential members to test for their connectedness.

A computer algorithm for identifying components might start from a randomly chosen point and trace all the other points to which it is directly connected. This same procedure can then be repeated for each of these points in turn, and so the component gradually increases in size through a 'snowballing' method. When no further points can be added to the component, its full membership has been identified. If any points remain outside the component, the same procedure can be repeated for them, so as to see what other components can be identified in the graph.

Components, then, are sets of points that are linked to one another through continuous chains of connection. The paths connecting points are traced through until the boundaries of the component are discovered. A 'connected graph', of course, simply comprises a single component. Other graphs typically consist of one or more separate components, together with a number of isolated points (see Figure 6.1). This idea is readily interpretable in sociological terms. The members of a component can, in principle, communicate with one another, either directly or through chains of intermediaries. Isolates, on the other hand, have no such opportunities. The pattern of components found in a graph – their number and size – can, therefore, be taken as an indication of the opportunities and obstacles to communication or the transfer of resources in the associated network. To this extent, then, they embody the ideas behind the 'topological regions' of the early field theorists. A basic step in the structural description of a network, therefore, is to identify the number and size of its components.

The simplest of algorithms to detect components in a graph would search all possible paths in order to discover the geodesics between points. The lengths of these geodesics will vary from a minimum of 1 (direct connection) to a maximum of $n-1$. In a graph of size 100, for example, the maximum possible path length would be 99. In large graphs, however, the longest geodesic in a component – its 'diameter' – is generally much shorter than this.[1] However, the diameter of a component will not generally be known before the boundaries of the component have been identified, and so such an algorithm must search all paths up to the maximum level of $n-1$ in the search for components.

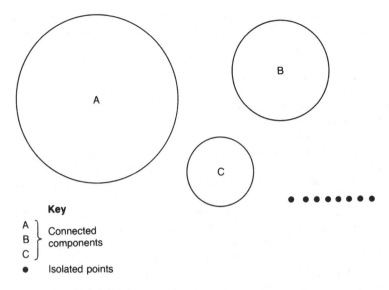

Figure 6.1   *Components in a network*

Because such a procedure is very time-consuming and inefficient, it is not practicable for most computing purposes. For this reason, social network packages generally use an alternative procedure. Components are discovered by building up 'spanning trees', using a back-tracking method from chosen points. The algorithm looks for any point that is connected to a starting point, and it then looks for any point that is connected to this additional point. This is repeated until no further connections can be found. The algorithm then back tracks along the chain that it has discovered until it is able to make a connection to a new point. It continues in the same way until it again comes to a halt. By repeated back-tracking of this kind, the boundaries of a component are discovered very efficiently and the procedure can search the remaining points for other components.

Components can be searched for in both undirected and directed graphs, but there are important differences between the two situations. In the case of directed graphs, two distinct types of component can be identified: 'strong components' and 'weak components'. A **strong component** is one in which the lines that make up the paths are aligned in a continuous chain without any change of direction. Any paths that do not meet this criterion are disregarded. The justification for this restriction is that the direction of a line is assumed to indicate the possible flow of some resource or facility, such as money, power, or information. It is only when the lines in a path run in a constant direction that this flow can continue without interruption. A strong component, then, represents a set of agents among whom such resources can easily and freely flow. An alternative, weaker interpretation can also be placed on directed lines. It can be assumed that the mere presence of a relationship, regardless of its direction, allows some possibility for communication. From this point of view, components can be identified from the semi-paths in the graph. Components in a directed graph that are identified in this way, disregarding the direction of the lines that make up the paths and taking account simply of the presence or absence of a connection, are termed **weak components**.

The distinction between strong and weak components does not, of course, exist in undirected graphs. In these situations the researcher is dealing with what might be called 'simple components': as no directions are attached to the lines, all paths constitute acceptable connections. Computer algorithms for identifying simple components in an undirected graph are, in principle, identical to those for identifying weak components in a directed graph. It is only when the question of direction has to be explicitly dealt with that the algorithms differ.

The result of a component analysis is a view of the graph as composed of one or more components (simple, weak or strong components) and a number of isolated points. Dense graphs are likely to show the dominance of a single large component, especially where the analysis is concerned with simple or weak components. In order to achieve a more fine-grained analysis, it is generally necessary to attempt to probe the internal structure of components.

Everett has proposed an extension of the component idea that aims to achieve such a fine-grained view of the texture of dense networks. His approach (1982, 1983a, b, 1984) is based on a graph theoretical concept that he terms the 'block'. There is a great deal of confusion over the word 'block', as it has been used in a number of radically different ways in social network analysis. To try to avoid some of this confusion, I propose to make some terminological innovations. For reasons that will soon become apparent, I shall refer to Everett's concept not as the 'block', but as the 'cyclic component'.[2]

The concept of the cyclic component depends on that of the cycle. A **cycle** is a path that returns to its own starting point, and, like a path, a cycle can be of any length. The cycles in a graph can be described by their length as 3-cycles, 4-cycles and so on. Putting this in its most general form, graph theorists can identify what

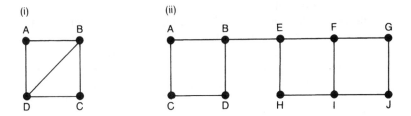

Figure 6.2 *Cyclic components*

Everett terms *k*-cycles, where *k* is any specified cycle length. A useful first step in the analysis of cycles is to decide on a maximum cycle length for consideration. Any cycle of greater length than this is ignored. If a maximum cycle length of 4 is chosen, for example, sociogram (i) in Figure 6.2 contains four cycles of length 4 (ABCDA, BCDAB, CDABC and DABCD) and six cycles of length 3 (ABDA, BDAB, DABD, BCDB, CDBC and DBCD).[3] At a maximum cycle length of 3, only the shorter cycles remain and points A and C are not connected by any cycle. Everett goes on to define a **bridge** as a line that does not itself lie on a cycle but that may connect two or more cycles.[4] Sociogram (ii) in Figure 6.2, for example, contains, at maximum cycle length 4, the bridge BE.

A **cyclic component** can be defined as a set of intersecting cycles connected by those lines or points that they have in common. The separate cyclic components of a graph, therefore, do not overlap with one another, though they may be connected by one or more bridges. Sociogram (ii) in Figure 6.2, for example, is not itself a cyclic component, it does, however, contain the cyclic components {A,B,C,D} and {E,F,G,H,I,J}. The latter set of points contains the line FI, which is common to the cycles EFIHE and FGJIF. It can be seen, therefore, that a cyclic component consists of a chain of intersecting cycles, where the intersections are lines or points common to the overlapping cycles.[5] The cyclic components of a graph are identified by removing from a graph all those lines that are bridges at the specified cycle length (termed the '*k*-bridges'). The sets of points that remain are the cyclic components.

Where an analysis of simple, weak or strong components results simply in the identification of components and isolates, an analysis of cyclic components generally produces more complex results. This is because the cyclic components will be connected to various points that are not themselves members of cyclic components. Everett (1982) has shown that the connected elements will fall into one of five categories:

1 **Cyclic components**.
2 **Hangers**. These are points that are connected to a member of a cyclic component, but which do not themselves lie on a cycle. Hangers simply 'hang' on to a cyclic component.
3 **Bridgers**. The points that are 'intermediaries' or 'waverers' between two or more cyclic components, but which are not members of any of them. A bridger, then, 'hangs' on to two or more cyclic components.
4 **Isolated trees**. These are chains of points (including dyads) that are not connected to any cyclic component. The members of these 'trees' are linked to one another in a non-cyclic way.[6]
5 **Isolates**. Those points that have no connections at all, i.e., those which have a degree of 0.

It can sometimes be difficult to give a substantive sociological interpretation to long paths of connection. This is a particular problem where long cycles tie large numbers of points together. There is, for example, a tendency for connected graphs to comprise a single, large cyclic component. Everett holds that, for most purposes, it is realistic to limit an analysis to relatively short cycles of length 3 or 4. At cycle length 3, for example, an analysis would be concerned simply with cyclic components built out of triads, to which a number of substantive interpretations can be given. At cycle length 4, an analysis would be concerned with those cyclic components that are built from either triads or 'rectangles'. If a researcher intends to use cycle lengths greater than 4, it is particularly important that the substantive sociological interpretation that is to be given to the mathematical structures should be both clear and meaningful.

An analysis of cyclic components can also be undertaken for directed graphs. The simplest way of doing this would be to disregard the directions that are attached to the lines. Such an analysis, based on the semi-paths in the graph, would identify 'semi-cycles'. These are cycles in which no account is taken of the direction of the lines. This does, of course, involve some loss of information, but the procedure allows the identification of what can be termed **weak cyclic components**. In order to analyse **strong cyclic components**, the information on directionality must be retained. Everett has recommended that this kind of analysis should, in fact, also include some of the semi-cycles. In a **directed cycle** the direction runs consistently through all the constituent lines. In Figure 6.3, for example, ABCA is a directed cycle. The path ABDA, on the other hand, involves a reversal of direction between A and D, and so is merely a semi-cycle. Everett defines a semi-cycle

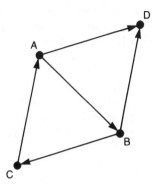

Figure 6.3   *Cycles and semi-cycles*

as being an 'acceptable semi-cycle' if points that do not lie on a directed cycle are, nevertheless, connected by two or more distinct directed paths. Thus, points A and D are not connected through a directed cycle, but they are connected through the directed paths ABD and AD. For this reason, ABDA is an acceptable semi-cycle.

In the identification of strong cyclic components, therefore, a computer algorithm must search for both the directed cycles and the acceptable semi-cycles of a graph. Using this procedure, all the cycles in a directed graph will be identifiable as directed, acceptable, or unacceptable, and an analysis of strong components would take account only of cycles of the first two types. Using these cycles alone, the strong cyclic components of the graph can be identified, and it will also be possible to distinguish between 'hangers-on' and 'hangers-off', according to the direction of the lines that connect them. The **hangers-on** are those hangers that direct a line towards a member of a strong cyclic component, while the **hangers-off** are those hangers to whom a member of the component directs a line.[7]

An alternative way to probe the internal structure of components is to see whether there are particular points that have a pivotal significance in holding components together. Hage and Harary (1983) have approached this, like Everett, through a concept that they designate as a 'block'. In their case, however, this term refers to those sub-graphs within simple components (or within the weak components of a directed graph) that have no 'cut-point'.[8] A **cut-point** is one whose removal would increase the number of components by dividing the sub-graph into two or more separate sub-sets between which there are no connections. In the graph component (i) shown in Figure 6.4, for example, point B is a cut-point, as its removal would create the two disconnected components shown in sociogram (ii). None of the other points is a cut-point.

Thus, cut-points are pivotal points of articulation between the elements that make up a component. These elements, together with their cut-points, are what Hage and Harary described as the 'blocks'. Once again, I wish to avoid the conceptual confusion which results from the varying usages given to the word 'block' and so, in what follows, I shall use the more descriptive term 'knot'. The component in Figure 6.4, then, comprises the two knots {A,B,C} and {B,D,E,F}. The various cut-points in a graph, therefore, will be members of a number of knots, with the cut-points being the points of overlap between the knots.[9]

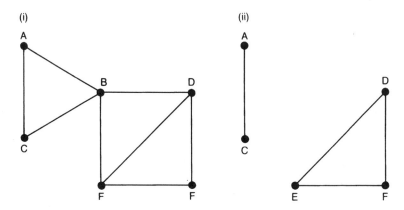

(i)   (ii)

Figure 6.4   *Knots and cut-points*

It is relatively easy to give a substantive sociological interpretation to the idea of a cut-point. It can, for example, be seen as indicating some kind of local centrality for the corresponding agent. Hage and Harary (1983) have argued that knots ('blocks' in their terminology) can be seen as being, for example, the most effective systems of communication or exchange in a network (see also Hage and Harary, 1991 and 1998 for applications of this view). Because they contain no cut-points, acts of communication and exchange among the members of a knot are not dependent upon any one member. There are always alternative paths of communication between all the points in a knot, and so the network that it forms is both flexible and unstratified.

The Contours of Components

I have looked so far at procedures for the identification of various kinds of components, and I have reviewed some proposals for analysing the elements that make up these components (the knots and cut-points) and those which lie outside the components (the hangers, bridgers, trees and isolates). In this and in the following section I will pursue the question of the internal structure of components more systematically. In this section I will assess how the 'contours' of components can be charted by identifying their 'cores', and in the following section I will look at the 'cliques' and 'circles' from which components are built.

I showed in Chapter 2 that the work of the Yankee City researchers involved an attempt to identify the core and peripheral members of what they called 'cliques'. This procedure can more usefully be applied to the internal structure of components. The contours of components can be disclosed by a procedure that is usually termed the 'nesting' of components, and that was briefly discussed in Chapter 3.[10] Nesting successive analyses of components involves using progressively stronger cut-off criteria for drawing the boundaries of components at each step of the analysis. When combined into a single picture, the result of such a procedure is a series of concentric bounded sets of points. The basic image in a nested analysis is that of a contour map or of a set of Russian dolls, each component being 'nested' within a larger component. A component is visualized as having a core of especially cohesive or intensely connected points, with the boundaries of the core being gradually extended to include more and more points as the cut-off level of cohesion or intensity is weakened. At the weakest level of connection, all connected points are included in a single component.

Figure 6.5 illustrates a simple case of nesting. The points in set A are the most tightly connected, and they comprise the core of their component. The boundary of set B is drawn with a weaker criterion

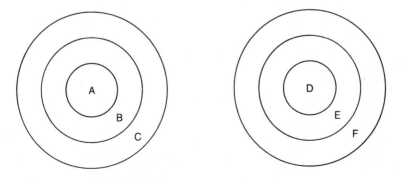

Figure 6.5 *Nested components*

of connection and so includes all the points of set A together with the additional points that are connected at this weaker level. Finally, set C has its boundary determined by the very weakest criterion of connectedness and so includes all connected points. Sets D, E and F in the second component can be interpreted in the same way. Thus, each of the components in a graph can be de-composed into its core elements and a contour diagram of the graph can be drawn.

Component detection algorithms treat all connections as binary data, as indicating simply the presence or absence of a relation. A valued graph, therefore, must be analysed by converting its actual values into binary, 1 or 0, values. This is done by comparing entries in the matrix for the valued graph with a 'slicing' or 'dichotomizing' threshold.[11] Entries above or below the specified threshold are dichotomized into binary values: those above it are given the value 1, and those below it are given the value 0. These binary values can then be used in the search for components. A valued adjacency matrix might, for example, contain entries that show the multi-plicities of the lines, and this matrix could be 'sliced' by choosing progressively stronger levels of intensity. By studying the components that are identified at each threshold level, the researcher can construct a contour diagram of nested components such as that shown in Figure 6.5. The boundaries of the components are drawn as concentric loops, and the diagram shows the 'peaks' of high intensity and the 'plains' of low intensity.

Two alternative methods of nesting have been proposed: one based on the use of the degrees of the points as a measure of cohesion, and the other based on the use of the multiplicities of the lines as a measure of intensity. The degree-based measure results in the identification of 'k-cores', while the multiplicity-based measure results in the identification of 'm-cores'.[12]

Seidman (1983) has proposed that the structure of components can be studied by using a criterion of minimum degree to identify areas of high and low cohesion. An analysis of the resulting k-core structure of a graph, he argues, is an essential complement to the measurement of density, which I have shown fails to grasp many of the global features of graph structure. A **k-core** is a maximal sub-graph in which each point is adjacent to at least k other points: all the points within the k-core have a degree greater than or equal to k.[13] Thus, a simple component is a '1k-core'. All its points are connected to one another and so have a degree of at least 1. To identify a 2k-core, all points with degree 1 are ignored and the structure of connections among the remaining points is examined. The 2k-core consists of those remaining connected points that have a degree of 2. A 3k-core is identified by deleting all points with a

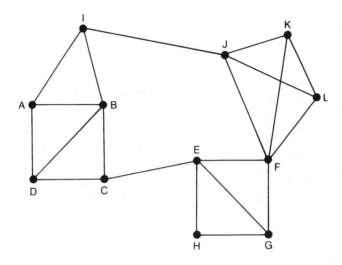

Figure 6.6 *A 3k-core*

degree of 2 or less, and so on. Figure 6.6 illustrates a 3*k*-core. In this sub-graph, all points have a degree of at least 3. Although there are two points with degree 4 (points B and J), there would be no 4*k*-core in this graph, as a *k*-core must have at least *k* + 1 members.

A *k*-core, then, is an area of relatively high cohesion within the whole graph. But it is not necessarily a maximally cohesive sub-graph – there may be areas of very high cohesion that are connected to one another rather loosely. In Figure 6.6, for example, the cohesive areas {E,F,G,H,J,K,L} and {A,B,C,D,E,I} are connected through the weaker links CE and IJ. *K*-cores, then, constitute areas of the component within which cohesive sub-groups, if they exist, will be found.[14]

Seidman also shows how the overall fragmentation of a network can be assessed by looking at what he calls the **core collapse sequence**. The points in a *k*-core can be divided into two sets: those that are in a *k* + 1 core and those that are not. The latter group Seidman terms the *k*-remainder. The remainder in any core comprises those points that will 'disappear' from the analysis when *k* is increased by 1. It is the disappearance of these less well-connected points that causes the core to 'collapse' as *k* is increased. Seidman proposes that the proportion of points that disappear from a core at each increase in *k* can be arranged in a vector (a simple row of figures) that describes the structure of local density within the component.[15]

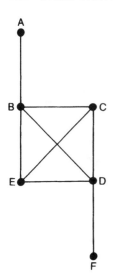

Value of k	Remainder	Remainder as proportion
0	0	0
1	2	0.3
2	0	0
3	4	0.6
4	No points left	

Figure 6.7   *Collapse of a k-core*

This can be illustrated through the sociogram in Figure 6.7. All six points are connected, and so the increase in k from 0 to 1 involves no loss of points. At $k = 1$ all points are contained in a core, but there is a remainder of 2 (points A and F) that will disappear when k is increased to 2. At $k = 2$, points B, C, D and E remain, each with a degree greater than or equal to 2. As these points are, in fact, mutually connected at degree 3, there is no remainder at $k = 2$. When k is increased to 3, however, the remainder is 4, as all points will disappear when k is increased to four. Arranging the sequence of remainders from $k = 0$ in a vector gives the following core collapse sequence: (0, 0.3, 0, 0.6).

The core collapse sequence gives a summary of the 'clumpiness' of the component. A slow and gradual collapse in the core, argues Seidman, indicates an overall uniformity in the texture of the network. An irregular sequence of values, as shown in Figure 6.6, shows that there are relatively dense areas surrounded by more peripheral points. The persistence of zero values in the vector up to high levels of k indicates a uniformity of structure within the component; the appearance and persistence of zero values after low levels of k indicates the existence of clumps of high density.

By contrast with k-cores, which are based around the degrees of the points, 'm-cores' are based around the multiplicities of the lines. The notion of an m-core describes the original nested components discussed by the GRADAP group.[16] An **m-core** can be defined as a maximal sub-graph in which each line has a multiplicity greater than or equal to *m*. An *m*-core is a chain of points connected by lines of the specified multiplicity. As in the case of a *k*-core, a simple component is a 1*m*-core, as all of its points are connected with a multiplicity of at least 1. In a 2*m*-core, lines of multiplicity 1 are ignored, and components are identified on the remaining lines. In a 3*m*-core, lines of multiplicity 1 and 2 are ignored, and so on. Figure 6.8 shows a simple 3*m*-core. All the points are connected through paths of multiplicity greater than or equal to 3, the weaker connections of the points to those outside the core being disregarded. As points B and C are connected by a line of multiplicity 4, they form a two-member 4*m*-core. It is the nesting of cores within one another that discloses the overall shape of the network.[17]

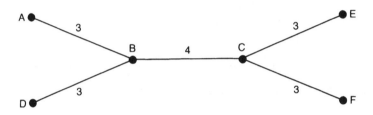

Figure 6.8   *A 3m-core*

Seidman's idea of the core collapse sequence can be extended to *m*-cores: indeed, the idea is far simpler to apply to them. This can be illustrated with the sociogram in Figure 6.9. Lines are progressively removed as the value of *m* is increased, and the remainder at each level of *m* is the number of points that will disappear when *m* is increased to *m* + 1. Two points disappear when *m* is increased from 1 to 2, but no further points disappear until *m* reaches 4. If *m* is increased to 5, all points will disappear, as the highest multiplicity in the graph is 4. Thus, the *m*-core collapse sequence for this component is: (0, 0.28, 0, 0.28, 0.43).

To complete this section it is necessary to consider the analysis of nesting in relation to cyclic components. Cyclic components can, of course, be identified in valued graphs by using an appropriate 'slicing' value. By varying the slicing criterion it is possible to arrive at an analysis of nested components – in this case, of nested cyclic components.[18]

Taken together, the various extensions of the basic idea of the simple component provide a powerful set of concepts for analysing the level of fragmentation in a network. They supplement the

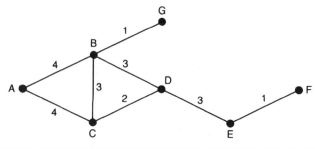

Value of *m*	*m*-cores	Remainder	Remainders as proportion
0	{A, B, C, D, E, F, G}	0	0
1	{A, B, C, D, E, F, G}	2	0.28
2	{A, B, C, D, E}	0	0
3	{A, B, C, D, E}	2	0.28
4	{A, B, C}	3	0.43
5		No points left	

Figure 6.9   *Collapse of an m-core*

measurement of density and help to overcome many of its limitations by highlighting the overall shape of the network. A full outline comparison of the global structures of networks of comparable size would involve measures of the overall density of the networks and their inclusiveness, the number and sizes of their components and their densities, and the nested structures of the components and their core collapse sequences.

Cliques and their Intersections

The concepts discussed so far in this chapter have gone some way towards formalizing the ideas of those early writers on social networks who talked about the 'cliques' discovered in the Hawthorne works and in Yankee City. But I have not yet considered the sociometric concept of the clique itself, which has arisen in discussions of the sociological applications of graph theory. There are a number of competing usages of the word 'clique', but the most widely held view is that its essential meaning is that of the 'maximal complete sub-graph' (Harary, 1969; Luce and Perry, 1949). That is to say, a **clique** is a sub-set of points in which every possible pair of points is directly connected by a line and the clique is not contained in any other clique.[19] As Figure 6.10 shows, a three member clique

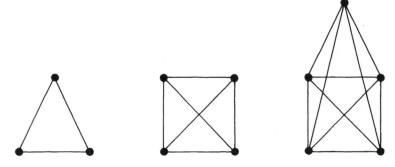

Figure 6.10   *Cliques of varying sizes*

contains three lines, a four member clique contains six lines, a five member clique has ten lines, and so on.[20] While a 'component' is maximal and connected (all points are connected to one another through paths), a 'clique' is maximal and complete (all points are adjacent to one another).

Doreian (1979: 51–2) has spelled out some of the formal properties of cliques. The basic consideration is that all cliques are maximal sub-sets of points in which each point is in a direct and reciprocal relation with all others. In an undirected graph all lines are, by definition, reciprocal relations, and so a clique detection procedure will consider all the lines in the graph. In directed graphs, however, this is not the case: its matrix is asymmetrical, and only the reciprocated lines should be considered. In directed graphs, therefore, network analysis identifies what might be called **strong cliques**. On the other hand, if the direction of the lines is disregarded and simply the presence or absence of a relation is considered, the analysis treats all lines as if they were reciprocated and results in the identification of **weak cliques**.[21]

This concept of the maximal complete sub-graph is rather restrictive for real social networks, as such tightly knit groups are very uncommon. For this reason, a number of extensions to the basic idea have been proposed.[22] The earliest of these extensions was the concept of the *n*-**clique**, which, it was claimed, is much closer to people's everyday understanding of the word 'clique'. In this concept, *n* is the maximum path length at which members of the clique will be regarded as connected. Thus, a 1-clique is the maximal complete sub-graph itself, the set in which all pairs of points are directly connected at distance 1. A 2-clique, on the other hand, is one in which the members are connected either directly (at distance 1) or indirectly through a common neighbour (distance 2).

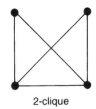

1-clique   2-clique   3-clique

Figure 6.11   *n-cliques of size 4*

The value of *n* which is to be used in an analysis is chosen by the researcher, and a progressive increase in the value of *n* results in a gradual relaxation of the criterion for clique membership (see Figure 6.11). A 3-clique, for example, is a looser grouping than a 2-clique. The maximum value that can be given to *n* is one less than the total number of points in the graph. In practice, however, most large connected graphs are joined into a single *n*-clique at much shorter path lengths than this.

N-cliques can be identified through the relatively simple matrix multiplication methods that are available in many spreadsheet programs or in specialist network analysis programs. Multiplying the adjacency matrix by itself, for example, produces a matrix of path distances. The square of the matrix shows all distance 2 connections, the cube of the matrix shows distance 3 connections, and so on. Matrix multiplication is, however, a rather inefficient method of clique detection, and most specialist network analysis programs use a variant of the back-tracking procedure used for component detection. Because of the ease with which this can be done, clique detection for undirected graphs is a feature that is built into most social network analysis programs.[23] It is possible to analyse *n*-cliques in a valued graph by applying a slicing criterion of the same kind as was discussed in the previous section. Such an analysis would generate a set of nested cliques for each level of *n*: nested 2-cliques, nested 3-cliques and so on.

There are two important limitations on the use of the *n*-clique idea. The first and most important is that values of *n* greater than 2 can be difficult to interpret sociologically. Distance 2 relations can be straightforwardly interpreted as those which involve a common neighbour who, for example, may act as an intermediary or a broker. Path lengths greater than 2, however, involve rather more distant and weak links. While long, weak chains of connection may be very important for the overall structure of the network, as Granovetter and the 'small world' analysts have argued, it is not at all clear that they are appropriate for the definition of cliques. The very idea of a clique seems to demand relatively close linkages. It is, therefore, difficult to justify the identification of n-cliques with values of n other than 1 or 2.

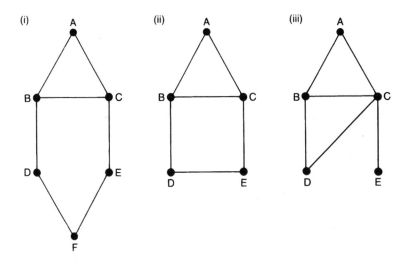

Figure 6.12   *Sub-graphs and 2-cliques*

The second limitation on the use of the n-clique concept is the fact that intermediary points on the paths of the n-clique may not themselves be members of the clique. For example, points A, B, C, D and E in graph (i) of Figure 6.12 form a 2-clique, but the distance 2 path that connects D and E runs through the non-member F. The 'diameter' of the clique – the path distance between its most distant members – may, then, be greater than the value of n that is used to define the clique. Thus, the set {A,B,C,D,E} comprises a 2-clique, but it has a diameter of 3. Both Alba (1973, 1982) and Mokken (1974) have taken up this problem and proposed some further extensions to the idea of the n-clique. Mokken has proposed that a more useful concept is one that would limit the diameter of the n-clique to n. That is to say, the researcher accepts, for example, distance 2 paths for the identification of clique members, but also requires that the diameter of the clique be no greater than 2. This concept he terms the **n-clan**. Graphs (ii) and (iii) in Figure 6.12 are, unlike graph (i), 2-clans.[24]

A different extension of the basic clique idea is that of the k-plex, proposed by Seidman and Foster (1978). Whereas the concept of the n-clique involves increasing the permissible path lengths that

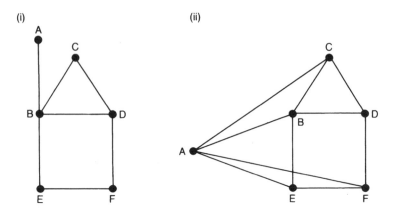

Figure 6.13   *A 3-clique and a 3-plex*

define the clique, the concept of the k-plex involves reducing the number of other points to which each point must be connected. Thus, the points in a k-plex are connected at distance 1, but not all points will be connected to one another. A **k-plex** is a set of points in which each point is adjacent to all except k of the other points.[25] Thus, if $k=1$, a 1-plex is equivalent to a 1-clique, and so it is a maximal complete sub-graph. Each member of the 1-plex is connected to $n-1$ other points. When k is equal to 2, all members in the 2-plex are connected to at least $n-2$ of the other members, but the 2-plex may not be a 2-clique. In Figure 6.13, graph (i) is a 3-clique, as all pairs of points are connected at distance 3 or less. It is not, however, a 3-plex, as A, C, E and F are each connected to fewer than three other members. Graph (ii) is both a 3-clique and a 3-plex.[26]

An important consideration in the analysis of k-plexes is that of the minimum size which the researcher will regard as acceptable for a plex. In particular, higher values of k ought to lead to a higher cut-off threshold for the size of acceptable k-plexes. When k takes a low value, k-plexes can be relatively small, but higher levels of k will produce trivial results unless the minimum size of the acceptable k-plexes is increased. The reason for this is that small sub-graphs at high levels of k will be only minimally cohesive. As a rule of thumb, the minimum size for an acceptable k-plex should be $k+2$. Nevertheless, the concept of the k-plex, considered as a generalization of the basic clique idea, seems to grasp more of the idea of cohesion than does the n-clique, especially when values of n higher than 2 are used.[27] As in the case of n-cliques and components, the basic idea of a *k*-plex can be extended to valued graphs by using a slicing criterion to analyse 'nested *k*-plexes'.

In any but the smallest graphs, there will be a considerable amount of overlap among the various *n*-cliques and *k*-plexes of which the graph is composed. Clique-analyses (of both *n*-cliques and *k*-plexes) will tend to produce long lists of overlapping cliques, and these results may be difficult to interpret. A relatively dense network will tend to comprise a large number of overlapping cliques, with many points being members of numerous different cliques. A graph with 20 points and a high density, for example, could contain approaching 2000 overlapping cliques. In these circumstances, the density of the overlap among cliques may be more significant than the composition of the cliques themselves. Alba (1982) has, therefore, proposed that social network analysts should use concepts that explicitly recognize this fact of overlap. Drawing on work undertaken with Kadushin and Moore (Alba and Kadushin, 1976; Alba and Moore, 1978; Kadushin, 1966, 1968), he argued that the concept of the 'social circle' can be used to grasp significant structural features of social networks.

This idea was devised by Kadushin from the initial insights of Simmel (1908), who first outlined the importance of the 'intersection of social circles'. The cohesion of a social circle is not founded on the direct 'face-to-face' contacts of its members, but on the existence of short chains of indirect connections that weld them together. Circles 'emerge' from interaction and may not be visible to their participants, as their boundaries are only loosely defined by the ramification of these indirect connections.

Alba's contribution was to formalize the idea of the circle in sociometric terms by relating it to other graph theoretical concepts. His basic argument is that overlapping cliques can be aggregated into **circles** if they have more than a certain proportion of their members in common. Alba suggests that the most appropriate procedure is to use a kind of 'snowballing' method in which cliques are aggregated into progressively larger, and looser, circles. The first step in an analysis of circles is to identify 1-cliques of size 3 (triads) and then to merge into a circle all of those cliques that differ by only one member. Put in a slightly different way, the criterion for identifying circles in the first step is that cliques are merged into a circle if two-thirds of their members are identical. The result of this first step, then, might be one or more circles, together with a number of separate cliques and isolated points. At the second step the remaining cliques might be merged with those circles with which there is a lower level of overlap. Alba suggests

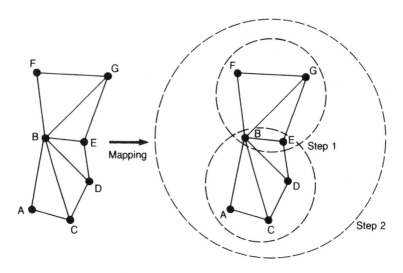

1-cliques: {A,B,C} {B,C,D} {B,D,E} {B,F,G} {B,G,E}
1st step circles: {A,B,C,D,E} {B,F,G,E}
2nd step circles: {A,B,C,D,E,F,G}

Figure 6.14   *Intersecting social circles*

that a one-third overlap in membership might be appropriate in this second step. The result of this aggregation will be a large circle or a set of smaller circles surrounded by a periphery of less well-connected cliques and points. Figure 6.14 shows a simplified analysis of social circles. Two circles are identified at step 1, but they are merged into a single circle at step 2. As in so many graph theoretical procedures, it is important to note that the level of overlap that is chosen for aggregation is arbitrary. The levels suggested by Alba were chosen on common-sense mathematical grounds, and it will be necessary for researchers to decide whether his suggestions make sense in specific applications.

The measurement of circles, therefore, takes the extent of the overlap between cliques as a measure of the distance between them. The particular way in which the cliques have been identified (as *n*-cliques or *k*-plexes, for example) hardly matters in this procedure, as the subtle differences in the procedures rapidly disappear during the process of aggregation. In practice, the end result of an aggregation into circles is barely affected by the initial clique detection method that is used.[28]

Components and Citation Circles

The sociology of science is one of the principle research areas in which a number of studies have invoked the idea of the social network. Crane's study (1972) of the 'invisible college' was one of the earliest pieces of research to use the idea of networks of communication among scientists as a way of explaining the growth of scientific knowledge. Crane's study involved the use of questionnaires to obtain information on patterns of communication and influence among rural sociologists, and she analysed such phenomena as co-publication and advice on areas of research specialization. Her concern was to outline the size and significance of the invisible college of collaborators in the research specialism, but few sociometric concepts were used to uncover its internal structure. Mullins (1973) adopted a different strategy. He looked at work in theoretical sociology and tried to discover the sub-groups of specialists that existed. Using material on education and career appointments as well as co-publication, he constructed sociograms for structural functionalist theory, small group theory, causal theory and a number of other areas.[29] Unfortunately, the boundaries of the research specialisms were not themselves derived from sociometric analyses, and so Mullins's work gives little idea of the overall structure of components and cliques in theoretical sociology.

Gattrell's work, however, is one of the few studies in this area to have adopted a rigorous sociometric approach to the discovery of network structure. Gattrell (1984a, b) has used the techniques of Q-analysis (see n. 17 above) to disclose the structure of components in research groups. It is unnecessary to discuss the details of this complex procedure, as Gattrell used it simply in order to construct a nested model of components, and his ideas can readily be translated into the terminology of this chapter.[30] Gattrell identified a set of geographical papers published between 1960 and 1978, which he regarded as the key elements in the literature on spatial modelling. Taking these papers as his population for study, he constructed a network of citation relations from their bibliographies and footnotes. Where the author of paper A cites the author of paper B, for example, a citation relation is directed from A to B. These citations can, therefore, be compiled into a binary matrix of directed lines. As the rows and columns of the matrix were ordered chronologically, by the date of publication, it was easy to assess any obvious shifts in citation patterns. If, for example, authors cited only relatively recent papers, the '1' entries in the matrix would lie close to the diagonal. The more scattered are the '1' entries, the more widespread in time are citations. Any clustering around the diagonal would show support for Price's hypothesis (1965) of the 'immediacy effect' in citation, but Gattrell found little support for this idea.

The main aim of Gattrell's paper was to examine the component structure of the citation data, and from his initial matrix he compiled two analyses. First, he analysed the structure of the network of papers cited (the rows), and, second, he analysed the structure of the citing papers (the columns). Two cited papers are regarded as being connected to one another if they are each cited in the same source, and a component comprises a set of papers that are connected through a continuous chain of such connections.[31] Where two cited papers have more than one of their citers in common, they are connected at a higher level of multiplicity, and it is possible to investigate the nesting of components at various levels of multiplicity.

Gattrell found that, at the lowest level, 49 of the papers were formed into a single large component. But at a multiplicity level of 6, this had shrunk to seven members. The seven papers in this component formed the core of the network. At the heart of this group were two highly cited papers by Hudson (1969) and Pedersen (1970). Hudson received 17 citations and Pedersen received 15 citations, but only eight of their citations were common to one another. Thus, Hudson and Pedersen formed a component of size 2 at multiplicity 8 (calculated from Gattrell, 1984b: 447). Gattrell concludes that:

> The general picture . . . is of a small group of highly cited papers, to which other literature is connected at lower . . . [multiplicity] levels. A small component of papers concerned with hierarchical diffusion emerges, and other papers are added to this nucleus as a result of their being cited by some of the sources that cite the seminal papers. (Gattrell, 1984b: 448)

The analysis of components and their cores, then, allows the investigation of the structure of influence in scientific research, such investigations pointing to the important role played by scientific cliques and circles in the promotion of particular ideas and approaches. The analysis of nested components in citation patterns highlights the 'star' cited papers and the extent to which there is any consensus over their star rating.

7

Positions, Roles and Clusters

The network concepts that have been discussed so far in this book have mainly been concerned with the particular patterns of direct and indirect contacts that agents are able to maintain with one another. They have been concerned with such things as the abilities of agents to join with one another in cohesive social groupings, their abilities to influence the actions of those particular others to whom they are connected, and so on. However, I have, at a number of points, alluded to the analysis of 'positions' rather than individual agents and their connections. Warner and Lunt (1942), for example, attempted to investigate the formation of distinct social positions, and Nadel (1957) argued that social roles were the central elements in social network analysis. The key concept in recent discussions of this problem is the idea of 'structural equivalence'. This involves a concern for the general *types* of social relations that are maintained by particular *categories* of agents. While two people may have direct connections to totally different individuals, the type of relations that they have with these others may, nevertheless, be similar. Two fathers, for example, will have different sets of children to whom they relate, but they might be expected to behave, in certain respects, in similar 'fatherly' ways towards them. The two men, that is to say, are 'structurally equivalent' to one another. They occupy the same social position – that of 'father' – and so are interchangeable so far as the sociological analysis of fathers is concerned. The idea behind structural equivalence, therefore, is that of identifying those uniformities of action that define social **positions**. Once the positions have been identified, the networks of relations that exist between the positions can be explored.

Social positions are occupied by agents who are 'substitutable' one for another, with respect to their relational ties (Burt, 1982; Sailer, 1978). They are, in certain important respects, interchangeable. Although social positions are manifest only in the particular relations that link specific agents, they cannot be reduced to these concrete connections. They involve more enduring relations that are reproduced over time. These enduring relations among social positions constitute a distinct area of structural analysis.

The Structural Equivalence of Points

It might appear, at first glance, that the analysis of structural equivalence is simply the analysis of social roles, but this is not the case. The example of the two fathers shows that the clearest cases of structural equivalence are, indeed, those that arise when people occupy institutionalized roles. The occupants of a clearly specified cultural role comprise a structurally equivalent category of agents: they do similar things in relation to similar others. But this is, of course, true only for fully institutionalized roles. If people do not act in conformity with standardized cultural expectations, but deviate or otherwise vary in the ways in which they perceive and enact their roles, very few uniformities of action may be found. In such circumstances, there will be no *position* of structurally equivalent agents corresponding to the culturally defined *role*. This is, no doubt, the case for many cultural roles, and the degree to which they are institutionalized into structured uniformities of action will be highly variable from one case to another.

Conversely, there may be structured uniformities of action that are neither culturally recognized nor identified in socially defined roles. Agents may occupy a distinct position in relation to other agents, acting in similar ways towards them, even though this fact is not recognized by the various participants. Indeed, this may be one of the ways in which new roles emerge: new forms of action arise and relations between more or less clearly defined categories of agents begin to crystallize long before people come to perceive what is going on and to give a name to it. In this sense, the identification of structurally equivalent categories of agents may be one basis for identifying emergent roles.

It is important, therefore, to see the concept of structural equivalence as applying to social positions *per se*, and not simply to roles or proto-roles. A social class, for example, could be identified in precisely these terms as a group of agents occupying an equivalent position with respect to the distribution of economic resources and, therefore, as having equivalent structurally determined interests and life chances in relation to the members of other classes.

The starting point for all formal discussions of structural equivalence has been the influential paper of Lorrain and White (1971). They built their approach around the concept of role, seeing the occupants of each role as being structurally equivalent to one another. Structurally equivalent agents, they argued, play the same part in the network or have similar linkages to the occupants of other positions and so are interchangeable one with another. They will have similar experiences or opportunities (Burt, 1987; Friedkin,

1984; Mizruchi, 1993). Lorrain and White's paper described some of the limitations of graph theory as a complete model for network structure and outlined an alternative strategy based on algebraic ideas. They argued that their approach had two major defining features that set it apart from other approaches to social network analysis. First, all points and their connections were handled simultaneously, rather than attention being limited to the particular lines, paths and cycles that connected them. Second, the approach did not remain with the adjacency matrix, but undertook a combined analysis of both the rows and the columns of the original incidence matrix. People and the organizations of which they were members, for example, could be analysed together rather than separately.

According to Lorrain and White, the overall pattern of connections in a network must be converted into a system of structurally equivalent positions by aggregating the individual points into larger sets of points. The underlying structure of the system is more apparent in the relations that exist between the sets than it is in the more numerous and more concrete relations that exist between the individual agents who make up these sets. Figure 7.1 shows Lorrain and White's view of the 'reduction' of a complex network to its 'block model' or 'image matrix'. The points of the original incidence matrix are re-arranged through a method of cluster analysis to form the structurally equivalent sets of the image matrix. In Figure 7.1, for example, the set $M1$ comprises those of the row points which are regarded as being structurally equivalent to one another, yet structurally divergent from those structurally equivalent points that make up set $M2$. The most fundamental features of a network,

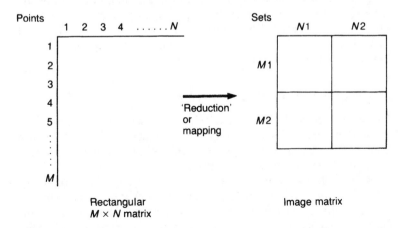

Figure 7.1   *A network and its block model*

argued Lorrain and White, are apparent in the relations among the sets, and the nature of these relations is shown by the values in the cells – the blocks – of the image matrix. The aim of much of White's subsequent work was to suggest how such block models might be produced.[1]

The concept of structural equivalence holds, in its strongest sense, that the members of a set are identical with one another as regards their relations to other members of the network. It is, however, very unusual to find agents that are perfectly equivalent in this strong sense. Most analysts of structural equivalence have, therefore, argued that the criterion needs to be weakened if it is to be of use in the study of real social networks. Instead of searching for those agents that are identical in their social relations, the aim is to identify those who are sufficiently *similar* to be regarded as structurally equivalent. Whatever the chosen measure of similarity, the researcher must decide on a cut-off threshold above which agents are to be regarded as being sufficiently similar to be, in effect, 'substitutable' for one another. This 'fuzzy' measure of structural equivalence is likely to be of greater use in real situations, though the cut-off level for identifying equivalence is, of course, a decision made by the researcher, and must be rigorously assessed for its substantive validity.

The major areas of disagreement among writers on structural equivalence concern the particular measure of 'similarity' that is to be used, the method of clustering by which points are to be grouped into sets, and the methods to be used for identifying the boundaries of the sets. In the next section, I will briefly review the main methods of cluster analysis which are available and, in the following section, I will outline in greater detail two particular approaches to structural equivalence. I will then return once more to the choice of clustering method and measure of 'similarity' through considering some alternative approaches.

Clusters: Agglomerative and Divisive

The words 'cluster' and 'clique' are often used interchangeably, as in the early discussions of sociometric 'cliques' in Old City and in Yankee City. Even some recent methodological commentators have not distinguished between the two ideas (see Lankford, 1974). I showed in the previous chapter, however, that the concept of the clique can be given a strict sociometric definition from which a whole family of related concepts can be derived. The concept of the cluster needs also to be clearly defined as a separate and very distinct idea. The intuitive idea of a cluster corresponds to the idea of an area of relatively high density in a graph. This idea of the cluster is applicable to relational and attribute data alike, and can be illustrated through scatter diagrams such as those in Figure 7.2. In a scatter diagram, the individual cases are plotted against the two variables which comprise the axes of the diagram. The scatter of the cases across the page gives an indication of how similar or different they are from one another in terms of these variables.

In each of the diagrams of Figure 7.2 there are two distinct clusters. In diagram (i), the clusters consist of points that are more 'similar' to one another than they are to other points. They form areas of high density in the overall scatter plot. While these clusters are apparent by simple visual inspection, computerized procedures are required for larger data sets. However, the researcher must then choose a particular method of cluster analysis. Most available methods would recognize the clusters in diagram (i), but not all would recognize such clusters as those of diagram (ii). The points in this diagram spread across elongated areas of the distribution, and points at opposite 'ends' of each cluster are quite 'distant' from one another. Clusters are defined in terms of their *contiguity* in the diagram and their *separation* from other clusters, but not all clusters will consist of points that are equally 'close' to one another in the scatter plot. Most techniques of cluster analysis assume compact 'spherical' clusters and would have great difficulty in finding the kinds of clusters depicted in diagram (ii).

Clearly, the boundaries of clusters cannot be drawn sharply. Diagram (iii) in Figure 7.2, for example, shows what might appear to be two large clusters, each of which contains a smaller cluster. But an alternative view is to see only the smaller clumps of points as being clusters. The composition of the clusters identified in a cluster analysis will depend on the density level that is chosen by the researcher, and on the assumptions made by the particular clustering method.

This arbitrariness in determining the boundaries of clusters indicates that clustering methods may be seen as using a variant of the nesting procedure. There is a hierarchical structure to clusters, which can be represented in 'dendrograms', or tree diagrams that show the clusters that exist at each level of similarity. This idea is illustrated in Figure 7.3. This diagram shows that points C and D are linked into a cluster at the first step in the analysis, points G and H are linked at the second step, points E and F at the third step, and points A and B at the fourth step. If the analysis stopped at this point, four clusters would have been identified. If the analysis is moved to a fifth step, however, points E, F, G and H are all identified as being members of a single cluster. Similarly points A,

(i)

(ii)

(iii)

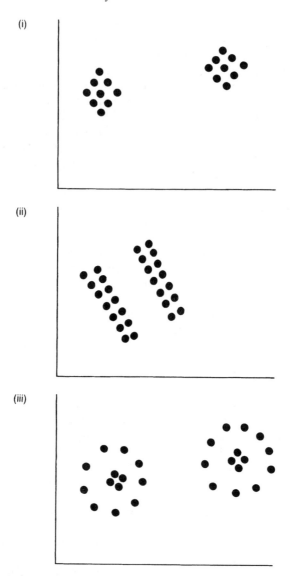

Figure 7.2   *Clusters*

B, C and D are clustered together at step six. Finally, at step seven, all points are aggregated into the same cluster. The number and composition of clusters found in any investigation will depend on the step at which the analysis is stopped.

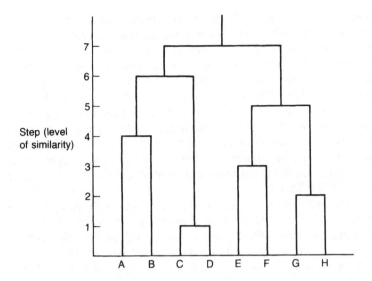

Figure 7.3   *A dendrogram*

Although these ideas have been illustrated through the more familiar type of attribute data, they are equally applicable to relational data. Here, for example, points might be clustered according to their path distance or density within a sociometric graph. The members of a cluster might be those that are similar to one another in terms of some graph theoretical criterion of closeness or distance from other points.

There are two principal families of cluster analysis methods: 'the agglomerative' and the 'divisive' (Bailey, 1976; Everitt, 1974). Each is hierarchical, in the sense that it 'nests' small clusters within larger clusters, but the principles that are used in constructing a hierarchy of clusters vary between the two cases. The discussion above was couched in terms of an agglomerative model in which individual points are gradually aggregated into larger and larger sets. Points are compared for their 'similarity' or 'distance' from one another, and are grouped together with those to which they are closest or most similar. Agglomerative methods can be of the 'single linkage' or the 'complete linkage' type (Johnson, 1967). In a **single linkage** method, points are fused into a cluster with their nearest neighbours. In a study of interlocking directorships, for example, enterprises might be merged into clusters on the basis of the number of directors that they have in common. Initially, the two closest points are fused into a cluster and later steps fuse successively more distant points and clusters. Two clusters would be fused, for example, if their most similar members were closer to one another than were any other pair of points in the set. A **complete linkage** method follows the same general approach, but measures the similarity between two clusters not by their closest but by their remotest members.[2] While the single linkage method tends to 'chain' points together into existing clusters, the complete linkage method is more likely to initiate new clusters at early stages in the analysis. The single linkage method, therefore, is less likely to identify the compact and homogeneous clusters of the kind found through complete linkage. In emphasizing the connections between clusters, the single linkage method can mask the existence of important divisions in the network (Alba, 1982: 55–6).

With both methods of agglomerative cluster analysis, it is for the analyst to decide on the level of similarity at which clusters are to be identified. In a connected graph, all points will, eventually, fuse into a single cluster, so the number and size of clusters identified will depend upon the cut-off threshold that is chosen. It follows that the choice of a cut-off threshold, as in so many areas of social network analysis, is a matter for the informed judgement of the researcher, though some measures of goodness of fit have been suggested as aids in this task.

In a divisive, or partitioning approach, the opposite strategy is followed. Starting from the graph as a whole, regarded as a single cluster, sub-sets are split off at reducing levels of similarity. There are two approaches to divisive clustering, the 'single attribute' and the 'all attribute' methods. **Single attribute** methods begin by differentiating those points that possess a particular indicator or value from those that do not, and the initial cluster is split into two on the basis of the possession or non-possession of this indicator. The same procedure is followed within each cluster at subsequent steps, in order to sub-divide each of them further.[3] The single attribute procedure, therefore, consists of a series of binary splits aimed at producing mutually exclusive sets of points. In an **all attribute** method, on the other hand, the first and subsequent splits are based on the average similarity of a set of points to all other points in the graph.

The methods of cluster analysis may seem a little vague in the abstract, but I hope that their general principles are clear. It should be apparent that the clusters that are identified in a particular graph will depend upon the choice of the method and the choice of the measure of similarity on which it works. The implications of this can be pursued by considering a particular approach that builds on the work of Lorrain and White (1971).

Block Models: CONCOR and BURT

The first workable algorithm for investigating structural equivalence along the lines that had been suggested by Lorrain and White was formulated by Breiger and Schwartz, two of White's students, who independently rediscovered the matrix clustering method proposed by McQuitty (1968).[4] Their algorithm, called CONCOR (standing for 'CONvergence of iterated CORrelations'), involves a rather complex and cumbersome procedure, although its general principles are fairly straightforward. The CONCOR algorithm operates on sociometric incidence matrices of cases and affiliations, and can be applied to the rows, to the columns, or simultaneously to both the rows and the columns of the matrix. Its general logic can, however, best be understood by following through the steps involved in an analysis of the rows alone. Such an analysis investigates the structural equivalences among the cases.

The first step in the analysis is to calculate the correlations between all pairs of cases in the matrix, measuring this by the similarity of the values that are contained in the row entries. For each pair of cases it is possible to measure their 'similarity' by the value of the Pearson correlation coefficient: two cases with exactly the same pattern of affiliations would show a correlation of $+1$, while a pair with completely different patterns of affiliation would have a correlation of -1. The result of this first step is a square case-by-case correlation matrix, a particular form of the adjacency matrix. The second step involves the use of a clustering procedure to group the cases into structurally equivalent sets, according to their measured similarity. If rows were either perfectly correlated or completely un-correlated, such a grouping would be easy. All values in the correlation matrix would be either $+1$ or -1, and a strong criterion of structural equivalence could be used to divide the matrix into two sets. The matrix would fall into two sets that were completely connected internally but had no connections with one another. Such a clustering would be possible for the data shown in Figure 2.6. As this kind of patterning is not normally the case with real data, a clustering method that works on a wider range of correlation values must be used as the basis for identifying 'fuzzy' sets of equivalent points.

CONCOR achieves a fuzzy clustering by converting the raw correlations into a tighter pattern. It does this by calculating, for each pair of cases, the correlation between their scores in the correlation matrix that has been constructed. That is, the correlations among the correlations scores are calculated and they are entered into a new correlation matrix. This process is repeated over and over again for each successive matrix – correlating the correlations of the correlations, and so on. Repeated correlations of this kind have been found to produce, eventually, a matrix in which all the cells will contain values of either +1 or −1. The iterated (repeated) correlations converge to a simple pattern and the rows can be partitioned into two clusters in much the same way as if a strong criterion of structural equivalence were being used. Each cluster constitutes a set of structurally equivalent cases.

Each of the two clusters can be divided into its constituent elements by using precisely the same method. To achieve this, the algorithm returns to the original matrix of raw values and divides this into two separate matrices, one for each of the clusters that have been identified. As in the first round of iterations, the raw group memberships within one of the clusters are converted into correlations, the correlations are correlated, and so on, until a pattern of +1 and −1 entries emerges within the cluster. At this point the cluster can be partitioned once more and the whole process repeated. Division and sub-division of clusters in this way can proceed for as long as the researcher wishes, though the larger the number of clusters, the more difficult it may be to interpret the final results.[5]

While the researcher must make an arbitrary decision about when to stop the process of division and sub-division within clusters, the emergence of a pattern of +1 and −1 values at each step does mean that there is a relatively unambiguous approximation to a strong criterion for identifying structural equivalence. The partitioning of the cases depends simply on the actual values that are produced in the final matrix.[6] Unfortunately, the reason why such a pattern should emerge is far from clear. This means that there is an unspecified, and partly obscure clustering principle at work in the CONCOR algorithm. It is the algorithm itself that, for reasons that are not entirely clear, produces the conversion of the raw data into structural equivalence categories. The clusters identified by CONCOR, therefore, are just as 'fuzzy' as those that might be produced through a procedure that does not result in such an elegant pattern.

This process of partitioning into clusters can be repeated for the columns of the original incidence matrix, so as to produce a separate grouping of the affiliations. If the cases were individuals and the affiliations were the organizations of which they were members, a partitioning of the organizations would cluster them according to similarities in their patterns of recruitment. For both the rows and the columns of the original incidence matrix, then, CONCOR can produce a hierarchical partitioning into structurally equivalent clusters – 'discrete mutually exclusive and exhaustive categories' (Knoke and Kuklinski, 1982: 73).

The clusters identified in these ways can be constructed into re-arranged image matrices of the type illustrated in Figure 7.1. It is possible to produce a square image matrix for the adjacency matrix of the cases or for the adjacency matrix of the affiliations. Each of the cells in the image matrix – they are termed the 'blocks' – contains a measure of the density of the connections between pairs of sets. If all density values were either 1 or 0, the pattern of relations would be clear. The 'zero-blocks' (the cells with density 0) would represent 'holes' in the network, the complete absence of connections; and the distribution of cells with density 1 would show the basic structure of the network. Such density patterns rarely occur in real data, and so a block modelling has to convert the actual range of density values into two categories of 'high' and 'low' values as approximations to the 1-blocks and zero-blocks. In the image matrix, the high values – those which are above a specified threshold value – are represented by 1, while low values are represented by 0. The most commonly used method for defining blocks with a high density is to take the average density of the whole matrix as a cut-off point: values at or above the mean are regarded as 'high', while those below it are 'low'. But this procedure, like so many in network analysis, involves a discretionary choice on the part of the researcher, and this choice must be grounded in theoretical or empirical considerations. It cannot be justified on any purely formal, mathematical principles alone. Friedkin (1998: 8) has also criticized the reliance on density as the sole measure of block formation.

Exactly the same procedure can be used to produce a block model for a combined analysis of the rows and columns. CONCOR will produce a clustering of the rows and a clustering of the columns and will then combine these into a single image matrix of the original rectangular incidence matrix.

Once a block model, an image graph containing only 1 and 0 values in its cells, has been produced, the researcher must attempt to interpret it. Interpretations of block models produced from rectangular, incidence matrices are extremely difficult to make, and Breiger and his associates, the originators of block modelling, have published no detailed analyses of such models. In the earliest analysis of an incidence matrix, Breiger, Boorman and Arabie (1975) re-analysed the *Deep South* data collected by Davis and his colleagues (1941) on the participation of 18 women in 14 social events.[7] To analyse these data, they computed separate row and column solutions and combined them into the block model shown in Figure 7.4.

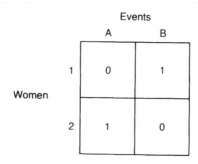

Figure 7.4   *A simple block model*

It can be seen that women in cluster 1 tend to meet in the events of cluster B and that women in cluster 2 tend to meet at the events of cluster A. The two clusters of women correspond closely to the two 'cliques' that had been identified by Homans (1951) in his commentary on the original data, but Breiger et al. did not go beyond this observation. Although they discuss the composition of the clusters, they give no attention to the pattern of block densities in the image matrix. In the same paper, they also re-analysed Levine's rectangular matrix of banks and corporations (Levine, 1972), but they again simply compare the separate row and column analyses with Levine's own analysis.

This failure on the part of the inventors of block modelling to analyse an incidence matrix in any detail suggests the existence of a fundamental difficulty in achieving the concurrent treatment of both rows and columns that was anticipated by Lorrain and White. A rectangular image matrix, if it is fairly simple, may give an initial and schematic overview of the network, but more detailed analyses can only be pursued by analysing the rows and the columns separately. An incidence matrix, then, must be analysed principally through the construction of separate block models for each of its constituent adjacency matrices. In these block models, those cells on the diagonal that contained a '1' would correspond to some kind of clique or social circle of the type discussed in the previous chapter. The other cells would show the presence or absence of connections between the various cliques and the other clusters that make up the graph.[8]

Breiger has shown how the CONCOR method can be applied in one of the central areas of social analysis. Using data on social mobility from Britain (Glass, 1954) and the United States (Blau and Duncan, 1967; Featherman and Hauser, 1978), he constructed a model of class structure in which the classes were defined as sets of occupations identifiable in a matrix of occupational mobility rates (Breiger, 1981, 1982). He sees this as an extension of Weber's (1920–21) claim that 'a structure of social classes exists only when the mobility chances of individuals within the classes cluster in such a way as to create a common nexus of social interchange' (Breiger, 1982: 18. See also Scott, 1996: ch. 2). CONCOR, he suggests, can be used to identify class boundaries. Breiger used inter-generational mobility matrices for adult males, the American matrices being 17×17 directed matrices of occupational categories and the British being 8×8 directed matrices. In each matrix, the cells contained the numbers of individuals moving from one category to another, the rows showed the 'origins' and the columns showed the 'destinations'. For the United States, Breiger (1981) concluded that there was a stable structure of eight classes over the period 1962–73, while for Britain he concluded that the earlier data (they related to 1949) could best be seen as reflecting a three-class structure. The central class boundaries in Britain separated manual from non-manual and the salaried 'middle class' from lower-level clerical and administrative jobs.

By far the easiest of matrices to analyse through block modelling are adjacency matrices with directed data – matrices where, for example, the rows represent relations 'sent' and the columns represent relations 'received'. A useful aid to the interpretation of this kind of data is the construction of arrow diagrams that show the relations among the clusters. This can be illustrated with the matrices in Figure 7.5, which show some hypothetical data on power relations.[9] In these matrices, the power relations are directed from rows to columns. The row entries in the original matrix, for example, would show over which other agents a particular agent exercises power. Conversely, the column entries would show to which other agents a particular agent is subordinate in a power relation. In the block models, agents are clustered according to both their exercise of power and their subordination to power, and the 1 and 0 entries in the image matrices show the densities of the power relations among the clusters.

In model (i) of Figure 7.5, members of cluster 1 exercise power over one another and also over members of cluster 2. This is shown by the entries of '1' in the relevant blocks. Members of cluster 2, however, exercise no power whatsoever, being completely subordinate to the power of those in cluster 1. This structure is summarized in the corresponding arrow diagram. In model (ii), on the other hand, there are two separate and self-regulating categories (clusters 1 and 3), and members of these clusters jointly exercise power over the

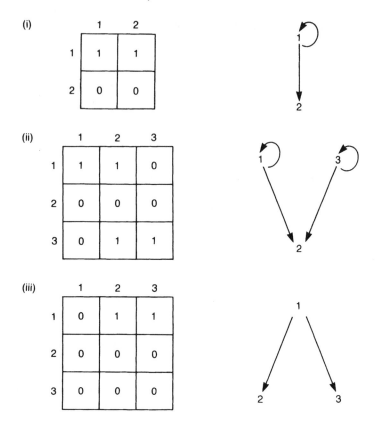

Figure 7.5   *Hierarchical block models*

members of cluster 2. Finally, in model (iii), cluster 1 dominates both cluster 2 and cluster 3, but there is little mutual exercise of power among the members of cluster 1 itself – the individual members of cluster 1 are each relatively autonomous agents.

Undirected matrices are, except in the most simple cases, rather more difficult to interpret, as the lack of any direction to the relations means that it is not possible to construct arrow diagrams to show their structures. Few such analyses have been published, and the application of block modelling to real and complex data sets of various kinds is essential if the value of the procedure is to be demonstrated.[10]

A fundamental problem with the CONCOR algorithm, as I have already suggested, is that it is not known exactly *why* it produces its solutions. The mathematical reasons for the convergence to a distribution of 1 and 0 entries are uncertain, and so an assessment of the validity of the results is difficult to make. This might seem to be a fairly damning criticism, but the fact that it does work and that it does seem to produce plausible models of small social networks helps to offset this criticism somewhat. There is, however, another difficulty, which suggests a further limitation on its applicability: CONCOR can identify structurally equivalent positions only *within* the components and sub-groups of a graph. If, for example, power relations were divided into distinct components within the network, CONCOR would not group together those who were dominant in the separate components as a single cluster of 'dominant' agents. Their equivalence as occupants of a position of dominance is masked, so far as CONCOR is concerned, by their sociometric division into separate components. Similarly, when a component is internally divided into relatively distinct cliques and circles, CONCOR will tend to identify only the dominant members within each of the sub-groups.

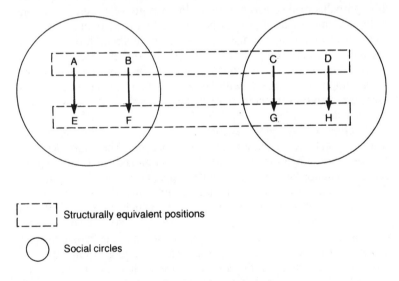

Structurally equivalent positions

Social circles

Figure 7.6 *Structural equivalence and social circles*

This can be illustrated through Figure 7.6, which shows a network in which A, B, C and D are structurally equivalent as dominant agents, and E, F, G and H are structurally equivalent as subordinate agents. An adequate clustering of the network into structurally equivalent positions should identify two clusters {ABCD} and {EFGH}. If, however, the agents are divided into two distinct social circles, as shown, CONCOR will tend to identify four clusters instead:

{AB}, {CD}, {EF} and {GH}. The conclusion to be drawn is that the CONCOR algorithm combines structural equivalence with conventional sociometric measures and so fails to produce a thoroughgoing analysis of structural equivalence.

These limitations of the CONCOR procedure have led Ronald Burt to advocate a different approach to structural equivalence, one which aims to avoid CONCOR's reliance on uncertain mathematical procedures. His approach differs from that of CONCOR both in the measure of similarity that is used and in the method of clustering. Having examined CONCOR in some detail, it will be fairly easy to understand how Burt's procedure operates and in what respects it is an improvement on CONCOR. Burt's procedure is implemented in his program STRUCTURE, and in order to distinguish it from the other procedures available in that program I shall term it 'BURT'.[11]

BURT uses a similarity measure based on path distances between pairs of points. Where CONCOR looked only at similarity in terms of direct contacts, BURT takes account also of indirect connections through paths of distance 2 or more in order to arrive at calculations of the minimum path distances between all pairs of points. The Burt measure of path distance also assumes that the strength of a relation declines with both the path distance and the significance of the path for the agent's overall pattern of contacts. This measure is based on the assumption that agents with large numbers of contacts are able to give less attention to their more distant ones.[12] Thus, the similarity measure used in BURT is a weighted distance measure.[13]

Structurally equivalent agents, in the strong sense, are those whose points are separated by zero distance. They are perfectly similar and substitutable. Burt has recognized that this strong criterion cannot be applied to most real data, and so he argued for the identification of weak structural equivalence through the use of a cut-off threshold of distance below which points would be regarded as structurally equivalent (Burt, 1980: 101ff.). While CONCOR's arbitrariness derives from an obscure mathematical procedure, BURT's arbitrariness has the virtue of being grounded in the informed judgement of the specialist researcher. BURT performs a hierarchical clustering of the distance matrix, using Johnson's (1967) aggregative single linkage method, and the researcher reads off the clusters that are found, if any, at the chosen cut-off level of distance.

Once a clustering has been produced by the BURT procedure, the investigation can proceed with the construction of a block model. If the densities in the image matrix are replaced by entries of 1 or 0, using the density of the whole network as a cut-off threshold, the resulting block model can be analysed in the same way as those derived from a CONCOR analysis. An image matrix that shows the density of connections among the clusters is a simplified mapping, a 'homomorphic reduction', of the concrete pattern of relations between agents, and Burt terms this a 'social topology'.

Burt argues that the departure from a strict measure of strong structural equivalence means that any analysis must be treated merely as a hypothetical model. Without some kind of statistical test of significance, he argues, researchers would be free to choose whichever cut-off threshold will produce the results that correspond most closely to their preconceptions. A significance test helps to introduce a degree of impartiality and objectivity to the assessment of block models. Burt's recommended test involves an examination of each cluster in order to measure how closely associated each of its members is with the other occupants of the cluster. The best solution, he argues, is that which optimizes this measure of association.[14]

Towards Regular Structural Equivalence

The CONCOR and BURT procedures are probably the most widely used methods for identifying structural equivalence, but a number of alternatives have been suggested. Although some of these have become relatively easily available, they have rarely been applied to real data, and their long-term value still remains to be assessed.

Where CONCOR takes account only of path distances of length 1 and BURT takes account of all connections, regardless of their path length, Sailer (1978) has proposed a procedure in which the researcher is given the choice of a path length to use. A path distance is chosen, and the similarity of connections between pairs of points is calculated at that chosen level. Sailer's measure, then, which he terms simply 'substitutability', is based on the 'neighbour-hood' of points. The degree of similarity between two points is measured in proportional rather than absolute terms, the number of contacts that they have in common at the specified path length being standardized by each point's adjacency. That is, the overlap between contacts is measured by the number of common connections expressed as a proportion of each point's total number of connec-tions at that distance. Each point, therefore, can be given a standar-dized measure of its similarity to each of the other points. Complete overlap in contacts produces a standardized score of 1, while complete absence of overlap gives a score of 0.[15] As in the CONCOR procedure, Sailer sees this as simply a first step in an iterative process. The matrix of similarities is treated as an initial estimate of the 'substitutability' of points, and the continued repetition of the method on each new set of estimates results in a convergence to a solution in which all values are either '1' or '0'. In this way, then, a block model can be produced for analysis. Sailer's procedure, however, fails to overcome the principal limitation of the CONCOR and BURT methods, which is that they cannot adequately handle networks that are divided into components or tight sub-groups of the kind illustrated in Figure 7.6 (see also Carrington and Heil, 1981; Wu, 1984).

An interesting attempt to overcome this sociometric limitation is REGE, an algorithm that is intended to detect 'regular' structural equivalence. This is defined as those equivalences that are regular across all the various sub-groups of a network (Reitz and White, 1989; White and Reitz, 1983; Winship and Mandel, 1984). The concept of regular equivalence is closer to the idea of the substitutability of agents by role or by function within a social system. Where CONCOR and BURT see points as being structurally equivalent when they have *identical* links to all the other points in the graph, REGE sees points as equivalent if they have *similar* links to points that are themselves structurally equivalent. Two points are regularly equivalent in relation to another set of points if the relation of one point to the points in that set is similar to the relation between the other point and the set. Each point has an identical relation with a counterpart in the same set, though this relation need not be with the same point or points. This can be illustrated by the obvious fact that all fathers are related to children, but they are not all related to the *same* children. White and Reitz argue, therefore, that the block models produced by REGE are *homomorphic* reductions, but not necessarily *isomorphic* reductions of their corresponding graphs.

The way in which REGE works can best be understood through the case of a directed matrix, although it is very difficult to understand the details of the procedure. The algorithm uses a partitioning method that looks at direct connections and also at the contacts of points adjacent to each pair. It begins by making estimates of the equivalence values between all pairs of connected points. These estimates are all initially set at 1, and they are revised with each round of calculation, which involves computing revised estimates of equivalences from the smallest in- and outdegrees for each pair of points. At the end of each round, therefore, there is a new matrix of estimated equivalences between pairs of points. The procedure is, ideally, continued until the revised estimates of equivalence no longer alter; that is, the computations are no longer resulting in any greater precision for the estimates. In practice, the researcher can choose to stop when it appears that further calculations will make little difference to the estimates. It has been suggested that the version of REGE implemented in UCINET produces optimum estimates after three rounds of calculation (see also Borgatti and Everett, 1989; Borgatti et al., 1989). This approach can be used only on directed data, though Doreian (1987) has suggested an adaptation that allows undirected data to be analysed. With a symmetrical matrix, as Doreian shows, the initial estimates are not altered by the calculation: the algorithm simply identifies all connected points as being regularly equivalent. Such matrices can be analysed only if they are divided into two asymmetrical matrices, which can then be jointly analysed by REGE. Doreian suggests using centrality scores to make this division, though Everett and Borgatti (1990) have suggested that any graph theoretical attribute could be used. If centrality is used, for example, one matrix would consist of the relations directed from more to less central points, while the other matrix contains the relations directed from less to more central points.

Despite its limitations, REGE is the first structural equivalence procedure to offer a true approximation to the regular structural equivalence described by Lorrain and White (1971). The substantive assumptions that it makes about the data are, however, obscured by complex mathematics, and it is difficult for a non-mathematician to assess whether these assumptions are valid and realistic. As with CONCOR, the fact that it *does* appear to work as expected on small-scale data is a powerful argument in its favour, but researchers must be aware that they are taking a certain amount on trust.

The aspiration of writers such as Nadel, it will be recalled, was to build a framework of sociological analysis in which positional analysis would complement more traditional sociometric concerns with cliques and components. The approaches to structural equivalence that have culminated in REGE have eschewed graph theory and so remain at one remove from these sociometric concerns. The approach of 'graph role analysis', on the other hand, tries to use the structural position of points as measured in graph theory as a basis for a measure of structural similarity (Zegers and ten Berghe, 1985). The procedure uses local dependency or geodesic matrices to calculate correlations between pairs of actors.[16] Structural equivalence is assessed in terms of how similar these measures are for the various points. A pair of points with, for example, similarly high betweenness scores might be recognized as being structurally equivalent in certain important respects. In order to avoid the obvious problem of regarding points as structurally equivalent only if they lie between the *same* points, the algorithm can compute whether they lie between points that are themselves similar in their betweenness scores. The particularly interesting feature of this procedure is that it begins to build a bridge between the relatively well understood concepts of graph theory and the rather less well understood measures of structural equivalence. Instead of conflating the approaches, as in CONCOR, it aims to theorize and to articulate their interdependence.[17]

Interlocks and Participations

Burt has pursued a long-standing interest in the question of interlocking directorships in the business world, but he has eschewed conventional clique-based approaches to their investigation. His earliest paper on this question (Burt, 1979) set out his aspiration to discover the linkages that occur between profitability and the structural location of enterprises in the corporate system, and his development of the idea of structural equivalence was specifically geared towards this issue of structural location.

His starting point was the hypothesis that many interlocks can be understood as 'cooptive mechanisms' through which enterprises absorb into their own leadership those people from other enterprises who might threaten their continued operations. Thus, the suppliers who create market 'uncertainty' are objects of 'cooptive interlocks' by those to whom they supply goods or capital. Financial institutions, for this reason, are of particular importance in corporate interlocking: 'The use of money as a general resource makes the actions of financial corporations a source of significant uncertainty, so that firms would be expected to establish cooptive interlocks with financial corporations so as to secure access to money when it is needed' (Burt, 1979: 416).

Drawing on his earlier discussions of 'positional' concepts (Burt, 1976, 1977a, b), Burt saw the firms that operated in each sector of the economy as structurally equivalent to one another – the economic sectors comprised positions in a social topology. Using input–output data at the sectoral level for the United States in 1967, Burt attempted to show in which inter-sector exchanges there existed the degree of uncertainty that would make cooptive interlocking a rational strategy. That is to say, he was interested in seeing whether the structure of constraining economic transactions was reflected in a parallel structure of interlocks. The idea of 'constraint' between sectors was operationalized in terms of competitive pressures: enterprises were more constrained by their transactions with oligopolistic sectors than they were by those with competitive sectors. Market constraint reduced the structural autonomy of enterprises, and interlocking reduces the effects of this constraint and so transforms the economic environment in which enterprises operate. Burt holds that 'structure in the two networks is a symbiotic phenomena [sic]: market structure patterning interlock structure and interlock structure repatterning market structure' (Burt, 1979: 433; see also Burt et al., 1980; Burt, 1982: chs 4 and 8).

Burt's data comprised two parallel directed adjacency matrices, in which the rows and columns corresponded to economic sectors. One matrix contained information on the economic transactions between sectors, while the other showed their patterns of inter-locking. The results of a block modelling of these data have not been directly reported, but Burt concluded that the two networks did mirror one another and that it was possible to identify a 'directorate tie market' – a structure of interlocks that provided a 'non-market' context for the regulating of commercial transactions (Burt, 1983b, c).[18]

Both the power and the limitations of the CONCOR procedure are apparent in an investigation of corporate shareholding which I undertook (Scott, 1986). The 250 largest British companies in 1976 were selected for study, and their largest shareholders were identi-fied from their share registers. This allowed the construction of a 250 × 250 incidence matrix of cross-shareholdings among the com-panies. In this matrix, the rows showed the companies as share-holders and the columns showed them as the targets of shareholding relations: shareholdings were directed from rows to columns. It was found that only 69 of the companies held controlling blocks of shares in other large companies, and that only 140 of them were targets of shareholdings by these 69. Thus, the effective data set was a 69 × 140 matrix. Centrality analysis showed that the Prudential Assurance was the most central shareholding participant, it having shareholdings in 88 of the 140 target enterprises. Similarly, Boots was found to be the most 'blue chip' of the targets – 18 of its 20 largest shareholders were among the 69 leading companies.

The main purpose of the analysis was to uncover some of the global features of the intercorporate network, using the CONCOR algorithm. The controlling companies were regarded as the major agents in the economy, and the research aimed to uncover whether they formed a unified group or were divided into rival and solidaristic coalitions. Analysis of components gave little indication that the enterprises were organized into coalitions, and the conclu-sion was drawn that the network was not fragmented into distinct corporate groupings. CONCOR, however, disclosed the existence of a number of structural positions in the network, among which hierarchical relations could be identified. A joint row and column

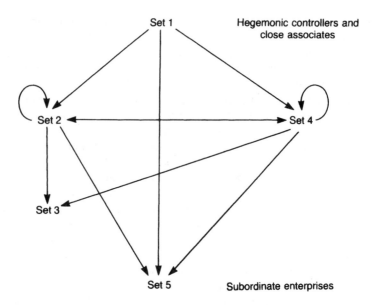

Figure 7.7   *The structure of financial hegemony in Britain*
(1976)

analysis suggested the existence of five sets of enterprises, which are shown in the arrow diagram of Figure 7.7.[19]

In Figure 7.7 the arrows indicate the direction of the shareholding links between the various sets that comprise the positions in the network. Sets 1, 2 and 4 together comprise the 'hegemonic controllers' of the economy, with set 1 being the dominant element in this grouping. Set 1 contained 20 enterprises and included large public sector corporations and merchant banks, and its members were the major shareholding participants in three of the other sets. It owed its position at the top of the corporate hierarchy to the fact that its members were controlled by wealthy families and by the state rather than by other companies. Set 2 contained 11 enterprises that were involved in one another's capital (indicated by the self-referencing arrows) and that were important participants in controlling sets 3, 4 and 5. Set 4 was rather similar to set 2 (comprising clearing banks, insurance companies and large private sector industrials), but it was distinguished by the fact that its members were less likely to be involved in joint control of the companies and consortiums that made up set 3. Set 5, containing 91 enterprises, comprised the subordinate enterprises that had virtually no role in the control of other enterprises.

As the British network was not internally fragmented, CONCOR was very effective in disclosing the structurally equivalent positions occupied by corporate enterprises. Using similar data for Japan, however, it was found to be less useful. The Japanese economy was strongly divided into discrete components, each of which operated as cohesive business groupings. These are the familiar *kigyoshudan* of the Japanese business system (Scott, 1991, 1997). Although there were structurally equivalent categories of dominant and subordinate enterprises, CONCOR divided these along the lines of the business groups (Scott, 1986: 186ff.). No single set of structurally equivalent hegemonic controllers was identified by CONCOR. Seven sets were identified in the network, three of them corresponding to the well-known Sumitomo, Mitsui and Mitsubishi business groups, and within each set could be seen a hierarchical division into hegemonic and subordinate enterprises. Thus, the Japanese economy looked very much like Figure 7.6, with the structurally equivalent positions being cross-cut by the social circles that represented the major business groupings.

8

Dimensions and Displays

The sociogram – the network diagram – was one of the earliest of techniques for formalizing social network analysis, and the drawing of sociograms has remained a crucial means for the development and illustration of social network concepts. They have been used extensively throughout this book for just that purpose. Centrality, for example, can be illustrated by sociograms in which a central point is the 'hub' of a series of radiating 'spokes' which connect it to the more peripheral points. But the conventional sociogram has certain limitations as a method of representing and displaying relational data. Principal among these is that its use is limited by the difficulties of drawing large graphs on a sheet of paper. With more than 10 or 20 points, even with networks having a relatively low density, the number of cross-cutting connections results in an un-interpretable thicket of lines.

In an attempt to overcome this limitation, various *ad hoc* extensions to the idea of the sociogram have been used as researchers have sought to complement their mathematical measures with some kind of diagrammatic representation. One common technique has been to construct the sociogram around the circumference of a circle, so that the pattern of lines becomes more visible (Grieco, 1987: 30). Figure 8.1 shows one example of this method from Scott and Hughes (1980). The circle is used simply as an arbitrary visual framework for organizing the data, and the order in which the points are arranged around the circle is determined only by the attempt to ensure a minimum of overlap among the lines that connect them. The researcher engages in a trial-and-error process of drafting and re-drafting until an aesthetically satisfactory solution is achieved.[1]

Such diagrams can often make the structure of a set of relations clearer, but they remain a rather arbitrary arrangement and they embody no specific mathematical properties. The points are arranged in arbitrary positions, and the drawn lengths of the various lines reflect this arbitrary arrangement. McGrath et al. (1997) have shown how sensitive data interpretation is to the particular visual configuration that is presented. In an experimental study, people could be led to identify differing numbers of sub-groups in the same network simply by presenting them with different spatial arrangements. This

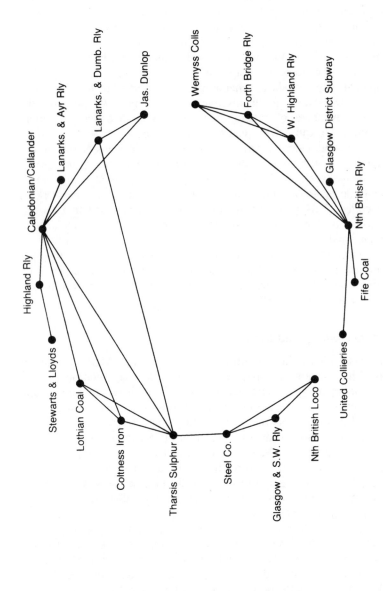

Figure 8.1 *Scottish companies: a circle diagram*

suggests that great care must be taken in choosing both the spatial framework and the criteria by which points are located within it. McGrath et al. conclude that if the researcher wishes to infer something about the actual sociometric properties of a network then the physical distance between points should correspond as closely as possible to the graph theoretical distances between them. This reinforces the long-standing desire of social network analysts to move away from metaphorical and illustrative diagrams and to produce more rigorous maps of social structure that, like geographical maps, retain the mathematical properties of the graph and allow new features to be discovered. Such maps would have the further advantage of making the data comprehensible and more meaningful to those who read the research reports.

The mathematical approach termed 'multidimensional scaling' embodies all the advantages of the conventional sociogram and its extensions (such as the circle diagram), but results in something much closer to a 'map' of the space in which the network is embedded. This is a very important advance, and one that returns to some of the central insights of field theory. Just as a two-dimensional map of the British Isles, for example, may allow its users to make new discoveries about the country, so long as they are familiar with the principles of map reading, so a sociogram produced through multidimensional scaling may allow the generation of new knowledge about the network under investigation.

Distance, Space and Metrics

The basic idea behind multidimensional scaling (MDS) is that of using the concepts of space and distance to map relational data.[2] Any model of space and distance in which there are known and determinate relations among its properties is termed a 'metric'. A metric framework has rather interesting characteristics so far as the mapping of relational data is concerned. If a configuration of points and lines can be made into a metric map, then it is possible to measure 'distances' and 'directions' in ways that differ from those of graph theory. In graph theory, the distance between two points is measured by the number of lines in the path that connects them. Distance, then, is measured as 'path distance'. The metric concept of distance is much closer to the everyday understanding of physical distance. In a 'Euclidean' metric, for example, the 'distance' from A to B, which is exactly the same as the distance from B to A, is measured by the most direct route that can be taken between them.[3] It is a distance that follows a route 'as the crow flies', and that may be across 'open space' and need not – indeed, it normally will not –

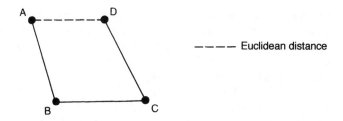

Figure 8.2   *Euclidean distance*

follow a graph theoretical path. In Figure 8.2, for example, the path distance between A and D is 3 lines, while the Euclidean metric distance is 2 centimetres.

MDS, at its simplest, is an attempt to convert graph measures such as path distance into metric measures analogous to physical distance.[4] Although the term 'Euclidean' may be unfamiliar and, indeed, rather daunting, it describes simply the most familiar, everyday concept of distance and space. It is, therefore, a particularly convenient model to use in social network analysis. A Euclidean map of social relations can be understood by analogy with atlases, maps and other familiar spatial models of everyday life.

MDS can take graph theoretical measures of the 'closeness' of points and can express these relations of closeness and distance in metric terms. This involves, more formally, the use of 'proximity data' to construct a metric configuration of points. The first step in such an analysis is to produce a case-by-case proximity matrix from graph theoretical measures. In this matrix, the values in each cell show how 'similar' or 'different' a pair of points are from one another. Proximity measures for relational data would include such things as the number or frequency of contacts between individuals, the size of shareholding relations between enterprises, the number of members in common between organizations, and so on. The metric properties of many of these values will be obscure, and it may not be known whether a particular measure conforms to the assumptions of a Euclidean metric. For this reason, they are often converted into correlation coefficients, which are known to conform to a Euclidean metric. Two points with identical patterns of connection in a graph will be perfectly correlated, and so the proximity measure for this pair will be 1. Such a measure is termed a similarity measure, as high values on the proximity measure indicate 'closeness'. In this case, the proximity matrix is said to contain data on 'similarities'. The other principal type of proximity measure is 'dissimilarity', in which low values indicate closeness. It is vitally important for researchers to be clear about whether they are using 'similarities' or 'dissimilarities' as the operation of particular MDS procedures may differ in each case.[5] Whichever type of data is used, the aim is to produce a metric configuration in which the pattern of metric distances corresponds to the pattern of proximities.

The way in which MDS can be used can most easily be illustrated by considering the mapping of a network of towns onto the two-dimensional page of an atlas. A matrix of road mileages between towns contains proximity measures of mileage that can easily be converted into centimetre distances between points on the page of the atlas. This 'scaling' would give a two-dimensional configuration in which distances are located along East/West and North/South dimensions. Such a map might not, however, have a perfect corres-pondence with the actual arrangement of towns in the country being mapped. Roads rarely follow the shortest and straightest routes between towns, and so road mileages will not be true Euclidean distances. Similarly, the map would take no account of the third dimension of height: the actual roads go up hill and down dale rather than running across perfectly flat plains. The atlas map, nevertheless, gives a reasonable and useful approximation, and its 'lack of fit' with any better solution can be assessed.

The construction of a simple physical map, then, gives a good insight into the outcome of a multidimensional scaling of relational data. The ways in which MDS works on relational data can also be understood by examining the geometrical principles that are used in map construction. These geometrical principles can be seen in the very simple case of drawing a map to show the correct spatial arrangement and locations of three towns from a knowledge only of the distances between them. This task corresponds, in fact, to a classic problem in old-fashioned school geometry, which was to draw a triangle when only the lengths of the three sides are known.

The solution to this geometrical problem is to see the corners of the triangle as the centres of circles whose radii correspond to the distances between the corners. Consider, for example, the case of a triangle with sides AB (length 3 cm), BC (length 4 cm) and AC (length 5 cm). The first step in constructing this triangle would be to draw any one of the lines, say AB. This line can be drawn at any position on the paper. Since it is known that AC measures 5 cm, it can be inferred that C must lie somewhere on the circumference of a circle that is centred on A and that has a radius of 5 cm. It is also known that C must lie on the circumference of a circle that is centred on B and that has a radius of 4 cm. The second step in constructing the triangle, therefore, is to draw these two circles and to identify the place at which they intersect. C can be positioned at

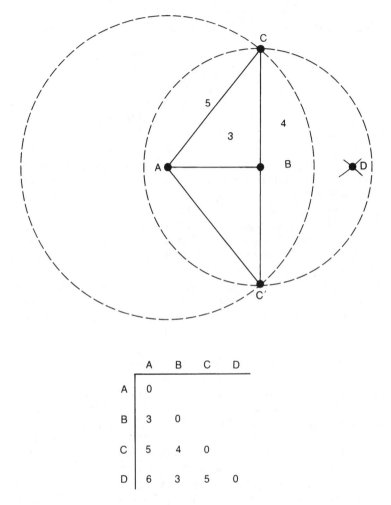

	A	B	C	D
A	0			
B	3	0		
C	5	4	0	
D	6	3	5	0

Figure 8.3 *Constructing a metric model*

the point of intersection, because it is only at this point that all three known distances will be correct. There are, in fact, two points of intersection, as shown in Figure 8.3, and so there are two possible locations for point C. For the moment it is sufficient simply to choose one of the two intersection points to represent the location of C. It does not matter which of these points is chosen, as the triangle ABC' is simply a mirror reflection of the triangle ABC. Here, then, is the solution to the problem of mapping three towns. If A, B and C represent the towns, and the given lengths of the lines AB, BC and AC represent the scaled mileages between them, then the triangle ABC is a simple two-dimensional map of the locations of the towns.

But what would have happened if C' had been chosen instead of C as the location for the third town? Would ABC' have been equally acceptable as a map? The triangle ABC' is simply an 'upside-down' version of the original map, and so there is no need to choose between ABC and ABC' as maps of the three towns. The choice does not matter in the slightest when one configuration is simply a perfect reflection of the other. Which configuration is taken as being the most useful will depend only upon the convenience of the user of the map. A physical map and its mirror image contain exactly the same information.

The same geometrical procedure can also be used for four or more points. If it is known that a point D lies 3 cm from B, 6 cm from A and 5 cm from C, its position can be plotted by drawing three additional circles centred on A, B and C. Once the initial choice of location has been made for point C, the position of D is uniquely determined by a single point of intersection for all these circles. (See Figure 8.3.) As a general principle, then, there is a unique configuration for a two-dimensional map once the positions of its first three points have been fixed.[6]

This piece of school geometry can be seen as giving a two-dimensional solution for the location of a set of points in a metric space. From the distance matrix shown in Figure 8.3, the two-dimensional configuration can be constructed. The two dimensions are the conventional horizontal (left/right) and vertical (up/down) dimensions of a flat piece of paper. In producing a map for an atlas, the configuration of points would normally be moved to a position in which the most northerly point is towards the top of the page and the most westerly point is towards the left of the page. In this way, the horizontal and vertical dimensions represent the known East/West and North/South dimensions. In MDS, this movement of the configuration is termed a 'rotation'. Only in the case of conventional mapping, however, does rotation generally involve aligning the configuration to known dimensions. More typically with the results of MDS, rotation is aimed at the *discovery* of meaningful dimensions. I shall return to this question of rotation later in the chapter.

MDS operates, in effect, in a very similar way to that I have described in this simple geometrical case. Although computer programs for MDS do not normally use such an inefficient method as the construction of circles, the end result is the same. The earliest forms of MDS were developed from Torgerson's (1952) pioneering work on psychometric scaling. In metric MDS, as I have shown, proximity data are used as if they were Euclidean distances. If dissimilarity measures are used, as in the case of the road mileage example, principles similar to the geometrical ones that I have described could be used to produce a metric map of the data. The raw data are treated as distance measures and they are plotted, to scale, on the final map. Algorithms for MDS use geometrical principles to ensure a 'fit' between the given proximity data and the final configuration of points in the map. The variety of approaches to metric MDS differ mainly in the details of their methods for generalizing the procedure to three or more dimensions.

Principal Components and Factors

An approach that conforms closely to this metric method of multi-dimensional scaling is principal components analysis (PCA). Principal components analysis is, in some texts, called 'factor analysis', though there are important differences between PCA and classical factor analysis. For present purposes, however, this distinction is not especially important, and the availability of principal components analysis as part of the factor analysis routine in SPSS has made it a widely used method of data analysis (Daultrey, 1976; Goddard and Kirby, 1976; Kim and Mueller, 1978; Kline, 1994).[7] The technique developed from early attitude and intelligence scaling methods, where researchers sought some underlying factor common to a number of specific measures of attainment or attitude. 'General intelligence', for example, was seen as a 'factor' underlying performance on a number of specific tests of logical reasoning. By extension, there may be two or more distinct 'factors' underlying any given set of data. PCA developed as a way of analysing a case-by-variable attribute matrix in order to discover one or more factors or components common to the variables. It is an attempt to use raw data to discover a set of coordinates or axes (the factors or dimensions) that can be used to plot a scatter diagram of the data. When relational data in a case-by-affiliation matrix are used, the scatter map is such that the spatial distance and compass direction from one point to another convey some real information about their relative positions.

The method of PCA can most easily be understood through its operation on a case-by-variable matrix of attribute data. A simple PCA algorithm would first convert the case-by-variable matrix into a variable-by-variable matrix that showed the correlations among the variables (the columns of the original matrix). Thus, the new matrix shows how well, or how badly, the variables are associated with one another. The next step is to search the matrix for those variables that are highly correlated with one another and to replace them with a constructed, artificial variable that measures their correlation with one another. Thus, a set of variables that are all mutually correlated at or above a specified level would be replaced by the constructed variable. This constructed variable is termed the first principal component. The next step would be to look for another set of variables that are correlated highly with one another, but that are not correlated with the first set. The constructed variable that replaces this set is the second principal component. By continuing in this way, principal components analysis aims to identify a set of un-correlated principal components that, taken together, account for all the variation to be found in the data. Such a complete analysis would continue until all possible components have been identified. Through this procedure, the original variable-by-variable correlation matrix is, in effect, converted into a variable-by-component correlation matrix.

The first principal component is the one that stands for the most highly correlated set of variables. The second principal component is, by definition, un-correlated with the first: it is 'orthogonal' to it. This independence means that the two components can be drawn at right-angles to one another as the axes of a two-dimensional scatter diagram. The same general principle holds for larger numbers of components, each dimension being orthogonal to, or un-correlated with, any of the others. It is, of course, more difficult to draw or to visualize three-dimensional scatter diagrams, and diagrams with more than three dimensions simply cannot be drawn. Nevertheless, the logic of the approach is the same, regardless of how many principal components are identified. It is normal in principal components analysis to search for the smallest number of principal components that is capable of explaining a high proportion of the variance in the data. In practice, any stopping point that falls short of a complete account of the variance is arbitrary, and it is normal for a researcher to stop when any additional principal component adds little more to the variance than has already been explained.

The starting point for PCA, therefore, is a variable-by-variable correlation matrix, constructed from the original case-by-variable matrix. From this matrix a variable-by-component matrix is constructed in which the cell entries show the 'loadings' computed for each variable against each component. The principal components are used as axes for a scatter diagram and the loadings are used to plot the position of each variable within these axes.

A complication arises from the possibility of 'rotation', which was touched on in the simple geometrical example discussed earlier. The purpose of the rotation of a configuration is to give a clearer picture of its structure. If the scatter of points seems to spread in a particular direction across the space, for example, it would make sense to rotate the configuration until the greatest spread in the points is aligned with the first component. In Figure 8.4, for example, diagram (ii) shows a rotation of the configuration to give a better alignment with the axes than in the un-rotated diagram (i). More generally, rotation procedures aim to produce a positioning of the configuration that gives the best possible alignment with the main axes. The outcome of a rotation program is a new variable-by-component matrix that contains a revised set of loadings for each variable.

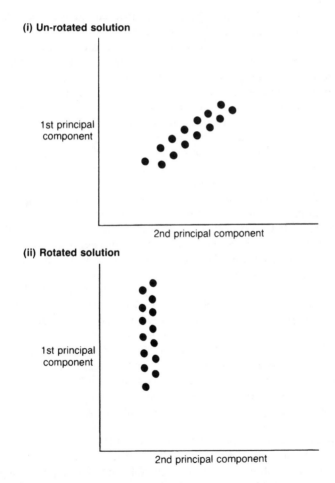

(i) Un-rotated solution

1st principal component

2nd principal component

(ii) Rotated solution

1st principal component

2nd principal component

Figure 8.4 *Rotation*

I have described the usual procedure of a PCA, which results in a scattering of the *variables* in a space defined by a set of dimensions. An alternative procedure, following a similar method, results in a scattering of the *cases*. In this procedure, the first step is to transpose the original case-by-variable matrix and to compute a case-by-case correlation matrix. From there on, the procedure is identical, although the units of analysis are cases instead of variables. The final result is a case-by-component matrix of loadings, from which a scattering of cases can be plotted. In some texts, this case-by-case analysis is termed 'Q-mode' principal components analysis in order to distinguish it from the usual, variable-by-variable 'R-mode' analysis.[8]

This distinction between Q-mode and R-mode analyses is mainly relevant when handling attribute data. The important point to bear in mind is that PCA in its normal, 'R-mode' operates on the *columns* of the original matrix. Thus, an investigation of a sociometric case-by-affiliation incidence matrix would result in an analysis of the affiliations. If the researcher wished to investigate the structure of relations among the cases, it would be necessary to transpose the matrix, so making the cases into the columns of the matrix, as in a Q-mode PCA. A persons-by-organizations incidence matrix, for example, can be directly analysed to produce an organizations-by-components matrix, or it can be transposed and analysed to yield a persons-by-components matrix.

In a direct analysis of such an incidence matrix of people and organizations, a PCA algorithm would investigate the organizations in order to find those that are most similar in terms of their membership. As with CONCOR, the correlation coefficient is used as a measure of proximity. The sets of similar organizations that are discovered are replaced by principal components, and the various organizations can be plotted as points in a space defined by the axes that correspond to the components. The Euclidean distance between the points in this scatter diagram would be a measure of the closeness of the organizations. A transposition of the original incidence matrix would allow an analysis of the cases to be made. As was seen with CONCOR and the other block modelling procedures discussed in the previous chapter, the 'column solution' and the 'row solution' produced from the same input data would be the 'dual' of one another. They are different but complementary representations of the same data.

It is possible to analyse an adjacency matrix using PCA, though with the symmetrical data matrix for undirected relations the row and column solutions would be identical with one another. In the case of a directed adjacency matrix, however, the two solutions would differ; one of them would correspond to the network created by the 'sending' of relations and the other to the network involving the 'receiving' of relations.[9]

Non-metric Methods

There are a number of limitations on the use of metric MDS and PCA in investigations of relational data. Many relational data sets are binary in form, indicating simply the presence or absence of a relation, and this type of data cannot be directly used to measure proximity. As I have shown, binary data must first be converted into measures, such as correlation coefficients, which do have metric properties. But this data conversion procedure may lead researchers to make un-warranted assumptions about their relational data. Even when the raw input data are valued, metric assumptions may not be appropriate. In particular, the use of ratio or interval measurement may not be appropriate. Two companies with four directors in common, for example, may not be twice as close to one another as two companies that have just two directors in common. While it may be realistic to consider the former as being 'closer' than the latter, it is difficult to be certain about *how much* closer they might be. Fortunately, some powerful MDS techniques have been developed that do not require the direct input of metric data, and these methods can be used in a much wider range of circumstances than their metric counterparts.[10]

These techniques of non-metric MDS, often called smallest space analysis, have become more widely available in standard computer packages. Non-metric MDS procedures work on a symmetrical adjacency matrix in which the cells show the similarities or dissimilarities among cases, using either correlation coefficients or actual valued data. The procedure does not convert these values directly into Euclidean distances, but takes account only of their rank order. That is to say, the data are treated as measures at the ordinal level. The non-metric procedures seek a solution in which the rank ordering of the distances is the same as the rank ordering of the original values.

This procedure can be illustrated with the data in Figure 8.5. The first step is to sort the cell values of the original matrix into descending order (from high to low). A new matrix is then constructed in which the original cell values are replaced by their ranks in the sorted distribution of values. In Figure 8.5, for example, the dissimilarity between A and B is the highest value in the original matrix and so is replaced by a value of 1 in the ordinal data matrix. The dissimilarity between A and C is the lowest of the six values,

(i) Original matrix (dissimilarities)

	A	B	C	D
A	0			
B	60	0		
C	10	40	0	
D	30	50	20	0

(ii) Matrix with ordinal data

	A	B	C	D
A	–			
B	1	–		
C	6	3	–	
D	4	2	5	–

(iii) Loadings: two-dimensional solution

	Dim. 1	Dim. 2
A	0.575	0.404
B	– 0.993	0.114
C	0.195	0.177
D	0.222	– 0.695

Figure 8.5   *Data for non-metric multidimensional scaling*

and so this is replaced by a value of 6 in the ordinal data matrix. It is then necessary to construct a matrix of Euclidean distances that have the same rank ordering as the original cell values.

These Euclidean distances can be used to draw a metric scatter plot similar to those produced by PCA. In this case, the rank order of the distances is the same as the rank order of the proximities, but no assumptions are made about the nature of the proximity data themselves. If the proximity measures did have metric properties, the procedure would, of course, produce a final matrix in which the values exactly matched those of the original matrix, allowing only for the scaling down of all values by the same amount. This is not the case in Figure 8.5, as the original data were not metric. While a variant of the simple geometrical method cannot be applied to the original data, it can be used on the values in the final matrix. The final matrix shows the 'best fit' metric distances for the non-metric data, and panel (iii) shows the loadings of the four points against the two dimensions of a two-dimensional solution.

How, then, can the matrix of Euclidean distances be calculated? The usual algorithm begins by computing a 'guess' of what these distances might be. This guess forms the initial or trial configuration, and the rank order of its distances is compared with that of the proximities. Successive trial-and-error refinements of the initial estimates lead to progressively better trial configurations. A configuration is accepted as an improvement over its predecessor if there is a better match between the distance and the proximity rank orderings. Eventually, one of the trial configurations will be found to have the best achievable fit with the original data.

In order to begin, therefore, a suitable trial configuration must be produced. The initial configuration itself can be randomly generated or, if something of the structure of the network is already known, estimated distances can be supplied by the researcher. The choice of method is immaterial, as the initial configuration is simply a starting point for the analysis and its accuracy, or inaccuracy, has no bearing upon the rest of the analysis. The only disadvantage of using a randomly chosen starting point is that the analysis may take slightly longer to complete, as a larger number of steps may be necessary before the final configuration is discovered. In fact, the widely used MINISSA algorithm normally produces an initial configuration from a principal components analysis.[11]

How is it known when a satisfactory final configuration has been produced? The rank ordering of the distances in the initial configuration must be compared with that for the original proximity data in order to see the disparity in ranking for each pair of points. This comparison shows in which direction, and by how much, the various points must be moved relative to one another in order to reduce the disparities. Where there is a large positive disparity in rank, for example, the points must be moved closer together than in the trial configuration. This comparison of disparities takes place with each successive configuration. The results of each step can be plotted into a diagram such as Figure 8.6 (i). In this diagram, termed a Shepard diagram after its inventor, the rank order of distances in a trial configuration are plotted against the rank order of dissimilarities in the original data. If the points are scattered widely about the diagram, there is a bad fit; but if they are clustered close to the 45° line, then the fit is better. A perfect fit is achieved when the points follow exactly the 45° line.[12] Gradually, by constant adjustment to reduce the disparities, a configuration is produced in which no changes can be made that do not worsen the fit. When this point has been reached, perhaps after quite a large number of steps, the best possible fit with the original data has been achieved.

I have so far written as if the number of dimensions is unproblematic. Indeed, the simple illustration in Figure 8.5 assumed a two-dimensional solution. In practice, the researcher must decide on the number of dimensions that should be used to plot the data. A

(i) A Shepard diagram

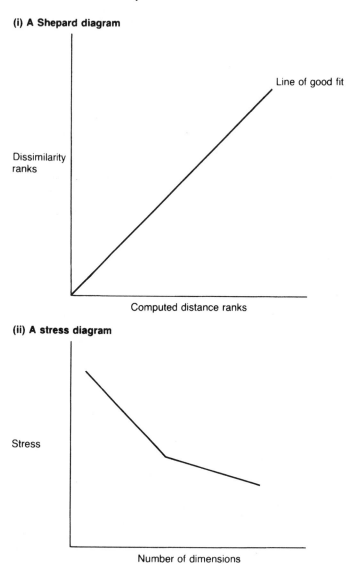

Figure 8.6   *Goodness of fit in non-metric multidimensional scaling*

Shepard diagram can be drawn for each dimensional solution, and a 'best fit' configuration can be discovered. There will, for example, be a best fit in two dimensions and another best fit in three dimensions. The Shepard diagrams give no indication of which solution is to be preferred.

Non-metric MDS does not, itself, determine the appropriate number of dimensions. The researcher must undertake a number of analyses for varying numbers of dimensions and then try to discover which of various dimensional solutions gives the best overall fit with the original data. This can be achieved by calculating a statistic called the 'stress'. This measures the average spread of points around the line of good fit in the Shepard diagram. By plotting the stress value for each dimensional solution, a diagram similar to that in Figure 8.6 will be produced. It can be seen that the stress initially decreases as the number of dimensions is increased, but that an 'elbow' point is eventually arrived at, and further increases in the number of dimensions produce no significant reductions in stress. When this plateau level has been reached, the best possible dimensional solution has been achieved. Further dimensions may reduce the stress, but not to any appreciable extent.

In addition to this comparison of stress values, it is also necessary to take account of the absolute level of stress in the preferred solution. If no solution is able to bring the stress below about 10 per cent, argues Kruskal (1964a), then the results should not be regarded as giving an adequate fit to the original data. Kruskal suggests that 5 per cent or lower indicates a good fit, while 10 per cent could still be regarded as a 'fair' fit. Stress values approaching 20 per cent are 'poor'. The stress value for the two-dimensional solution of the data in Figure 8.5 is 0.

The idea of 'dimensions' in a metric space is not the only concept of dimensionality that has been proposed in social network analysis. Atkin (1974) has proposed an idea of dimensionality based on his Q-analysis. In Q-analysis, the dimensionality of a point is one less than its row or column solution in the incidence matrix. According to Atkin, this figure gives the number of dimensions that are needed to represent the point adequately. Thus, a director who sits on the boards of four companies, for example, must be represented in three dimensions. From this point of view, however, each case in a network will have its own dimensionality, and these may differ from the dimensionality of the whole network.

While this approach has the virtue of being rooted in ideas close to those of graph theory, its value in relation to more familiar ideas is uncertain. Freeman (1983), therefore, has rejected the Q-analytic idea of the dimensionality of a graph and proposes, instead, to combine graph theory with the geometrical dimensions discovered through MDS. The dimensionality of a graph, he argues, is the minimum number of dimensions that are necessary to embed the graph in a space with a good fit. His criterion of good fit is, however, stronger than that of Kruskal, and involves the achievement of a stress value of 0.

The two-dimensional scatter plot drawn on a flat sheet of paper is familiar and comprehensible, but the number of dimensions that gives the best fit, at an adequate absolute level, will often be more than two. In these cases, it is not possible to draw the final configuration on a flat sheet of paper. Perspective drawing or cartographical techniques may be used to indicate a third dimension, but such representations can rarely be more than illustrative. (See the work of Levine, 1972, discussed below.) A substantial improvement over pencil and paper methods is to use computer graphics to display a three-dimensional configuration, but this procedure runs into similar problems if more than three dimensions have to be used. The most common solution for results in larger numbers of dimensions is to display on paper successive two-dimensional 'slices' through the configuration. In a three-dimensional solution, for example, the configuration can be represented on paper as three separate two-dimensional views of the overall configuration: dimension 1 with dimension 2, dimension 2 with dimension 3, and dimension 1 with dimension 3.

Using the output from an MDS program, a configuration of points can be plotted within a space defined by the number of dimensions discovered. It is then that the process of interpretation can begin. There are two issues for interpretation: the meaning of the dimensions and the significance of the spatial arrangement of the points. In an atlas map, for example, the dimensions can, in general, be treated unambiguously as the East/West and North/South dimensions of ordinary geographical space. With models of social networks, however, the initial task of the analyst will be to arrive at a sociological interpretation of the dimensions. It may be decided, for example, that one dimension reflects the economic resources of individuals, while another reflects their political affiliations. Rotation of the configuration may often help in interpreting the dimensions. It is also necessary to give some meaning to the spatial arrangement of the points themselves. A common procedure is to group the points together, using the output from a cluster analysis of the original data. Points within clusters are encircled by contour lines, and a hierarchical clustering approach would allow the construction of a contour map of the points. A cluster analysis of Euclidean distances of the kind proposed by Burt, for example, could be used to plot the clusters on a Euclidean MDS solution. Alternatively, the results of multiplicity- and degree-based analyses of graph components and their cores can be mapped onto an MDS solution. Whereas the 'contour maps' of nested components that were discussed in Chapter 6 were drawn in arbitrary positions on the page, those associated with an MDS solution may represent a more 'natural' arrangement of the data. Figure 8.7 shows a simple example of this procedure.

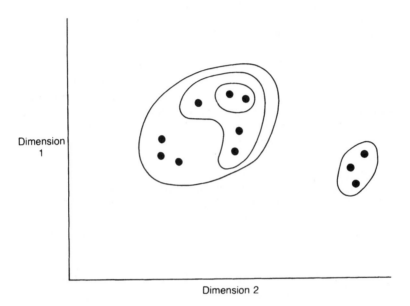

Figure 8.7 *A multidimensional scaling configuration*

Having produced such a diagram as that shown in Figure 8.7, a researcher can search for some characteristic common to the points in the cluster, as these are the distinct neighbourhoods of the space. Thus, a full interpretation involves identifying the clusters and then using the dimensions to give some meaning to their position in relation to one another. It should be noted that this process of interpretation is a creative and imaginative act on the part of the researcher. It is not something that can be produced by a computer alone. The researcher remains in control of the process and is responsible for arriving at any interpretations that are to be placed upon the results. Indeed, there is no guarantee that the dimensions will be capable of substantive interpretation: they may be mere artefacts of the methods of sampling or analysis. There has been much debate in psychology, for example, over the question of whether IQ testing reflects a real factor of general intelligence or simply reproduces features of the process of testing.

Advances in Network Visualization

MDS and associated technologies have done much to integrate the concepts of graph theory with spatial ideas. However, the results of these analyses – particularly for large social networks – can often show simply a dense thicket of points and lines that cannot easily be visually inspected. For this reason, a number of social network analysts have explored the possibilities of marrying MDS with powerful techniques of structural modelling that can help to visualize and explore network structure in more intuitive ways.

One of the earliest attempts to do this was that of Klovdahl (1981, 1986, 1989), whose VIEW-NET program drew on molecular modelling methods and aimed to use simple three-dimensional 'ball and stick' representations of points and lines. The output from this program, however, has not yet generated easily interpretable representations of large networks.

Krempel (1994) has tried to move beyond this by developing methods for simplifying complex structures and so highlighting their essential features. His method involves the use of a simple – and arbitrarily chosen – geometric shape as a framework for organizing the features of a network. The circle diagram illustrated in Figure 8.1 is, of course, a simple example of this kind of procedure, and Krempel uses the circle as the basis of his own work. Krempel generalizes this approach by devising an algorithm that uses graph theoretical measures to produce a best fit for the relational data to the circle shape – much as a regression line gives the best linear fit for a scatter of points. Thus, measures of distance or centrality can be used in place of aesthetic criteria to determine the location of points around a circle. Where the data consist of more or less distinct sub-graphs, these can each be analysed as separate circles within a larger circle. The known shape of the circle gives the mind a familiar structure for interpreting the overall features of the actual network.[13] Krempel sees this procedure as producing an 'underlying structure' for a particular configuration of relations.

This procedure offers great possibilities for large-scale data sets. It is possible to compress the lower-level circles of an analysis into macro-points that represent a whole sub-graph. A sociogram of the macro-points can then be produced, giving a simplified and clearer model. A researcher can choose any particular part of this sociogram for fuller investigation and can decompress a macro-point in order to examine its internal structure. A Krempel diagram, then, is a hierarchy of nested circles, with the amount of detail shown depending on which of the circles are compressed and which are decompressed.

Freeman (1996a) has tried to develop some general principles for network visualization, and he has devised and adapted a number of physical science methods for use in the analysis of social networks. He holds that, at the very least, points and lines should be colour-coded or otherwise distinguished in order to bring out their relational properties, that the layout should be organized around the most important structural features of the data, and that time-dependent aspects of a network should be brought out by animation procedures.

Freeman's particular interest is in using molecular modelling techniques from chemistry on social network data. In these techniques, points and lines are represented by three-dimensional balls and sticks, and a number of programs are available that allow this to be undertaken by computer rather than as a physical model. He has made a great deal of use of MOVIEMOL, an animation program that shows dynamic changes in structures (chemical or social) over time. This program, however, limits the placement of points, as it assumes that the laws of chemistry should govern where points are located. At present, it is difficult to modify it for social network data, though Freeman (1996b) has found it to be useful in analysing changes in small networks.

A more flexible modelling program is MAGE.[14] This allows for greater flexibility in the placing of points (for example, by taking an MDS output file) and can plot lines by their intensity or multiplicity. By using the program in conjunction with web-based VRML viewers (integral to or easily added to web browsers such as Internet Explorer and Netscape), it is possible to rotate a network model around its various dimensions and to zoom in and out to explore it in greater detail. MAGE is also able to show some changes over time, though it does this as a sequence of stills rather than as a continuous flow. It is possible that further developments could involve morphing procedures to produce something approaching a true animation.

Elites, Communities and Influence

One of the earliest uses of multidimensional scaling to be undertaken in sociology was the 1960 community study carried out by Edward Laumann (1966). This study has subsequently been enlarged and extended through a series of related investigations of community power and elite structure. The research originated in Laumann's Harvard doctoral thesis, which was produced under the supervision of Homans and showed the influence of both Parsons and Harrison White. The research brought together the advanced sociometric concerns of the Harvard researchers with the general theoretical framework of Parsonian systems theory, directing these methods and theories to the investigation of community structure. The particular direction that was taken in data analysis, however, derived from the work of Louis Guttman, whom Laumann met at Michigan. It was through the influence of Guttman that Laumann decided to use the techniques of non-metric MDS to analyse his relational data.

Laumann's starting point was Bogardus's notion of 'social distance', which was developed in various papers from the 1920s onwards (see the summary in Bogardus, 1959). Laumann interprets the idea of social distance as referring to the patterns of differential association that are found among the occupants of occupational positions. It is an 'objective' measure of how much, or how little, the occupants of various social positions associate with one another in community life. Laumann contrasts this 'objective' concept of social distance with the 'subjective' feelings of social distance that agents may experience and that are expressed in their adoption of positive or negative attitudes towards one another. Thus, Laumann's work is firmly within the tradition of thought that moved sociometric concerns from the psychological, or 'subjective' level to the sociological level of relational association. His aim was to arrive at an operational measure of 'objective' social distance and then to use MDS to convert this into a metric map of the social structure.

Laumann drew a sample of white male residents in two urban areas in Boston, Massachusetts, aiming to achieve a high degree of occupational diversity in his sample. His concern was to undertake a *positional* study of the kind discussed in the last chapter, as his units of analysis were to be the occupational positions rather than the individuals themselves. The responses of occupants of each occupational position to his questions on such matters as friendship choices, kinship and neighbouring, were aggregated to produce summary measures for each position.

The initial analysis involved the use of five occupational categories: top professional and business, semi-professional and middle business, clerical and small business, skilled manual, and semi- and un-skilled manual. These five social positions were used in the construction of a number of position-by-attribute incidence matrices containing frequency data, and these data matrices were analysed as conventional contingency tables. This statistical analysis showed that friendship choices were largely confined to occupational equals, while other social relations were more likely to involve people in different occupational positions.

The truly innovatory part of Laumann's work, however, was his use of MDS to discover whether there was a hierarchy inherent in patterns of differential association (Laumann, 1966: ch. 6). Conventional studies of the occupational hierarchy were based on 'prestige' rankings, where popular assessments of the standing of particular occupations were used as measures of their status. Laumann rejected such approaches for their reliance on 'subjective' appraisals, and he sought to use actual patterns of association – of social distance – to construct a hierarchy. Fifty-five occupational positions taken from the Duncan (1961) index were used and were constructed into a 55 × 55 incidence, or 'joint occurrence' matrix for each of seven social relations. The separate matrices were summed into a single incidence matrix of differential association, and the standardized frequency values in the matrix were treated as similarity measures. The greater the frequency with which members of one occupational position interacted with members of another, the 'closer' they were to one another in social space.[15]

The results from Laumann's analysis suggested that a three-dimensional solution gave the best fit with the original data. The 55 occupational positions were plotted in a three-dimensional space, and contour lines were drawn around those that were close to one another on the Duncan prestige index (Laumann, 1966: Figure 6.3, which gives a fold-out picture of the configuration). Little in the way of detailed information is given about this rather arbitrary clustering, which seems to build in the very 'prestige' assumptions that Laumann was seeking to escape. Nevertheless, his interpretation of the model is informative. He sees the first, and most important, dimension as one of prestige. Scores on this dimension correlated at 0.824 with the Duncan index. It seems that patterns of differential association did, indeed, follow the pattern described in earlier studies of prestige. But the pattern could not be understood in simple one-dimensional terms. The other two dimensions were, however, less easy to interpret, and Laumann failed to produce any satisfactory interpretation for his second dimension. The third dimension he tentatively saw as contrasting entrepreneurial occupations with salaried and bureaucratic occupations.

This approach to community structure was extended in Laumann's later study of Detroit, undertaken in 1966 (Laumann, 1973). Laumann aimed to explore the friendship relations that existed between various social positions, using a sample of 1013 white males. This work continued the positional focus of the earlier research, but extended it from occupational positions to other social positions. This style of research had much in common with Warner's pioneering positional studies, but Parsons (1951) was the specific theoretical point of reference.

The main analyses were those of the ethno-religious and occupational networks of friendship. Laumann initially analysed ethnicity and religion separately, but discovered that a better MDS solution was achieved if they were combined into a single relation. Twenty-two ethnic groups and 15 religious groups were combined into 27 ethno-religious groups, for which dissimilarity measures were calculated from the friendship choices of their members. His three-dimensional solution (Laumann, 1973: Figure 3.3) showed a strong first dimension, which separated out the Protestants, the Catholics and the Jews. The second dimension seemed to measure economic standing, and it correlated well with family income, while the third dimension measured frequency of church attendance. Thus, the ethno-religious groups were structured by the three dimensions of religion, income and church attendance. Catholics, for example, were differentiated into high and low income groups and were, independently, differentiated by the frequency of their church attendance. The identifiable clusters of positions in the social space frequently had an ethnic basis to them.

The occupational analysis in Laumann's study involved 16 occupational groups, and a two-dimensional solution was found to give the best fit. His discussion of these data largely confirms the results of the earlier study. The first dimension, he again concluded, was status or prestige (it correlated with income and educational attainment), and a second dimension divided the entrepreneurial from the bureaucratic.

Working with Pappi, Laumann has further extended his analysis of community structure to the level of the 'elite', drawing on the work of Hunter (1953) and Dahl (1961) and their investigations of community power (Laumann and Pappi, 1973, 1976). They studied the small town of Julich in western Germany, to which they gave the pseudonym 'Altneustadt'. This was a rapidly expanding town during the 1950s and 1960s, and communal divisions had emerged between established and newcomer groups, divisions that had their political foci in, respectively, the Christian Democratic Union and the Social Democratic Party. The study was, again, positional in approach. Although individual occupants of positions were sampled, it was the relations between the positions that were important. The social positions on which they focussed were the 'highest positions of authority' in each of the Parsonian A, G, I and L institutional sub-systems. Forty-six occupants of these positions were interviewed, each being asked to name which of the other 45 they considered to be most influential in the town. There was a high degree of consensus over this: 'Herr K' received 46 votes as the most influential person and, as he had nominated himself for this position, the researchers clearly had to take the diagonal of the data matrix seriously. Laumann and Pappi looked at interactions among the 46 people in three kinds of social relationship: business and professional relations, 'social, expressive' relations (e.g., those rooted in education, religion and residence) and community affairs relations (political coalitions and alignments).

Sociometric choices were plotted for each of these relations, but, as the researchers were interested in the presence or absence of a relation rather than in its direction, these were converted into symmetrical matrices. The geodesic matrices were used for nonmetric MDS, and two-dimensional solutions were produced for each type of relation. The interpretation placed upon the resulting structures was that location towards the centre of the configuration of points could be taken as an indicator of 'integrative centrality' in the community structure. Taking the 'community affairs' network, which showed the political structure of the community, the central zone of the structure comprised an 'inner circle' of influentials in the power structure. Figure 8.8 shows a simplified version of the Laumann and Pappi map of the community power structure in Julich. Points are seen as arranged in zones of decreasing centrality, and lines of political division could be drawn that separated those groups with opposed views on each of five key community issues. This combination of centrality with issue division resulted in the identification of a number of distinct segments in the community power structure.

MDS has proved a useful technique for furthering certain types of investigations of community power and highlighting the existence of local elites. It has also been used most impressively in an investigation of national-level elites. Where Laumann and Pappi used a reputational method for discovering local elites, Levine (1972) has used interlocking directorships in business to identify a national economic elite.

Levine was one of the original network investigators in the new wave of Harvard researchers and he pioneered the use of MDS rather than graph theory as a technique for social network analysis. Using data from the 1966 Patman enquiry into bank operations in the United States, he investigated the top 100 industrial corporations and their connections with 14 banks in three cities. Seventy of these industrials had bank interlocks and so Levine constructed a 70×14 incidence matrix to show the number of directors in common between each pair of enterprises. The number of directors in common was taken as a measure of 'preference', or similarity, between the enterprises. The incidence matrix was analysed in order

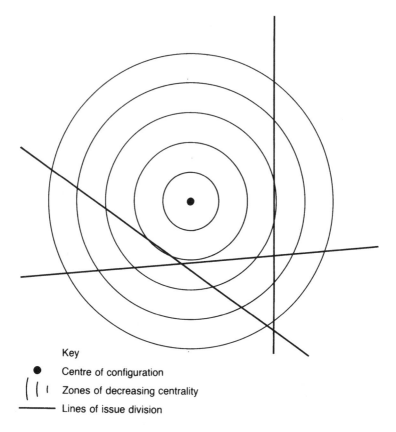

Key

●   Centre of configuration

((ɩ   Zones of decreasing centrality

————   Lines of issue division

Figure 8.8   *Community elite structure*

to produce a joint space in which both the banks and the industrials could be located.

The results from Levine's analysis showed that a three-dimensional solution gave the best fit with the original data, and Levine was able to give a sociological interpretation to two of these dimensions. The first, and most important dimension appeared to reflect a regional structuring of the data, separating out the New York, Pittsburgh and Chicago enterprises. No interpretation could be given to the second dimension, but Levine held that the third dimension separated the banks from the industrials. His results are summarized in Figure 8.9.

Levine's view was that the structure could be seen as forming a sphere around the centre of the joint space. The structure of the sphere comprises an onion-like arrangement of layers or concentric

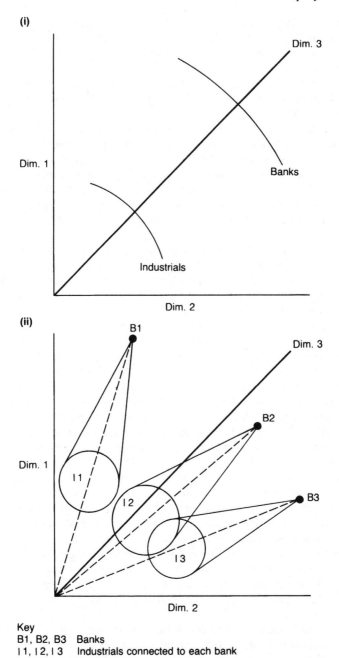

Figure 8.9 *Multidimensional scaling and bank interlocks*

shells. Looking along the third dimension, industrial enterprises are located on various inner shells of this sphere while banks are located on outer shells in the same dimension. This pattern is shown in diagram (i) of Figure 8.9. The exact location of the enterprises on the shells was described by the first and second dimensions, showing that both banks and industrials were regionally differentiated around their respective shells.

The centre of this spherical configuration, argued Levine, is the position that would be occupied by isolated enterprises – those without any interlocks. These enterprises were excluded from his data set and so, in the final configuration, the centre was empty.[16] Those clusters of industrial enterprises that were interlocked with particular banks – the groups that Marxist writers have described as financial interest groups – can be seen as sectors or 'wedges' in the sphere, as shown in diagram (ii) of Figure 8.9. If a line is drawn from each bank to the centre of the sphere, each line, or vector,[17] is the central axis of that bank's sector of the sphere. The distance in space that an industrial enterprise lies from the bank, measured along this vector, is an indication of its closeness to the bank, and the angle between this vector and that which connects the industrial company to the centre of the sphere is a measure of how peripheral the industrial is within its wedge.

Although describing the overall configuration of bank–industry interlocks as a sphere, Levine also described the wedges associated with each bank as their 'spheres of influence'. The rationale for this terminology was that the two terms relate to differing viewpoints on the same structure. Viewed from the standpoint of each bank, there are spheres of connection around them. Looking at its interlocked enterprises from the standpoint of the apex of the conical wedge that it forms (see Figure 8.9), a bank would see these enterprises as arrayed in a circular pattern around it. But these bank spheres of influence intersect with one another in such a way as to produce the overall spherical configuration of the joint space. Looking at the overall structure, the bank spheres appear as conical wedges of the larger sphere of intercorporate relations. Levine equates this difference in viewpoint with the difference between a geocentric and a heliocentric view of the stellar universe. Instead of remaining at the level of the ego-centric spheres of particular banks, Levine proposes a shift of viewpoint to see the socio-centric features of the overall structure itself.

The final question considered by Levine was that of how best to represent his three-dimensional configuration on a flat two-dimensional sheet of paper. Figure 8.9 used the trick of perspective drawing to achieve this, but the limitations of this method have already been indicated. To improve his presentation, Levine turned to the cartographic projection methods used by geographers to map the three-dimensional structure of the earth onto a flat surface. He rejected the idea of using any of the two-dimensional views produced by the MDS procedure itself, as these produced particularly undesirable distortions. Such views are based on a 'parallel projection', a view from infinity. This projection is rarely used by cartographers because of the distortions that it involves. This is shown in Figure 8.10, where the peak and base of a mountain appear as separate points in a parallel projection. In a parallel projection the vertical separation of the peak and the base produces a horizontal and lateral separation of them in the resulting map.

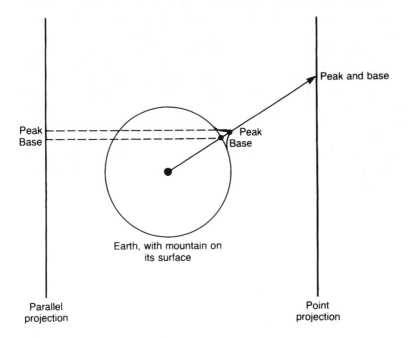

Figure 8.10 *Alternative projections*

To solve this problem, Levine proposed a form of 'point projection' from the centre itself. In cartography, this is termed a gnomonic projection. In this projection, all points on the same radius are mapped to the same position on the page. Thus, as shown in Figure 8.10, the peak and base of a mountain appear as a single point. An adequate representation of Levine's data would show clearly the association between particular banks and their linked industrials – they should appear as clear clusters on the page. A gnomonic projection, argues Levine, satisfies this requirement. Each bank appears at the dead centre of its cluster, and the industrials on the inner shells of the sphere are brought closer to those banks on the outer shells to which they are connected. In this way, the separate 'bank spheres of influence' are retained in the map of the overall structure. The gnomonic projection of the configuration is shown in Levine (1972: Figure 10).

Levine's work serves as an important indicator of both the promise and the achievement of the methods of social network analysis. It was one of the pioneering studies, carried out by one of the first generation of the new group of Harvard network analysts, yet it remains, perhaps, the most advanced example of how social network analysis can proceed in a substantive application. In Levine's work, ego-centric and socio-centric concerns are integrated into a coherent model of the embeddedness of networks in a multidimensional space. It points the way forward in offering a framework in which the principal concepts of graph theory – density, centrality and social circles of all kinds – can be allied with positional concepts describing regional and industrial sectors and can be displayed in sophisticated and easily comprehended diagrams. My aim in this book has been to offer some clarification of the leading theoretical ideas that must figure in this kind of methodological and theoretical synthesis.

Social Network Packages

At a number of places in this book I have mentioned the availability of different procedures in social network analysis software. The purpose of this Appendix is to turn to the main programs which are easily accessible to researchers and to try to indicate their principal features. I will discuss, from a user's point of view, the four major packages that are available for personal computers: GRADAP, STRUCTURE, UCINET and PAJEK.

GRADAP

GRADAP is the 'Graph Definition and Analysis Package'. It was originally developed for use on certain CDC Cyber mainframe computers, but a PC version was produced in 1988. Minor improvements have been made to the program, but essentially the same version is still available.[1] The program runs on a minimum specification PC, but requires a mathematical co-processor (integral on most 486 and all Pentium machines). The program runs with a minimal memory requirement as it builds overlay files on the hard disk. It runs directly from DOS or in a DOS window in Windows (any version). The manual is comprehensive, but its 580 pages manage to avoid telling the user in simple terms how to actually run the program.

GRADAP is not interactive, but runs in batch mode. The program was designed to be compatible with SPSS data files and command language, and it operates in very much the same way as SPSS, with an input 'program file' and separate data files. The instructions and data are read from input files, and, if all goes well, the user is presented with the opening screen and a lot of hard disk activity before being informed that the run has been completed. (Rather confusingly, the opening screen says that it is 'loading' the program, even when analysis is well under way.) The input command file contains the instructions for running the program's procedures. The commands are written in a style that follows closely the language and syntax of SPSS. The command file has separate 'PROCEDURE', 'OPTION' and 'STATISTICS' lines to specify exactly which analyses are to be undertaken.

The results are written to a new output file. This is a normal text file that can be printed or viewed on the screen. GRADAP operates in the wide 132 column format, rather than the 80 column screen format, and so it is necessary to print in a small (and non-proportional) font if the output is to be readable. The output file contains all the calculations and listings that were requested in the input command file.

The basic data required for a GRADAP analysis comprise a point set and a line set. The first comprises a list of the points in the network, together with information on their characteristics (the 'pointinfos'). Examples of pointinfos would be the names of the people represented by the points or their responses to items on a questionnaire or interview schedule. The line set lists each line by the two points at its ends, allowing a direction to be assigned by identifying one point as the 'head' and the other as the 'tail'. As in the point set, 'lineinfos' can be added to each line, showing, for example, the type of relation, its place and duration, and so on. Further details on the format of the GRADAP data files can be found in Chapter 3 above.

For any analysis to be possible, the graph must be built up from the point and line data. The user declares a name for the graph and refers to it by this name. Behind the scenes, GRADAP converts the raw data into internal system files – five for each graph. These are given the DOS extension '.GSF', but they need not normally concern the user once they have been created.[2] Once this graph file has been created, further analysis can be carried out on the same graph system files by using the command 'USE GRAPH *name*' in an input command file, where 'name' is the name given to the graph. When this command is used, GRADAP automatically invokes the system files and operates on them. The system files can be backed up or archived with the command 'SAVE GRAPH *name*'. This writes the system files to a single large file. Working system files can be reconstructed from this file by using the command 'GET GRAPH *name*'.[3]

The main general purpose procedures for undertaking social network analysis in GRADAP are SUBGRAPHS, CENTRALITY, ADJACENCY and DISTANCE. The chosen procedure must be named in an input command file after the graph and task have been specified, or immediately following another completed procedure. The PROCEDURE line specifies the particular analyses that are required. It is followed by an OPTION line and, in some cases, a STATISTICS line that specifies exactly how the particular procedure is to be implemented.

SUBGRAPHS comprises a set of routines for the identification of cliques, components and 'blocks' (i.e., cyclic components), in directed and in undirected graphs, and the user can set various minimum sizes and distances. The available options make it possible to specify how detailed the output should be and where it should be listed. For each sub-graph that is identified, the output normally shows its size and density and, if chosen, a list of its members.

CENTRALITY is used to calculate the local and global centralities of the various points and the density and overall centralization of the whole network. A number of alternative measures of point centrality and graph centralization can be chosen. Using the STATISTICS line allows such topics as spread and attenuation to be explored.

ADJACENCY constructs the adjacency matrix, taking account of the multiplicity of the lines, and the available options specify whether the matrix itself is listed along with details on the neighbourhood of each point and, in directed graphs, the indegrees and outdegrees of the points. The STATISTICS line for this procedure allows the user to specify how points are to be sorted for output (for example, by name or by reference number).

Finally, DISTANCE constructs the distance matrix and derives such measures as the 'reachability' of points and their sum, median and mean distances from other points. The STATISTICS line determines how the matrix is to be sorted and whether the diameter and various other parameters for the network as a whole are to be calculated.

The adjacency and distance matrices can be printed to files for analysis by other packages, such as those concerned with multidimensional scaling or cluster analysis. These procedures themselves are not available in the GRADAP program. The program is, however, compatible with dBase and INGRES database formats.

For all its power, GRADAP is somewhat cumbersome and is not especially user-friendly. It has all the disadvantages of having been a pioneer, and it is unfortunate that its developers have been unable to produce a newer version of the program. It is, however, systematically rooted in graph theory and offers a wide range of measures with intuitively understandable listed output.

STRUCTURE

STRUCTURE began its life in 1975, when Ronald Burt produced it for his own work on structural autonomy. He has since expanded the original program into a powerful suite of programs.[4] It is currently available in two different forms: a Basic Edition, which runs on almost any PC, and a Virtual Memory Edition, which requires a 386 or better computer with 1 Mb RAM and 5 Mb free disk space. The Basic Edition of the program is limited in the size of network (85 actors) that it can handle because it works exclusively in RAM, whereas the Virtual Memory Edition swaps data back and forth to the hard disk and so can deal with much larger networks (999 actors with 53 Mb free work space on your hard disk). With the growth in the size of hard disks in recent years, the Virtual Memory Edition should be a possibility for many users. On-line and printed manuals are available. There is an ASSISTANT program for use in preparing command files and the JEDIT program for handling data files.

Like GRADAP, STRUCTURE runs in batch mode, rather than interactively, and so it is necessary to set up an input command file, a data file and an output file. The Basic program is loaded by typing 'STRUC' at the DOS prompt – there is no Windows version – and then, when prompted, entering the name of the input command file. This file tells STRUCTURE which data file to use, the particular analyses to perform, and the name of the output file in which the results are to be stored. To run the Virtual Memory Edition, it is necessary to type 'VSTRUC', and this presents the user with a menu system that allows a degree of interactive use.

The command file is simply a text file that can be produced in any text editor, with a word processor, or with ASSISTANT. The file comprises a number of separate command lines, and the ASSISTANT program helps to compile these. (It also has in-built procedures for help in testing equivalence hypotheses and undertaking Monte Carlo analyses.) The core lines in a command file are those that contain the DATA, NETWORK and ANALYZE commands. These name the data file, describe the data, and set out the particular procedures to use in the analysis. At its simplest, then, a command file contains just these three lines. More complex analyses can be undertaken by building sequences of these three lines, each ANALYZE command telling the program to carry out the analysis requested. An ANALYZE command on its own, however, simply performs default calculations, and the line will normally be preceded by specific commands and options. The main procedures are CLIQUES, POWER, POSITIONS and AUTONOMY and the options include those for calculating density and other graph parameters. Data files are simple matrices and can be produced like a command file or with a spreadsheet or database package that is capable of writing an output matrix. It is also possible to use GRADAP to produce matrices for direct input to STRUCTURE. The JEDIT program, however, is a useful alternative to this.

The program itself is based around Burt's ideas on cohesion, structural equivalence, prominence, range and brokerage. This means that it departs somewhat from the assumptions of graph theory that underpin GRADAP and UCINET. The POSITIONS command, for example, is used to undertake analyses of structural equivalence, while AUTONOMY explores structural autonomy and constraint.[5] The program can also be run in an error-detection mode that checks the syntax of commands and the format of the data files. This prevents the program from going into a lengthy run and then crashing because of a syntax error deep in the command file. I have not fully tested the program for speed on varying networks, but the Basic Edition is faster than the Virtual Memory Edition on small networks. This difference is largely because of the time that is taken up in setting-up the virtual memory files. There is, then, a slight time penalty in using the Virtual Memory Edition on small data sets, but this is more than outweighed by the possibilities that it offers for analysing large data sets.

STRUCTURE is easy to use and well supported, but it lacks the comprehensive range of graph theoretical procedures found in the other programs. It makes up for this in the power of its specialized procedures for positional analysis.

UCINET

UCINET was produced by a group of network analysts at the University of California, Irvine (UCI). The current development team is Stephen Borgatti, Martin Everett and Linton Freeman.[6] It began as a set of modules written in BASIC, progressed to an integrated DOS program, and is now available as a Windows program. It is a general purpose, easy to use, program that covers the basic graph theoretical concepts, positional analysis and multidimensional scaling. It is, in my opinion, the best of the currently available programs and the one that is most accessible for the novice user. The program will run on virtually any modern PC, so long as it has at least 1.5 Mb of RAM. Memory is important, as the program operates in virtual memory wherever appropriate, trading off speed against the ability to handle large data sets. It can handle up to 500 points for basic clique procedures, though procedures such as multidimensional scaling can be run only on smaller networks.

UCINET 5.0 data files are the same as those for Version 4.0, but they differ slightly from those used by Version 3.0. These data files are in matrix format and consist of simple alphanumeric files. The rows in a data file represent the rows in an incidence or adjacency matrix, but a header row contains details on the number of rows and columns and the labels to be used for them. The program contains in-built procedures for converting earlier UCINET data files, and it will also convert STRUCTURE and NEGOPY files into UCINET format. In addition to exporting in various formats, a number of conversion utilities are provided to allow UCINET to feed, almost seamlessly, into other social network analysis programs.

As well as a series of commands for file management and setting program options, the menu bar has four principal options: DATA, TRANSFORM, NETWORK and TOOLS. The DATA and TRANSFORM options together allow most of the basic data management tasks to be carried out: inputting, transforming and exporting are all handled in this way.

The easiest way to produce data files is by using the intuitive and built-in, spreadsheet-style data entry system, which is accessible from the DATA menu or from a button on the tool bar. This uses a linked list format that shows, for each point, the code numbers of all the other points to which it is connected. As well as entering and editing through the UCINET spreadsheet, it is possible to import (and export) data from EXCEL worksheets. The data file can be edited after the initial data entry, and various permutations and transformations can be performed on it so as to identify subsets for further analysis. For example, the rows and the columns can be permutated, sorted, or transposed, or the weightings of lines can be altered. This latter procedure – termed 'dichotomizing' the matrix – makes it easy to prepare a series of data files for use in the analysis of, for example, nested components.

The principal social network analysis procedures are found under the NETWORK menu, where there are sub-menus for COHESION, COMPONENTS, CENTRALITY, SUB-GROUPS, ROLES & POSITIONS, and various more specialized procedures. COHESION gives access to basic line calculations of paths, distances and geodesics, and a separate PROPERTIES menu allows the calculation of density. CENTRALITY is the venue for all the various measures of degree, closeness, betweenness and other approaches to centrality and prominence. The SUBGROUPS menu gives access to a number of powerful techniques for the detection of *n*-cliques, *n*-clans and *k*-plexes, while the COMPONENTS option detects simple components, cyclic components and *k*-cores. Complementing these graph theoretical measures are the measures for structural equivalence that are found under ROLES & POSITIONS. Here it is possible to run both CONCOR and REGE, as well as other algorithms for positional analysis. Finally, the TOOLS option is used for metric and non-metric multidimensional scaling, cluster analyses, factor analysis and correspondence analysis. The output from these procedures can be plotted on screen as scatter diagrams or dendrograms. These will be quite suitable for many purposes, though proper visual inspection of sociograms means transferring the output into a more specialist program.

PAJEK

PAJEK – the word is Slovenian for spider – was specifically devised to handle very large data sets. Produced by Vladimir Batagelj and Andrej Mrvar, it was released at the end of 1996 and has been periodically up-dated. As development is still in progress, it is still not in official release form.[7]

The program is a Windows program that displays its results and workings in a main window and various subsidiary windows. The equivalent to the DATA and TRANSFORM options in UCINET are called FILES and NET in PAJEK. The FILES menu has options to read, edit or sort data files – which are similar in format to UCINET data files – and can be either the adjacency matrices themselves or the results of partitioning or clustering the data. Using commands available from NET, the networks can be transposed or reduced. This is also the place where the command to detect components is hidden away. A number of other menus allow a variety of partitioning and clustering options that are specifically designed to reduce the size of very large networks and make them more amenable to analysis. A large network can be analysed and partitioned, for example, and then the partitions can each be analysed separately and in greater detail.

PAJEK does not contain the vast array of network measures contained in UCINET or GRADAP, but it does allow some powerful processing of large networks. For many users, however, the most interesting parts of the program will be the various options found under the DRAW menu. It is here that the user can gain access to procedures for the two-dimensional and three-dimensional drawing of sociograms on screen. PAJEK uses a spring embedding procedure, similar to MDS, and the resulting sociogram can be coloured and labelled to bring out its central characteristics. Options are available to spin and rotate the sociogram for inspection from a variety of angles, and points can be moved easily by dragging with the mouse. All aspects of these manipulations can be controlled in great detail. The sociograms created can be exported in a variety of formats, including Postscript (for printing), MOL for molecular modelling and VRML for web viewing.

Although the documentation of the program is rather limited, PAJEK will be extremely useful to those who are analysing large data sets (thousands of points can, apparently, be handled efficiently) and those who are looking for an easy and accessible way to produce network visualizations. The program has massive potential for future development. One particularly striking feature is the macro facility, an advance on the command files of GRADAP and UCINET, that allows operations to be recorded and stored for later use. This points the way for other programs that will, increasingly, have to build in at least a rudimentary macro language for controlling the way that the program operates.

Other Software

KRACKPLOT Devised by David Krackhardt, together with Cathleen McGrath and Jim Blythe, the program is distributed by Analytical Technologies.[8] Data input files can be produced by converting UCINET files or directly in a text editor. It is specifically designed to draw data on screen and can produce circle diagrams and MDS displays. Points can be labelled and they can be moved under mouse control. Sociograms can be displayed, printed, or saved in GIF format.

NETIMAGE Produced by Linton Freeman.[9] It is a small program that produces camera-ready images of graphs. It comes as a series of programs that allow it to run under Windows, UNIX or LINUX. When the main program is run, a window displays the sociogram. Data input can be UCINET output files or simple text files.

NEGOPY This is one of the original network analysis programs, produced by Bill Richards.[10] It runs under DOS or from Windows. The program handles up to 1000 points and 20,000 lines. It specializes in the detection of sub-graphs that have similarities with both cliques and positions. A related program from the same source (MULTINET) allows various forms of structural equivalence and specializes in the handling of ego-centric data. A version is under preparation that will allow the import of UCINET and KRACKPLOT files.

Conclusion

Ultimately, the choice of which of the main programs to use will be a matter of personal preference, and, perhaps, of personal finance. GRADAP seems to handle fairly large data sets on basic computers more easily, and it is based around the familiar tenets of graph theory. STRUCTURE is slightly more user-friendly, thanks to the ASSISTANT program, and it allows for simulation testing using 'Monte Carlo' runs, but it has only a limited range of general purpose procedures. PAJEK is still in its development stage, but handles very large data sets, and is easy to use. UCINET has many powerful features, and the current version, running interactively under Windows, is fast and efficient with a very wide range of measures available.

New programs are appearing all the time, often based around innovative – and sometimes unfamiliar – methods and measures. It is well worth checking these out, so long as you are clear about what they are trying to do. Most can be discovered from the INSNA home page and following through its connections.[11] Many new programs are announced through the SOCNET information service.[12]

Notes

Notes to Chapter 1   Networks and Relations

1 This distinction draws on earlier arguments of Wellman (1980) and of Berkowitz and Heil (1980).

2 But see also the interesting attempts of Abell (1986) to apply the techniques of graph theory to the analysis of sequential patterns of action. While this is not, in itself, an example of social network analysis, graph theory is fundamental to the analysis of social networks.

3 The choice of four friends to name, though common, is quite arbitrary. The general point applies no matter how many friends may be specified in the question.

Notes to Chapter 2   The Development of Social Network Analysis

1 Moreno first used his sociogram at a conference in 1933. Its use was reported in the *New York Times* of 3 April 1933.

2 Balance theory rests on the assumption that individuals will find imbalance uncomfortable and so will act to establish or re-establish some kind of balance. This psychological assumption is, of course, contestable. Graph theory itself is a purely mathematical framework and its application does not require this psychological assumption.

3 The position outlined in Cartwright and Harary (1956) is more complex than this, as they define balance not simply in terms of triads, but in terms of any 'cycle' of lines. The notion of a cycle is explored further in Chapter 6 below. The later work of Davis (1967) showed, in fact, that balance could be assessed by taking account only of triads, which have, he argued, a structural significance of the kind recognized by Simmel.

4 This might be taken to support the idea that all cohesive groups define their identities by contrasting themselves with an out-group of aliens or outsiders, whether real or imaginary. See Erikson (1966).

5 Davis misleadingly talks of these sub-groups as 'cliques' and 'clusters', but they are neither cliques nor clusters in the sense that it has become customary to define these terms. For this reason, I have used the general term sub-group to outline his position. The terms clique and cluster will be defined in Chapters 6 and 7.

6 Mayo's own wider-reaching accounts of the work can be found in Mayo (1933, 1945).

7 As will be apparent from my discussion in Chapter 6, the substantive concept of 'clique' used by the Hawthorne researchers is different from, and far looser than, concepts defined in purely sociometric terms.

8 The Arensberg and Kimball (1940) study of rural Ireland had also been

supervised by Warner at Harvard and was closely related to the Yankee City study.

9 As remarked in note 5, this idea does not correspond to the sociometric concept of the clique. Warner's sociological idea might as appropriately be termed a social 'set' or a 'crowd'.

10 This is not a purely circular process, as it is possible to have individuals from each of the six classes who were, for example, members of a clique with predominantly class 1 membership.

11 From this positional analysis of stacked matrices they proceed to the construction of image graphs – again, a pioneering and undeveloped attempt at techniques that would not become common place for another 30 years. Developments of this approach are discussed in Chapter 7 below.

12 Homans uses the word 'order' instead of the more meaningful term 'direction'.

13 Their analysis of 18 women is, in fact, merely an illustrative selection from their data on over 60 cliques in Old City.

14 Homans's presence at Harvard, where many of the original researchers still worked, means that some credence must be given to this statement. It is contradicted, however, by the actual report of Roethlisberger and Dickson (1939).

15 Despite his opposition to Parsons's theoretical position, the distinction between the 'internal' and the 'external' is very similar to that employed by Parsons and which became the basis of a distinction between the external 'A' and 'G' functions and the internal 'I' and 'L' functions. As I note below, Parsons drew his concepts from reflections on the small group research of Robert Bales (1950).

16 Homans builds further on this model by introducing hypotheses about norms, status and leadership. Some of this is illustrated through case studies, but none is specifically sociometric.

17 Bott was not a member of the Department, but was a close associate of its members.

18 'Interpersonal order' is probably a better term, as the phrase 'personal network' can easily be confused with that of the ego-centric network. The latter idea is discussed below and in Chapter 4.

19 This is the same distinction as is found in Parsons and in much sociology of the 1950s and 1960s. See the related view in Lockwood's discussion of Parsons in Lockwood (1956). The distinction was re-discovered by Habermas (1968). It was also related to Homans's distinction between the internal and external systems.

20 This view of multiplexity and the 'stacking' or combining of relational data has been central to Mitchell's mathematical concerns.

21 Mitchell also gives brief mention to the 'frequency' of a relation, but this is best seen as a measure of activation rather than of the relations themselves.

22 INSNA is an international group for the exchange of information and mutual intellectual support. It publishes a newsletter, *Connections*, and was involved in the foundation of the journal *Social Networks*. Its website can be found at http://www.heinz.cmu.edu/project/INSNA This site holds back copies of the newsletter and links to other social network sites.

23 This model of attenuation is based on the well-known observation that a whispered message passed along a line of people will gradually become distorted. In Granovetter's model, the amount of information that flows is reduced with each step in the chain, so those who are far removed from the

source are unlikely to receive much accurate information about the job opportunity.

24 It is preferable to see the relational or structural approach of network analysis as *complementary* to cultural approaches, rather than as something that can incorporate and replace them. See White (1992a, 1993), and the discussion between White and Brint (Brint, 1992; White, 1992b).

Notes to Chapter 3   Handling Relational Data

1 Even if it is physically 'square', having the same number of rows and columns, it is logically rectangular.

2 There can, of course, be three-mode or, more generally, *n*-mode data, depending on the number of separate sets of points that there are. There are, however, no readily available and tested methods for handling these more complicated forms of data.

3 The incidence matrix is, in effect, a one-column vector.

4 Computational procedures that operate directly on an incidence matrix are an exception to this argument. Some of these procedures analyse the rows and some the columns of the matrix, while others analyse both the rows and the columns simultaneously. In such cases, it is necessary to make sure that the appropriate set of agents is made the target of the analysis. If the particular procedure analyses only the columns (as is often the case), the matrix may need to be transposed in order to analyse the agents which have been designated as 'cases' in the original matrix. Certain other exceptions to this claim that the distinction between cases and affiliations is arbitrary will be noted in later chapters.

5 The 'binary' data referred to here and throughout the book involves the use of binary *digits* to indicate the presence or absence of a relation. This does not involve any attempt to represent the strength of a relation as a binary *value*. Thus, a relation that has a value of 3 (there are three common affiliations between the two cases) is represented in binary form simply as '1' (a relation is present) and not as the binary numeral 11. This should not normally cause any confusion, and so I follow the normal practice of referring simply to the distinction between binary and valued data.

6 If complex data have been reduced to simpler data, it is possible to return to the original data and to transform them into a different form of simpler data. However, it is not possible to convert raw undirected data, for example, into valued or directed data without drawing on information about values or direction which was not coded into the original, undirected matrix.

7 Most word processors save their documents in a proprietary format, and it will be necessary to save the file in text or ASCII format. Such a file contains nothing but the codes corresponding to letters and numbers. See Roistacher (1979).

8 The numbers and letters that are used to refer to the cells of the spreadsheet need not be used as data labels, especially if the data are separately labelled and annotated. The numbers and letters are there simply so that there is an unambiguous way to refer to any cell in the spreadsheet. Unfortunately the convention on spreadsheets is the opposite of that for matrices: in referring to the cells of a spreadsheet, columns come before rows. Such is life!

9 Some tasks can be undertaken with a database program such as ACCESS, though these are not especially suitable for social network analysis purposes. It is important to note that the relational database is not, as it might appear, a database for relational data. The word 'relational' is being used in two distinct senses.

Some of the principles of database construction are well covered in Brent (1985).

10 STRUCTURE and UCINET require header lines that describe the format of the data. These lines are added above the data, before exporting it, to give information about the number of rows and columns and the type of data.

11 There is a slight ambiguity over the meaning of the word 'line' in graph theory. The relation between company 1 and company 2, for example, can be described as consisting of three lines (each created by a different director) or of a single line with a 'value' of 3 attached to it. The second usage is preferable for most purposes.

12 The distinction between 'tail' and 'head' is arbitrary in undirected networks. In directed networks, lines are described as directed from the tail to the head: the head of the line is where the arrow head of the sociogram points. Figure 3.4 shows that the tail corresponds to the row elements and the head to the column elements.

13 These terms have been widely used in discussions of elites (Scott, 1999). It was Laumann et al. (1983) who recently showed their more general relevance to the issue of sampling.

14 See the systematic comparisons on this basis in Stokman et al. (1985).

15 When a positional approach is used and all cases above a cut-off threshold are selected for study, we are not dealing with a sample in the strict sense. Taking all cases that qualify might be termed quasi-enumeration. It is not a complete enumeration, as links to those outside the 'slice' are ignored. For a proposal on data selection in large-scale corporate networks which avoids this problem, see Berkowitz et al. (1979).

16 The directors do not constitute an independently drawn sample, and this circularity precludes the use of many conventional statistical tests, which assume, for example, the probability sampling of cases.

17 PAJEK, discussed in the Appendix, makes great promises for the handling of very large data sets.

18 Density, which will be discussed more fully in the following chapter, can be calculated from the mean number of connections held by agents in a network.

19 The question of popularity in sociometric studies is one form of the measurement of 'centrality' in network analysis. This measure will be discussed in Chapter 5.

20 The initial choice of respondents is, of course, important in a snowball sample if bias is to be avoided.

Notes to Chapter 4   Points, Lines and Density

1 Points are sometimes referred to as 'vertices' or 'nodes', and lines are sometimes termed 'edges' or 'arcs'. There is no real advantage in using these alternative words, and so I retain the simplest usage.

2 'Graph diagram' is the general term, 'sociogram' is the term used for a graph diagram of a social network as opposed to that drawn, for example, for an electrical wiring network. As this book is concerned with sociological applications of graph theory, I shall sometimes use the two terms interchangeably.

3 A valued graph is sometimes, rather misleadingly, called a 'network'. This terminology is best avoided, as all graphs should be seen as models of networks. Some writers distinguish 'signed graphs', where the relations are characterized as positive or negative, as was seen in the case of balance theory in Chapter 2. It

seems more appropriate, however, to see the signed graph as a kind of valued graph in which the values are positive or negative binary digits. Alternatively, it could be seen as the compound graph constructed from two simple graphs, one with positive values and one with negative values.

4 In a square matrix, the row sum and the column sum for a particular point will be the same. If only the lower half of the matrix is available, the row and column sums cannot be calculated unless the remaining values are included. Those social network programs which accept data as a lower half matrix will perform these adjustments automatically.

5 Schoolteachers taught us that all measurements must have a unit attached to them. In graph theory, the 'line' is generally the unit. That is, we could say that the distance between two points is 'three lines'. This unit is not, however, normally given.

6 Note, however, that points C and A are directly connected by a line.

7 To complete the interrelated formulae, the actual number of lines is equal to half the sum of the degrees, and so density can also be expressed as $\Sigma d_i/n(n-1)$, where d_i is the degree of point i.

8 Inclusiveness, the proportion of points which are actually connected, can sometimes be more meaningfully expressed as a percentage, but this is not appropriate for small numbers.

9 See the recent discussions of this question in Sharkey (1989, 1990) and Timms (1990).

10 The GRADAP program allows a calculation of density based on multiplicity weightings, but it has no other density measures for valued graphs.

11 More general arguments on the significance of size can be found in Blau (1977a, b), Rytina (1982) and Rytina and Morgan (1982).

12 Morgan and Rytina (1977) outline some problems and limitations with this approach, and Granovetter (1977) has replied to them.

13 Wellman gives his calculations as percentage figures, and I have converted them to the base defined earlier in this chapter.

14 Wellman assumed that all relations were symmetrical: if a respondent said that intimate A was close to intimate B, then it was assumed also that intimate B was close to intimate A. Note that this analysis deals only with relations as *perceived* by respondents, and not, necessarily, with the actual links among intimate associates. The work, therefore, is directly in line with some of the phenomenological assumptions of the earliest studies of balance theory.

15 A British study which looks at reciprocity in support through kinship networks is Werbner (1990).

Notes to Chapter 5   Centrality and Centralization

1 This relative measure is calculated by the formula degree/$(n-1)$, as every point can be connected to a maximum of $n-1$ other points.

2 See also Marsden (1982). Burt has developed the idea of the intermediary as the *tertius gaudens*, the third party that benefits from the conflict or separation of two others. Anthonisse (1971) has proposed a measure called the 'rush', which is closely related to Freeman's notion of betweenness. The rush measure is implemented in the GRADAP package.

3 As a proportion, this varies from 0 to 1, with a score of 1 showing that the pair of points are completely dependent on Y for their connections.

4 The measurement of centrality, then, depends upon the solution of a set of

simultaneous equations. This measure was originally applied in Bearden et al. (1975), where r_{ij} was measured by the number of interlocks between two companies. This research is discussed later in this chapter.

5 β is a weighting attached to the raw measured centrality score, it is not a multiplier.

6 See also the application of the idea in Stokman et al. (1985).

7 It is possible that the 'positional' approaches discussed in Chapter 7 could be allied with the Stokman and Snijders approach to produce more reliable discriminations.

8 In a directed graph the 'in' and 'out' distances will differ and so the maximum column entry will be the 'in-separation' and the maximum row entry will be the 'out-separation'.

9 Note that, in this case, point B is also equidistant from all other points. This will not be the case in all graphs.

10 Note that, while it may not be possible to identify a unique absolute centre, all the actual or imaginary centres identified through Christofides's procedure will have the same mathematical properties. It is, therefore, possible to use the idea of the absolute centre in calculating other measures.

11 If a graph has a unique actual point of minimum eccentricity, then this will be its absolute centre. If there are two such points with equal eccentricity, as in sociogram (iv) of Figure 5.4, then there will be a unique absolute centre located mid-way between them. If there are more than two points with minimum eccentricity, then there may be no unique absolute centre to the graph. Unfortunately, the Christofides algorithm is not available in any of the standard social network analysis packages.

12 This digression is not essential for the newcomer to social network analysis, who may prefer to proceed directly to the next section.

13 In two dimensions, it could be said that its area would be $c(1.5)^2/3$, or $0.75c$.

14 The ratio of the circumference to the diameter of a circle is a constant, π. The ratio of the circumference to the diameter in a graph, as those concepts have been defined here, does not appear to be a constant.

   I have glossed over the issue of the units in which the volume of a graph is to be measured. As all distances in graph theory are measured in 'lines', this should be the basis of the measure. Volume would, then, be measured in 'cubic lines'.

15 The distinction between strong and weak ties in corporate networks was later systematized in the work of Stokman et al. (1985) as that between 'primary' and 'loose' interlocks.

16 It is arguable that, in this second case, the weighting should also have been based on the size of the recipient board, as the weighting is an attempt to measure the salience of the interlock for the board to which the directors are sent. Further considerations of the Bonacich measure can be found in Mizruchi and Bunting (1981) and in Mariolis and Jones (1982).

17 This idea of a cluster will be examined in Chapter 7.

18 The idea of a 'component' as a connected part of a graph will be more formally defined in the next chapter. For the purposes of the present discussion, its general meaning should be clear.

19 A comparative survey of this and related work can be found in Scott (1997). Useful theoretical discussions are Mizruchi and Galaskiewicz (1994) and Brass and Burckhardt (1992). Mizruchi (1992) provides a related extension of this work into corporate political donations.

Notes to Chapter 6   Components, Cores and Cliques

1 This is one of the implications of the so-called 'small world' phenomenon. See Milgram (1967), Erickson (1978), Lin et al. (1978), Kilworth and Bernard (1979).

2 Everett (1982) suggests that his approach to 'blocking' is similar to that used in analyses of structural equivalence. In fact, the procedures are radically different and must be distinguished. Structural equivalence is discussed in the following chapter.

3 As with the identification of paths, there may be a number of identical cycles, depending on which point is made the starting point for naming the cycle. In counting the number of cycles in a graph, this double counting must be reckoned with. In what follows, I shall not normally distinguish the identical cycles and will name them simply by an arbitrarily chosen starting point. Sociogram (i) of Figure 6.2, for example, has only three distinct cycles: ABCDA, ABDA and BCDB.

4 Everett claims that his concept of a bridge is similar to that used by Granovetter (1973) to describe the 'weak' ties which connect 'strongly' tied sub-groups.

5 It should be noted that all pairs of points in a cyclic component will be connected through a cycle, though many of these may be longer than the cycle length used to define the cyclic component. The cyclic component {E,F,G,H,I,J} in Figure 6.2 is built from 4-cycles, but points E and J, for example, are connected only through a cycle of length 6.

6 This is important, as a cycle in an undirected graph must connect at least three points. Thus, a dyad can never be a cyclic component.

7 In case the analysis still results in the identification of a single large component, Everett argues for the use of a further *ad hoc* procedure for fragmenting the structure of the graph. He argues that it is possible, for example, to take account only of reciprocated directed lines, where A directs a line to B and B directs a line to A. These are the strongest lines in the graph, and an analysis which takes account of these alone should, he argues, identify the strongest structural features of the graph. This procedure is implemented in UCINET by reading a directed (asymmetrical) matrix as if it were undirected. The program disregards all unreciprocated lines.

8 This idea of the 'block', unlike that of Everett, is based on earlier usage in graph theory.

9 Where a knot consists simply of two points connected by a line, the line is termed a 'bridge' between the other knots of which its points are members. This notion of a bridge is very different from that of Everett and from the idea that was introduced by Schwartz and his colleagues and that was discussed in the previous chapter. It is an unfortunate fact in social network analysis that words are so often used in contradictory ways to describe different concepts.

10 The term 'nested components' was first introduced by the GRADAP team for a particular procedure, but it has a far wider application.

11 The term 'slicing' is the most descriptive of the procedure involved, though 'dichotomizing' is the term used in the UCINET manual. Everett refers to the procedure as 'compression'.

12 I am here generalizing Seidman's concept (1983) of the core in such a way that the general concept is no longer defined by Seidman's *k* parameter. This is elaborated in the following discussion.

13 It is important to note that the degree in this procedure is measured only in relation to the other members of the core, not in the graph as a whole.

14 I shall examine the cohesive sub-groups themselves in the following section. Seidman specifically points to the parallels between his conceptualization of k-cores and Granovetter's work (1973) on weak ties.

15 Note that while the minimum degree (k) is calculated only for points within the core, the proportion of points disappearing is based on the total number of points in the graph as a whole. This ensures that the vector is, to a certain extent, standardized for the size of the graph.

16 I have invented the term 'm-core' to parallel Seidman's notion of the k-core. This terminology also has the advantage of keeping clear the distinction between the component itself and the cores of which it is composed.

17 What I have termed m-cores are the basis of Atkin's method of Q-analysis, developed as an alternative to graph theory. In Q-analysis, it is possible to construct a matrix of Q-nearness, in which the Q-nearness of two points is, confusingly, one less than the multiplicity of the line connecting them. Thus, a component of points which are all 2-near to one another would correspond to a $3m$-core (see Atkin, 1974, 1977, 1981; Beaumont and Gattrell, 1982; Doreian, 1980, 1981, 1983). The application of Q-analysis is discussed in the Appendix of Scott (1986).

18 In the terminology which has evolved in this chapter, these would be k-cyclic m-cores, where k is the cycle length and m is the multiplicity.

19 A pair of connected points is a clique in only a trivial sense, and clique analysis should normally be concerned only with cliques of size 3 or more.

20 The formula linking the number of points to the number of lines is that which is used to identify the total possible number of lines in calculating density. It is $n(n-1)/2$, where n is the number of points. This defines the sequence of so-called 'triangular numbers'.

21 In practice, a number of clique detection programs simply will not work on directed graphs. The terminology of strong and weak cliques is an innovation of my own, designed to parallel the distinction between strong and weak components.

22 A further reason for relaxing the strict idea of clique membership was that, during the 1940s and 1950s, it proved difficult to discover algorithms that could identify them in an efficient way. Greater mathematical knowledge and improvements in computing have now removed this obstacle.

23 There was a fault in UCINET Release 3.0 which meant that its clique detection algorithm simply did not work. This was rectified in later release 5. The program GROUP reads UCINET files and has a number of clique detection procedures.

24 A technique for the identification of n-clans is available in UCINET. Mokken (1974) also introduced the concept of the n-club, a component with maximum diameter n. This can usefully be seen as a further extension of the idea of the simple component, though little analysis in this direction has been attempted. Note that a weak component is both an n-clan and an n-club in which the value of n is just large enough to connect the maximum number of points.

25 The concept of the k-plex is constructed along similar lines to that of the k-core, also developed by Seidman, both concepts being degree-based. Unfortunately, the letter k does not mean the same thing in the two concepts. In a k-core it is the minimum degree of points in the core; in a k-plex it is the number of points to which a point need not be connected.

26 In fact, graph (ii) is a 2-clique rather than merely a 3-clique.

27 Seidman and Foster develop a further concept, following Mokken's suggestion of limiting the diameters of sub-graphs. They extend the k-plex idea and identify what they call a 'diameter-n k-plex'. This is defined as a group in which each point is connected to at least $k-1$ of the other points at a distance of n or less. The concept of a diameter-2 k-plex, in particular, seems a very fruitful extension to the clique idea. Unfortunately, the k measure is, again, used in a different sense, and so comparisons must be made with care. (See Seidman and Foster, 1978: 69–70.)

28 The identification of circles might be seen, in a general sense, as a particular kind of clustering method. But in this book I have restricted the idea of the cluster to those sub-graphs which are found through specific hierarchical methods. Circles, cliques and plexes group points on the basis of the degree of their mutual connections, while hierarchical clustering methods take account of their whole pattern of connections to the rest of the network. In this sense, hierarchical clustering is closely linked to the identification of structural equivalence, which is reviewed in the following chapter.

29 Chapter 10 in Mullins (1973) is a study of social network analysts. It includes a data matrix but no sociogram.

30 In fact, Gattrell goes beyond this, but I do not intend to pursue these issues here. The interested reader can consult Beaumont and Gattrell (1982) and then read Gattrell's studies.

31 It is important to note that this does not mean that every paper is directly connected to every other in the component. He is not concerned with cliques. The data simply show the existence of a chain of connections.

Notes to Chapter 7 Positions, Roles and Clusters

1 As in so many areas of social network analysis, there are confusing problems of terminology here. Reseachers following Lorrain and White have used the word 'block' to refer both to the sets or clusters of points and to the cells of the image matrix. Further confusion arises from the fact, pointed out in Chapter 6, that graph theorists have used the word 'block' to refer to a number of totally different and un-related ideas. Having eschewed the word 'block' in that chapter, I limit its use in this chapter to describe the cells of image matrices. The sets of points, for reasons set out in the following section, I refer to as 'clusters'.

2 There are other forms of agglomerative cluster analysis, but these are the most common. An intermediate approach is the median distance method used in the UCLUS algorithm. This takes neither the smallest nor the greatest distance between clusters as a measure of similarity. Instead it takes the median distance. Anderberg (1973) has provided an intermediate 'average linkage' method. See also Allen (1980).

3 Some writers suggest using χ^2 to select the criterion at each step.

4 The most elaborated account of this method can be found in Boorman and White (1976), Breiger et al. (1975) and White et al. (1976). The original method was discussed in McQuitty (1968) and McQuitty and Clark (1968).

5 It has also been suggested that it is unfruitful to divide the matrix into sets that contain fewer than three points, as, in most matrices a set of size 2 will be only a trivial case of structural equivalence.

6 In practice, it has been found that the process can be halted before all values converge to $+1$ or -1. It has been suggested that little is gained from the extra

computing time in setting the convergence criterion higher than +0.9 and −0.9. The version of CONCOR implemented in UCINET allows the investigator to make this choice of convergence criterion. When such a decision is made, however, an arbitrary element is, of course, introduced into the procedure.

7 The Breiger et al. (1975) analysis relates not to the original Davis et al. data (1941), but to the re-analysis of the original data given in Homans (1951).

8 When the actual density of a block is 1.0, the block will be a 1-clique. When it is less than 1, however, the block will not form a 1-clique, and it may not even form an *n*-clique. This is hardly surprising, as CONCOR is specifically presented as an alternative to clique detection methods. If CONCOR simply identified cliques, its cumbersome procedures would hardly be worthwhile.

9 More complex, but comparable, real data sets are discussed in Breiger (1979).

10 Further sources on CONCOR and block models can be found in Light and Mullins (1979), Arabie et al. (1978) and Schwartz (1977). CONCOR is extended in Bonacich and McConaghy (1979). See also Carrington et al. (1980).

11 This discussion draws on Burt (1980, 1982) and Burt and Schott (1990). White's latest work has moved in a similar conceptual direction to Burt. See White (1992a, b).

12 Burt terms this the 'frequency decay' assumption. The STRUCTURE program allows alternative assumptions to be used at the choice of the researcher.

13 BURT calculates 'Euclidean' distances, which I shall discuss in the following chapter.

14 The actual test recommended by Burt involves performing a principal components analysis on the 'co-variance matrix' of each cluster. The loading of a point on the first component is taken as a measure of its association with the other members of the cluster. This test may seem a little obscure unless the methods of principal components analysis are understood. They are discussed in the following chapter, and readers may prefer to return to this section after reading the relevant part of that chapter. Burt's approach is criticized in Faust and Romney (1985).

15 As each point has a different number of contacts, the matrix of similarities will not be symmetrical.

16 The correlation calculated is not a normal Pearson correlation coefficient, but one which incorporates some of the Euclidean assumptions of Burt's method.

17 For an attempt to specify the relations between structural equivalence and conventional graph theoretical concerns, see Everett et al. (1990).

18 Burt has combined structural equivalence with multidimensional scaling (MDS) to produce a topology of United States markets in Burt (1988) and Burt and Carlton (1989). MDS will be discussed in the following chapter.

19 A small sixth set with very weak links to the rest of the network is excluded.

Notes to Chapter 8   *Dimensions and Displays*

1 KRACKPLOT, described in the Appendix, has a procedure for constructing these circle diagrams, though the order in which the points are arranged has still to be determined by the researcher.

2 Multidimensional scaling can also be used to disclose features of attribute data, but this is beyond the scope of this book.

3 Euclidean metrics have additional properties that need not detain us here. Basically, a Euclidean metric allows the use of all the familiar additive arithmetic operations (addition, subtraction, multiplication and division) and it conforms to

the principles of conventional school geometry (e.g., Pythagorus's theorem). Metric models other than the Euclidean have been proposed, but they have not been especially important in social network analysis. One such model is the curved space 'Reimannian' metric, in which Pythagoras's and other familiar theorems do not apply.

4 This characterizes metric multidimensional scaling. The slightly different non-metric approach to multidimensional scaling is discussed later in this Chapter. A procedure that, for most practical purposes, seems to produce similar results to MDS is spring embedding (Kamada and Kawai, 1989). Although this is used in the PAJEK program (see Appendix), its basis has not yet been worked through in the secondary literature.

5 'Dissimilarities' are sometimes termed 'differences'.

6 There is an exactly similar problem of reflection with respect to the position of A. If the original line had been drawn as BA rather than AB (i.e., running in the opposite direction), ABC would be reflected around the line BC. The curious reader may experiment for her- or himself.

7 It is important not to confuse the concept of 'component' used in principal components analysis with the graph theoretical idea of a 'component'. In graph theory a component is a particular kind of segment in a graph; in principal components analysis, a component is a 'dimension' or 'factor'.

8 It is important not to confuse Q-mode analysis with the Q-analysis of Atkin which was touched on in Chapter 6 and to which I refer later in this chapter.

9 With a non-symmetrical adjacency matrix it is often possible to produce a combined row and column solution that shows the joint space occupied by the cases.

10 See Coxon (1982) and Kruskal and Wish (1978). The original sources on non-metric multidimensional scaling include Shepard (1962), Kruskal (1964a, b), Guttman (1968) and Lingoes and Roskam (1973).

11 As an initial configuration is simply generated for testing, its source does not matter. Thus, a metric procedure can be used to generate this initial configuration.

12 Strictly speaking, this is an over-simplification, but it corresponds to the general principles used in testing goodness of fit. The most general principle is that the relation between the data ranks and the distance ranks be 'monotonic' – i.e., the line moves up and to the right in a constant way, though not necessarily at 45° to the axes.

13 UCINET and KRACKPLOT are able to construct simple circle diagrams, but Krempel's own algorithm is not yet generally available.

14 UCINET comes with conversion procedures for transforming its own output data files into the format required by MAGE and by many other molecular modelling programs.

15 Although square, the matrix was asymmetrical, as the columns were the occupations of respondents and the rows were the occupations of those with whom they claimed to interact. The data were, in this sense, directed from columns to rows. Laumann, therefore, used the asymmetric variant of the Guttman–Lingoes program, the version normally used for rectangular incidence matrices.

16 Note that it is fundamentally incorrect to try to equate 'centrality' in the sphere with any of the ideas of network centrality discussed in Chapter 5. In fact, the 'centre' in Levine's analysis is exactly the opposite of that discussed in relation

to the work of Laumann and Pappi. The reason for this is that Levine used similarity data, while Laumann and Pappi used dissimilarities. In Levine's analysis, the centre is the zero point of least similarity. Paradoxically, Levine's 'centre' contains the most 'peripheral' points, and the position of the banks towards the outer layers of the sphere supports the Bearden et al. (1975) view of bank centrality.

17 A vector, in this context, is simply a line drawn through the configuration.

Notes to Appendix   Social Network Packages

1 GRADAP, Release 2.10 (dated 10 February 1992). Available from iec ProGAMMA, PO Box 841, 9700AV, Gröningen, The Netherlands; fax: +31-50-363687; e-mail gamma.post@gamma.rug.nl. Price $795 for disks and manual. Further information on GRADAP can be found through the internet on http://www.gamma.rug.nl/files/p315.html

2 The GRADAP commands use the general term 'graph' to refer to the whole collection of files associated with a particular data set. This allows them all to be referenced by a single name. The term is, however, stretched beyond its technical meaning in graph theory, where it refers to the mathematical model of a network. GRADAP's concept might better be referred to as a 'graph file'.

3 'UNLOAD' can be used in place of 'SAVE', and 'RELOAD' in place of 'GET'.

4 STRUCTURE, Basic Edition, Release 4.2. Available from Center for the Social Sciences, 420 West 118th Street, 8th Floor, Columbia University, NY 10027, USA, free of charge. The Basic Edition can be downloaded from http://www.columbia.edu/cu/css/download.htm, and the on-line manual can be downloaded from Burt's web site at Chicago University: http://www.uchicago.edu/fac/ronald.burt/teaching/strucmanual.pdf

5 These ideas are discussed in Burt (1982).

6 UCINET Version 5.0 (dated February 1999). Available from Analytical Technology, 11 Ohlin Lane, Harvard, MA 01451, USA; fax: +978-456-7373. Price $150 ($100 upgrade from Version 4.0; $40 to students). The UCINET website is at http://eclectic.ss.uci.edu/~lin/ucinet.html

7 PAJEK can be downloaded free from http://vlado.mat.uni-lj.si/vlado/vlado.htm Brief manuals can also be downloaded. Batagelj can be contacted at the Department of Mathematics, University of Ljubljana, Jadranska 19, 1000 Lubljana, Slovenia; fax: +386-66-217-281; e-mail vladimir.batagelj@uni-lj.si

8 For address see note 6 above. Version 3.0 costs $125 ($39 for students). Information can be obtained from http://www.heinz.cmu.edu/~krack

9 The official name uses upper and lower case and spells the name NetImage. It can be downloaded free from http://tarski.ss.uci.edu/netim.html

10 Version 4.302 (November 1995). A small demo and the full manual can be downloaded free of charge, and the full program can be ordered from http://www.sfu.ca/~richards/negopy.htm

11 The INSNA home page is at http://www.heinz.cmu.edu/project/INSNA

12 To subscribe to this service send an e-mail to listserv@nervm.nerdc.ufl.edu The message should say simply 'SUBSCRIBE SOCNET Your Name', replacing 'Your Name' with your own name.

Bibliography

Abell, P. (1986) *The Syntax of Social Life*. Oxford: Oxford University Press.

Alba, R.D. (1973) 'A Graph Theoretic Definition of a Sociometric Clique', *Journal of Mathematical Sociology*, 3.

Alba, R.D. (1982) 'Taking Stock of Network Analysis: A Decade's Results', *Research in the Sociology of Organizations*, 1.

Alba, R.D. and Kadushin, C. (1976) 'The Intersection of Social Circles: A New Measure of Social Proximity in Networks', *Sociological Methods and Research*, 5.

Alba, R.D. and Moore, G. (1978) 'Elite Social Circles', *Sociological Methods and Research*, 7.

Allen, M.P. (1980) 'Cliques Versus Clusters in Corporate Networks'. Paper presented to the Pacific Sociological Association, San Francisco.

Anderberg, M.R. (1973) *Cluster Analysis for Applications*. New York: Academic Press.

Anthonisse, J. (1971) *The Rush in a Directed Graph*. Amsterdam: University of Amsterdam Mathematical Centre.

Arabie, P., Boorman, S.A. and Levitt, P.R. (1978) 'Constructing Blockmodels: How and Why', *Journal of Mathematical Psychology*, 17.

Arensberg, C.M. and Kimball, S.T. (1940) *Family and Community in Ireland*. London: Peter Smith.

Aron, R. (1964) *German Sociology*. Glencoe: Free Press.

Atkin, R. (1974) *Mathematical Structure in Human Affairs*. London: Heinemann.

Atkin, R. (1977) *Combinatorial Connectivities in Social Systems*. Basle: Birkhauser.

Atkin, R. (1981) *Multidimensional Man*. Harmondsworth: Penguin.

Bailey, F.G. (1969) *Stratagems and Spoils*. Oxford: Basil Blackwell.

Bailey, K.D. (1976) 'Cluster Analysis', in Heise (ed.), 1976.

Bales, R.F. (1950) *Interaction Process Analysis*. Reading, MA: Addison–Wesley.

Banck, G.A. (1973) 'Network Analysis and Social Theory', in Boissevain and Mitchell (eds), 1973.

Barnes, J.A. (1954) 'Class and Committee in a Norwegian Island Parish', *Human Relations*, 7.

Barnes, J.A. (1969) 'Graph Theory and Social Networks', *Sociology*, 3.

Barnes, J.A. (1974) *Social Networks*. Module in Anthropology, No. 26. Reading, MA: Addison–Wesley.

Barnes, J.A. and Harary, F. (1983) 'Graph Theory in Network Analysis', *Social Networks*, 5.

Bavelas, A. (1948) 'A Mathematical Model for Group Structure', *Applied Anthropology*, 7.

Bavelas, A. (1950) 'Communication Patterns in Task-Oriented Groups', *Journal of the Acoustical Society of America*, 22.

Bearden, J., Atwood, W., Freitag, P., Hendricks, C., Mintz, B. and Schwartz, M.

194   *Social network analysis*

(1975) 'The Nature and Extent of Bank Centrality in Corporate Networks'. Paper to the American Sociological Association.

Beauchamp, M. (1965) 'An Improved Index of Centrality', *Behavioural Science*, 10.

Beaumont, J.C. and Gattrell, A.C. (1982) *An Introduction to Q-Analysis*. Norwich: Geo Publications.

Berkowitz, S.D. (1982) *An Introduction to Structural Analysis*. Toronto: Butterworths.

Berkowitz, S.D. and Heil, G. (1980) 'Dualities in Methods of Social Network Analysis'. Discussion Paper, University of Toronto Structural Analysis Program.

Berkowitz, S.D., Carrington, P.J., Corman, J.S. and Waverman, L. (1979) 'Flexible Description for a Large Scale Corporate Data Base', *Social Networks*, 2.

Blau, P.M. (1977a) *Inequality and Heterogeneity*. New York: Free Press.

Blau, P.M. (1977b) 'A Macrosociological Theory of Social Structure', *American Journal of Sociology*, 83.

Blau, P.M. and Duncan, O.D. (1967) *The American Occupational Structure*. New York: John Wiley.

Bogardus, E.S. (1959) *Social Distance*. Yellow Springs, OH: Antioch Press.

Boissevain, J. (1974) *Friends of Friends*. Oxford: Basil Blackwell.

Boissevain, J. and Mitchell, J.D. (eds) (1973) *Network Analysis*. The Hague: Mouton.

Bonacich, P. (1972) 'Technique for Analysing Overlapping Memberships', in Costner (ed.), 1972.

Bonacich, P. (1987) 'Power and Centrality: A Family of Measures', *American Sociological Review*, 52.

Bonacich, P. and McConaghy, M. (1979) 'The Algebra of Blockmodelling', in Schuessler (ed.), 1979.

Boorman, S.A. and White, H.C. (1976) 'Social Structure from Multiple Networks, II', *American Journal of Sociology*, 81.

Borgatti, S. and Everett, M.G. (1989) 'The Class of All Regular Equivalences: Algebraic Structure and Computation', *Social Networks*, 11.

Borgatti, S., Boyd, J. and Everett, M.G. (1989) 'Iterated Roles: Mathematics and Applications', *Social Networks*, 11.

Bott, E. (1955) 'Urban Families: Conjugal Roles and Social Networks', *Human Relations*, 8.

Bott, E. (1956) 'Urban Families: The Norms of Conjugal Roles', *Human Relations*, 9.

Bott, E. (1957) *Family and Social Network*. London: Tavistock.

Boyd, J.P. (1969) 'The Algebra of Group Kinship', *Journal of Mathematical Sociology*, 6.

Brass, D.J. and Burckhardt, M.E. (1992) 'Centrality and Power in Organizations', in Nohira and Eccles (eds), 1992.

Breiger, R.L. (1979) 'Toward an Operational Theory of Community Elite Structure', *Quality and Quantity*, 13.

Breiger, R.L. (1981) 'The Social Class Structure of Occupational Mobility', *American Journal of Sociology*, 87.

Breiger, R.L. (1982) 'A Structural Analysis of Occupational Mobility', in Marsden and Lin (eds), 1982.

Breiger, R.L., Boorman, S.A. and Arabie, P. (1975) 'An Algorithm for Blocking Relational Data, with Applications to Social Network Analysis', *Journal of Mathematical Psychology*, 12.

Brent, E.E. (1985) 'Relational Database Structures and Concept Formation in the Social Sciences', *Computers and the Social Sciences*, 1.

Brint, S. (1992) 'Hidden Meanings: Cultural Content and Context in Harrison White's Structural Sociology', *Sociological Theory*, 10.

Buckley, W. (1967) *Sociology and Modern Systems Theory*. Englewood Cliffs, NJ: Prentice–Hall.

Bulmer, M. (1985) 'The Rejuvenation of Community Studies? Neighbours, Networks, and Policy', *Sociological Review*, 33.

Burt, R.S. (1976) 'Positions in Social Networks', *Social Forces*, 55.

Burt, R.S. (1977a) 'Positions in Multiple Network Systems, Part One', *Social Forces*, 56.

Burt, R.S. (1977b) 'Positions in Multiple Network Systems, Part Two', *Social Forces*, 56.

Burt, R.S. (1979) 'A Structural Theory of Interlocking Corporate Directorates', *Social Networks*, 1.

Burt, R.S. (1980) 'Models of Network Structure', *Annual Review of Sociology*, 6.

Burt, R.S. (1982) *Towards a Structural Theory of Action*. New York: Academic Press.

Burt, R.S. (1983a) 'Studying Status/Role-Sets Using Mass Surveys', in Burt and Minor (eds), 1983.

Burt, R.S. (1983b) *Corporate Profits and Cooptation*. New York: Academic Press.

Burt, R.S. (1983c) 'Firms, Directors and Time in the Directorate Tie Network', *Social Networks*, 5.

Burt, R.S. (1987) 'Social Contagion and Innovation: Cohesion Versus Structural Equivalence', *American Journal of Sociology*, 92.

Burt, R.S. (1988) 'The Stability of American Markets', *American Journal of Sociology*, 94.

Burt, R.S. (1992) *Structural Holes*. New York: Cambridge University Press.

Burt, R.S. and Carlton, D.S. (1989) 'Another Look at the Network Boundaries of American Markets', *American Journal of Sociology*, 95.

Burt, R.S. and Minor, M.J. (eds) (1983) *Applied Network Analysis*. Beverly Hills, CA: Sage Publications.

Burt, R. and Schott, T. (1990) *STRUCTURE 4.1 Reference Manual*. New York: Columbia University Press.

Burt, R.S., Christman, K.P. and Kilburn, H.C. (1980) 'Testing a Structural Theory of Corporate Cooptation: Interlocking Directorate Ties as a Strategy for Avoiding Market Constraints on Profits', *American Sociological Review*, 45.

Carrington, P.J. and Heil, G.H. (1981) 'COBLOC: A Hierarchical Method for Blocking Network Data', *Journal of Mathematical Sociology*, 8.

Carrington, P.J., Heil, G.H. and Berkowitz, S.D. (1980) 'A Goodness-of-Fit Index for Blockmodels', *Social Networks*, 2.

Cartwright, D. and Harary, F. (1956) 'Structural Balance: a Generalisation of Heider's Theory', *Psychological Review*, 63. Reprinted in Leinhardt (ed.), 1984.

Cartwright, D. and Zander, A. (eds) (1953) *Group Dynamics*. London: Tavistock.

Christofides, N. (1975) *Graph Theory: An Algorithmic Approach*. New York: Academic Press.

Coleman, J.S., Katz, E. and Menzel, H. (1966) *Medical Innovation: a Diffusion Study*. Indianapolis: Bobbs–Merrill.

Cook, K.S. (1977) 'Exchange and Power in Networks of Interorganisational Relations', *Sociological Quarterly*, 18.

Cook, K.S. (1982) 'Network Structure from an Exchange Perspective', in Marsden and Lin (eds), 1982.

Cook, K.S. and Whitmeyer, J.M. (1992) 'Two Approaches to Social Structure: Exchange Theory and Network Analysis', *Annual Review of Sociology*, 18.

Costner, H. (ed.) (1972) *Sociological Methodology, 1973*. San Francisco: Jossey Bass.

Coxon, A.P.M. (1982) *The Users Guide to Multidimensional Scaling*. London: Heinemann.

Crane, D. (1972) *Invisible Colleges*. Chicago: University of Chicago Press.

Dahl, R.A. (1961) *Who Governs?* New Haven, CT.: Yale University Press.

Daultrey, S. (1976) *Principal Components Analysis*. Norwich: Geo Abstracts.

Davis, A., Gardner, B.B. and Gardner, M.R. (1941) *Deep South*. Chicago: University of Chicago Press.

Davis, J.A. (1967) 'Clustering and Structural Balance in Graphs', *Human Relations*, 20. Reprinted in Leinhardt (ed.), 1984.

Davis, J.A. (1968) 'Structural Balance, Mechanical Solidarity, and Interpersonal Relations', *American Journal of Sociology*, 68.

Doreian, P. (1979) *Mathematics and the Study of Social Relations*. London: Weidenfeld & Nicolson.

Doreian, P. (1980) 'On the Evolution of Group and Network Structure', *Social Networks*, 2.

Doreian, P. (1981) 'Polyhedral Dynamics and Conflict Mobilisation in Social Networks', *Social Networks*, 3.

Doreian, P. (1983) 'Levelling Coalitions in Network Phenomena', *Social Networks*, 4.

Doreian, P. (1987) 'Measuring Regular Equivalence in Symmetrical Structures', *Social Networks*, 9.

Duck, S. and Perlman, D. (eds) (1985) *Personal Relationships*, vol. 1. Beverly Hills, CA: Sage Publications.

Duncan, O.D. (1961) 'A Socio-economic Index for all Occupations', in Reiss (ed.), 1961.

Emerson, R.M. (1962) 'Power–Dependence Relations', *American Sociological Review*, 27.

Emerson, R.M. (1964) 'Power–Dependence Relations: Two Experiments', *Sociometry*, 27.

Emirbayer, M. (1997) 'Manifesto for a Relational Sociology', *American Journal of Sociology*, 103.

Emirbayer, M. and Goodwin, J. (1994) 'Network Analysis, Culture, and the Problem of Agency', *American Journal of Sociology*, 99.

Erickson, B.H. (1978) 'Some Problems of Inference from Chain Data', in Schuessler (ed.), 1978.

Erickson, B.H. and Nosanchuk, T. (1983) *Understanding Data*. Toronto: McGraw Hill.

Erickson, B.H., Nosanchuk, T.A. and Lee, E. (1981) 'Network Sampling in Practice: Some Second Steps', *Social Networks*, 3.

Erikson, K.T. (1966) *Wayward Puritans*. New York: John Wiley.

Everett, M.G. (1982) 'A Graph Theoretic Blocking Procedure for Social Networks', *Social Networks*, 4.

Everett, M.G. (1983a) 'EBLOC: A Graph Theoretic Blocking Algorithm for Social Networks', *Social Networks*, 5.

Everett, M.G. (1983b) 'An Extension of EBLOC to Valued Graphs', *Social Networks*, 5.

Everett, M.G. (1984) 'An Analysis of Cyclically Dense Data Using EBLOC', *Social Networks*, 6.

Everett, M.G. and Borgatti, S. (1990) 'A Testing Example for Positional Analysis Techniques', *Social Networks*, 12.

Everett, M.G., Boyd, J.P. and Borgatti, S. (1990) 'Ego-Centered and Local Roles: A Graph Theoretic Approach', *Journal of Mathematical Sociology*, 15.

Everitt, B. (1974) *Cluster Analysis*. London: Heinemann.

Fararo, T.J. and Sunshine, M.H. (1964) *A Study of a Biased Friendship Net*. Syracuse, NY: Syracuse University Press.

Faust, K. and Romney, A.K. (1985) 'Does "Structure" Find Structure? A Critique of Burt's Use of Distance as a Measure of Structural Equivalence', *Social Networks*, 7.

Featherman, D.L. and Hauser, R.M. (1978) *Opportunity and Change*. New York: Academic Press.

Festinger, L. (1949) 'The Analysis of Sociograms Using Matrix Algebra', *Human Relations*, 2.

Festinger, L. (1957) *A Theory of Cognitive Dissonance*. Evanston, IL: Row Peterson.

Festinger, L., Riecken, H.W. and Schachter, S. (1959) *When Prophecy Fails*. New York: Harper and Row.

Fischer, C.S. (1977) *Networks and Places: Social Relations in the Urban Setting*. New York: Free Press.

Fischer, C.S. (1982) *To Dwell Among Friends*. Chicago: University of Chicago Press.

Frank, O. (1978a) 'Sampling and Estimation in Large Networks', *Social Networks*, 1.

Frank, O. (1978b) 'Estimation of the Number of Connected Components in a Graph by Using a Sampled Sub-graph', *Scandinavian Journal of Statistics*, 5.

Frank, O. (1979) 'Estimation of Population Totals by Use of Snowball Samples', in Holland and Leinhardt (eds), 1979.

Frank, O. (1988) 'Random Sampling and Social Networks: A Survey of Various Approaches', *Mathematiques, Informatique et Sciences Humaine*, 26.

Frankenberg, R. (1966) *Communities in Britain*. Harmondsworth: Penguin.

Freeman, L.C. (1979) 'Centrality in Social Networks: I. Conceptual Clarification', *Social Networks*, 1.

Freeman, L.C. (1980) 'The Gatekeeper, Pair Dependency and Structural Centrality', *Quality and Quantity*, 14.

Freeman, L.C. (1983) 'Spheres, Cubes, and Boxes: Graph Dimensionality and Network Structure', *Social Networks*, 5.

Freeman, L.C. (1996a) 'Visualizing Social Networks', http://carnap.ss.uci.edu/vis.html

Freeman, L.C. (1996b) 'Using Molecular Modelling Software in Social Network Analysis: A Practicum', http://eclectic.ss.uci.edu/~lin/chem.html

Freeman, L.C., White, D.R. and Romney, A.K. (eds) (1989) *Research Methods in Social Network Analysis*. New Brunswick, NJ: Transaction Books, 1992 edn.

Friedkin, N.E. (1981) 'The Development of Structure in Random Networks', *Social Networks*, 3.

Friedkin, N. (1984) 'Structural Equivalence and Cohesion Explanations of Social Homogeneity', *Sociological Methods and Research*, 12.

Friedkin, N. (1998) *A Structural Theory of Social Influence*. New York: Cambridge University Press.

Galtung, J. (1967) *Theory and Methods of Social Research*. London: George Allen & Unwin.

Gattrell, A.C. (1984a) 'Describing the Structure of a Research Literature: Spatial Diffusion Modelling in Geography', *Environment and Planning, B*, 11.

Gattrell, A.C. (1984b) 'The Growth of a Research Speciality', *Annals of the Association of American Geographers*, 74.

Glass, D.V. (1954) *Social Mobility in Britain*. London: Routledge and Kegan Paul.

Goddard, J. and Kirby, A. (1976) *An Introduction to Factor Analysis*. Norwich: Geo Abstracts.

Granovetter, M. (1973) 'The Strength of Weak Ties', *American Journal of Sociology*, 78.

Granovetter, M. (1974) *Getting a Job*. Cambridge, MA: Harvard University Press.

Granovetter, M. (1976) 'Network Sampling: Some First Steps', *American Journal of Sociology*, 81.

Granovetter, M. (1977) Reply to Morgan and Rytina, *American Journal of Sociology*, 82.

Granovetter, M. (1979) 'The Theory-Gap in Social Network Analysis', in Holland and Leinhardt (eds), 1979.

Granovetter, M. (1982) 'The Strength of Weak Ties: A Network Theory Revisited', in Marsden and Lin (eds), 1982.

Grieco, M. (1987) *Keeping It in The Family*. London: Tavistock.

Guttman, L. (1968) 'A General Non-Metric Technique for Finding the Smallest Co-ordinate Space for a Configuration of Points', *Psychometrika* 33.

Habermas, J. (1968) 'Labour and Interaction: Remarks on Hegel's Jena Philosophy of Mind', in Habermas, 1974.

Habermas, J. (1974) *Theory and Practice*. London: Heinemann.

Hage, P. and Harary, F. (1983) *Structural Models in Anthropology*. Cambridge: Cambridge University Press.

Hage, P. and Harary, F. (1991) *Exchange in Oceania: A Graph Theoretic Analysis*. Oxford: Oxford University Press.

Hage, P. and Harary, F. (1998) *Island Networks: Communication, Kinship, and Classification Structures in Oceania*. Cambridge: Cambridge University Press.

Harary, F. (1969) *Graph Theory*. Reading, MA: Addison–Wesley.

Harary, F. and Norman, R.Z. (1953) *Graph Theory as a Mathematical Model in Social Science*. Ann Arbor, MI: Institute for Social Research.

Harary, F., Norman, R.Z. and Cartwright, D. (1965) *Structural Models*. New York: John Wiley.

Heider, F. (1946) 'Attitudes and Cognitive Orientation', *Journal of Psychology*, 21. Reprinted in Leinhardt (ed.), 1977.

Heise, D.R. (ed.) (1976) *Sociological Methodology, 1975*. San Francisco: Jossey Bass.

Heise, D.R. (ed.) (1977) *Sociological Methodology, 1978*. San Francisco: Jossey Bass.

Helmers, H.M., Mokken, R.J., Plijter, R.C. and Stokman, F.N. (1975) *Graven Naar Macht*. Amsterdam: Van Gennep.

Holland, P. and Leinhardt, S. (eds) (1979) *Perspectives on Social Networks*. New York: Academic Press.

Homans, G.C. (1941) *English Villagers of the Thirteenth Century.* Cambridge, MA: Harvard University Press.

Homans, G.C. (1951) *The Human Group.* London: Routledge and Kegan Paul.

Homans, G.C. (1961) *Social Behaviour.* London: Routledge and Kegan Paul.

Honigmann, J.J. (ed.) (1973) *Handbook of Social and Cultural Anthropology.* Chicago: Rand McNally.

Hudson, J.C. (1969) 'Diffusion in a Central Place System', *Geographical Analysis*, 1.

Hunter, F. (1953) *Community Power Structure.* Chapel Hill, NC: University of North Carolina Press.

Johnson, S.C. (1967) 'Hierarchical Clustering Schemes', *Psychometrika*, 32.

Kadushin, C. (1966) 'The Friends and Supporters of Psychotherapy', *American Sociological Review*, 31.

Kadushin, C. (1968) 'Power, Influence and Social Circles: A New Methodology for Studying Opinion Makers', *American Sociological Review*, 33.

Kamada, T. and Kawai, S. (1989) 'An Algorithm for Drawing General Undirected Graphs', *Information Processing Letters*, 31.

Katz, F. (1966) 'Social Participation and Social Structure', *Social Forces*, 45.

Kerr, C. and Fisher, L.H. (1957) 'Plant Sociology: The Elite and the Aborigines', in Komarovsky (ed.), 1957.

Kilworth, P.D. and Bernard, H.R. (1979) 'A Pseudo-model of the Small World Problem', *Social Forces*, 58.

Kim, J. and Mueller, C.W. (1978) *Introduction to Factor Analysis.* Beverly Hills, CA: Sage Publications.

Kline, P. (1994) *An Easy Guide to Factor Analysis.* London: Routledge.

Klovdahl, A.S. (1981) 'A Note on Images of Networks', *Social Networks*, 3.

Klovdahl, A.S. (1986) 'VIEWNET: A New Tool For Network Analysis', *Social Networks*, 8.

Klovdahl, A.S. (1989) 'Urban Social Networks: Some Methodological Problems and Prospects', in Kochen (ed.), 1989.

Knoke, D. and Burt, R.S. (1983) 'Prominence', in Burt and Minor (eds), 1983.

Knoke, D. and Kuklinski, J.H. (1982) *Network Analysis.* Beverly Hills, CA: Sage Publications.

Kochen, M. (ed.) (1989) *The Small World.* Norwood, NJ: Ablex.

Köhler, W. (1925) *The Mentality of Apes.* New York.

Komarovsky, M. (ed.) (1957) *Common Frontiers of the Social Sciences.* Glencoe, IL: Free Press.

König, D. (1936) *Theorie der endlichen und unendlichen Graphen.* New York: Chelsea, 1950 edn.

Krempel, L. (1994) 'Simple Representations of Complex Networks: Strategies for Visualizing Network Structure', http://www.mpi-fg-koeln.mpg.de/~lk/algo5a/algo5a.html

Kruskal, J.B. (1964a) 'Multidimensional Scaling by Optimizing Goodness of Fit to a Nonmetric Hypothesis', *Psychometrika*, 29.

Kruskal, J.B. (1964b) 'Nonmetric Multidimensional Scaling: A Numerical Method', *Psychometrika*, 29.

Kruskal, J.B. and Wish, M. (1978) *Multidimensional Scaling.* Beverly Hills, CA: Sage Publications.

Lankford, P.M. (1974) 'Comparative Analysis of Clique Identification Methods', *Sociometry*, 37.

Laumann, E.O. (1966) *Prestige and Association in an Urban Community*. Indianapolis: Bobbs–Merrill.

Laumann, E.O. (1973) *Bonds of Pluralism*. New York: John Wiley.

Laumann, E.O. and Pappi, F.U. (1973) 'New Directions in the Study of Community Elites', *American Sociological Review*, 38. Reprinted in Leinhardt (ed.), 1984.

Laumann, E.O. and Pappi, F.U. (1976) *Networks of Collective Action*. New York: Academic Press.

Laumann, E.O., Marsden, P.V. and Prensky, D. (1983) 'The Boundary Specification Problem in Network Analysis', in Burt and Minor (eds), 1983.

Laumann, E.O., Marsden, P.V. and Prensky, D. (1989) 'The Boundary Specification Problem in Network Analysis', in Freeman et al. (eds), 1989.

Layder, D. (1992) *New Strategies in Social Research*. Cambridge: Polity Press.

Lee, N.H. (1969) *The Search for an Abortionist*. Chicago: University of Chicago Press.

Leinhardt, S. (ed.) (1977) *Social Networks: A Developing Paradigm*. New York: Academic Press.

Leinhardt, S. (ed.) (1984) *Sociological Methodology, 1985*. San Francisco: Jossey Bass.

Levine, J.H. (1972) 'The Sphere of Influence', *American Sociological Review*, 37. Reprinted in Scott (ed.), 1990.

Lewin, K. (1936) *Principles of Topological Psychology*. New York: McGraw Hill.

Lewin, K. (1951) *Field Theory in the Social Sciences*. New York: Harper.

Light, J.M. and Mullins, N.C. (1979) 'A Primer on Blockmodelling Procedures', in Holland and Leinhardt (eds), 1979.

Lin, N. (1982) 'Social Resources and Instrumental Action', in Marsden and Lin (eds), 1982.

Lin, N., Dayton, P.N. and Greenwald, P. (1978) 'Analysing the Instrumental Use of Relations in the Context of Social Structure', *Sociological Methods and Research*, 7.

Lingoes, J.C. and Roskam, E.E. (1973) 'A Mathematical and Empirical Analysis of Two Multidimensional Scaling Algorithms', *Psychometrika*, 38.

Lockwood, D. (1956) 'Some Remarks on *The Social System*', *British Journal of Sociology*, 6.

Lorrain, F. and White, H.C. (1971) 'Structural Equivalence of Individuals in Social Networks', *Journal of Mathematical Sociology*, 1.

Luce, R.D. and Perry, A. (1949) 'A Method of Matrix Analysis of Group Structure', *Psychometrika*, 14.

Mariolis, P. (1975) 'Interlocking Directorates and Control of Corporations', *Social Science Quarterly*, 56.

Mariolis, P. and Jones, M.H. (1982) 'Centrality in Corporate Networks: Reliability and Stability', *Administrative Science Quarterly*, 27.

Marsden, P.V. (1982) 'Brokerage Behaviour in Restricted Exchange Networks', in Marsden and Lin (eds), 1982.

Marsden, P.V. and Lin, N. (eds) (1982) *Social Structure and Network Analysis*. Beverly Hills, CA: Sage Publications.

Mayhew, B.H. and Levinger, R. (1976) 'Size and the Density of Interaction in Human Aggregates', *American Journal of Sociology*, 82.

Mayo, E. (1933) *The Human Problems of an Industrial Civilization*. Cambridge, MA: Macmillan.

Mayo, E. (1945) *The Social Problems of an Industrial Civilization*. London: Routledge and Kegan Paul, 1946 edn.

McCallister, L. and Fischer, C.S. (1978) 'A Procedure for Surveying Social Networks', *Sociological Methods and Research*, 7.

McGrath, C., Blythe, J. and Krackhardt, D. (1997) 'Seeing Groups in Graph Layouts', http://www.andrew.cmu.edu/user/cm3t/groups.html

McQuitty, L. (1968) 'Multiple Cluster Types and Dimensions for Interactive Columnar Correlation Analysis', *Multivariate Behavioural Research*, 3.

McQuitty, L. and Clark, J.A. (1968) 'Clusters from Interactive Columnar Correlation Analysis', *Educational and Psychological Measurement*, 28.

Meek, R.L. and Bradley, I. (1986) *Matrices and Society*. Harmondsworth: Penguin.

Milgram, S. (1967) 'The Small World Problem', *Psychology Today*, 1.

Mintz, B. and Schwartz, M. (1985) *The Power Structure of American Business*. Chicago: University of Chicago Press.

Mitchell, J.C. (1969) 'The Concept and Use of Social Networks', in Mitchell (ed.), *Social Networks in Urban Situations*. Manchester: Manchester University Press.

Mizruchi, M.S. (1982) *The American Corporate Network, 1904–1974*. Beverly Hills, CA: Sage Publications.

Mizruchi, M.S. (1992) *The Structure of Corporate Political Action: Interfirm Relationships and their Consequences*. Cambridge, MA: Harvard University Press.

Mizruchi, M.S. (1993) 'Cohesion, Equivalence, and Similarity of Behaviour: A Theoretical and Empirical Assessment', *Social Networks*, 15.

Mizruchi, M.S. (1994) 'Social Network Analysis: Recent Achievements and Current Controversies', *Acta Sociologica*, 37.

Mizruchi, M.S. and Bunting, D. (1981) 'Influence in Corporate Networks: An Examination of Four Measures', *Administrative Science Quarterly*, 26.

Mizruchi, M.S. and Galaskiewicz, J. (1994) 'Networks of Interorganizational relations', in Wasserman and Galaskiewicz (eds), 1994.

Mizruchi, M. and Schwartz, M. (eds) (1987) *Intercorporate Relations*. Cambridge: Cambridge University Press.

Mokken, R.J. (1974) 'Cliques, Clubs and Clans', *Quality and Quantity*, 13.

Moreno, J. (1934) *Who Shall Survive?* New York: Beacon Press.

Morgan, D. and Rytina, S. (1977) 'Comment on "Network Sampling: Some First Steps" by Mark Granovetter', *American Journal of Sociology*, 83.

Mullins, N.C. (1973) *Theories and Theory Groups in Contemporary American Sociology*. New York: Harper and Row.

Nadel, S.F. (1957) *The Theory of Social Structure*. London: Cohen and West.

Nash, K. and Scott, A. (eds) (1999) *The Blackwell Companion to Political Sociology*. Oxford: Basil Blackwell.

Newcomb, T. (1953) 'An Approach to the Study of Communicative Acts', *Psychological Review*, 60.

Niemeijer, R. (1973) 'Some Applications of the Notion of Density', in Boissevain and Mitchell (eds), 1973.

Nieminen, V. (1974) 'On Centrality in a Graph', *Scandinavian Journal of Psychology*, 15.

Nohira, N. and Eccles, R.G. (eds) (1992) *Networks and Organizations*. Boston, MA: Harvard University Press.

Park, R.E., Burgess, E.W. and McKenzie, R.D. (1925) *The City*. Chicago: University of Chicago Press.

202   *Social network analysis*

Parsons, T. (1937) *The Structure of Social Action.* New York: McGraw Hill.
Parsons, T. (1951) *The Social System.* Glencoe, IL: Free Press.
Parsons, T., Bales, R.F. and Shils, E. (1953) *Working Papers in the Theory of Action.* Glencoe, IL: Free Press.
Pedersen, P.O. (1970) 'Innovation Diffusion Within and Between National Urban Systems', *Geographical Analysis,* 2.
Price, D.J. de Solla (1965) 'Networks of Scientific Papers', *Science,* 149.
Rapoport, A. (1952) 'Ignition Phenomena in Random Nets', *Bulletin of Mathematical Biophysics,* 14.
Rapoport, A. (1958) 'Nets with Reciprocity Bias', *Bulletin of Mathematical Biophysics,* 20.
Reiss, A.J. (ed.) (1961) *Occupations and Social Status.* New York: Free Press.
Reitz, K.P. and White, D.R. (1989) 'Rethinking the Role Concept: Homomorphisms on Social Networks', in Freeman et al. (eds), 1989.
Roethlisberger, F.J. and Dickson, W.J. (1939) *Management and the Worker.* Cambridge, MA: Harvard University Press.
Roistacher, R.C. (1979) 'Acquisition and Management of Social Network Data', in Holland and Leinhardt (eds), 1979.
Rose, M. (1975) *Industrial Behaviour.* Harmondsworth: Allen Lane.
Rytina, S. (1982) 'Structural Constraints on Interpersonal Contact', in Mardsen and Lin (eds), 1982.
Rytina, S. and Morgan, D. (1982) 'The Arithmetic of Social Relations', *American Journal of Sociology,* 88.
Sabidussi, G. (1966) 'The Centrality Index of a Graph', *Psychometrika,* 31.
Sailer, L. (1978) 'Structural Equivalence: Meaning and Definition', *Social Networks,* 1.
Schuessler, K.F. (1978) *Sociological Methodology, 1979.* San Francisco: Jossey Bass.
Schuessler, K.F. (1979) *Sociological Methodology, 1980.* San Francisco: Jossey Bass.
Schwartz, J.E. (1977) 'An Examination of CONCOR and Related Methods for Blocking Sociometric Data', in Heise (ed.), 1977.
Scott, J. (1986) *Capitalist Property and Financial Power.* Brighton: Wheatsheaf.
Scott, J. (ed.) (1990) *The Sociology of Elites,* vol. 3. Cheltenham: Edward Elgar.
Scott, J. (1991) 'Networks of Corporate Power', *Annual Review of Sociology,* 17.
Scott, J. (1996) *Stratification and Power: Structures of Class, Status and Command.* Cambridge: Polity Press.
Scott, J. (1997) *Corporate Business and Capitalist Classes.* Oxford: Oxford University Press.
Scott, J. (1999) 'Studying Power', in Nash and Scott (eds), 1999.
Scott, J. and Hughes, M. (1980) *The Anatomy of Scottish Capital.* London: Croom Helm.
Seidman, S.B. (1983) 'Network Structure and Minimum Degree', *Social Networks,* 5.
Seidman, S.B. and Foster, B.L. (1978) 'A Note on the Potential for Genuine Cross-Fertilisation between Anthropology and Mathematics', *Social Networks,* 1.
Sharkey, P. (1989) 'Social Networks and Social Service Workers', *British Journal of Social Work,* 19.
Sharkey, P. (1990) 'Social Networks and Social Service Workers: A Reply to Timms', *British Journal of Social Work,* 20.
Shepard, R.N. (1962) 'The Analysis of Proximities', Parts 1 and 2, *Psychometrika,* 27.

Simmel, G. (1908) *Soziologie*. Berlin: Duncker and Humblot, 1968 edn.

Smith, R.M. (1979) 'Kin and Neighbours in a Thirteenth Century Suffolk Community', *Journal of Family History*, 4.

Snijders, T.A.B. (1981) 'The Degree Variance', *Social Networks*, 3.

Sonquist, J.A. and Koenig, T. (1975) 'Interlocking Directorships in the Top US Corporations', *Insurgent Sociologist*, 5.

Stacey, M. (1969) 'The Myth of Community Studies', *British Journal of Sociology*, 20.

Stokman, F.N., Ziegler, R. and Scott, J. (1985) *Networks of Corporate Power*. Cambridge: Polity Press.

Timms, E. (1990) 'Social Networks and Social Service Workers: A Comment on Sharkey', *British Journal of Social Work*, 20.

Torgerson, W.S. (1952) 'Multidimensional Scaling 1. Theory and Method', *Psychometrika*, 17.

Useem, M. (1984) *The Inner Circle*. New York: Oxford University Press.

Van Poucke, W. (1979) 'Network Constraints on Social Action: Preliminaries for a Network Theory', *Social Networks*, 2.

Warner, W.L. and Lunt, P.S. (1941) *The Social Life of a Modern Community*. New Haven, CT: Yale University Press.

Warner, W.L. and Lunt, P.S. (1942) *The Status System of a Modern Community*. New Haven, CT: Yale University Press.

Wasserman, S. and Galaskiewicz, J. (eds) (1994) *Advances in Social Network Analysis*. Beverley Hills, CA: Sage Publications.

Weber, M. (1920–21) *Economy and Society*. Berkeley, CA: University of California Press, 1968 edn.

Wellman, B. (1979) 'The Community Question: The Intimate Networks of East Yorkers', *American Journal of Sociology*, 84.

Wellman, B. (1980) 'Network Analysis: From Metaphor and Method to Theory and Substance'. Discussion Paper, University of Toronto Structural Analysis Program. Revised version in Wellman and Berkowitz (eds), 1988.

Wellman, B. (1982) 'Studying Personal Communities', in Marsden and Lin (eds), 1982.

Wellman, B. (1985) 'Domestic Work, Paid Work and Network', in Duck and Perlman (eds), 1985.

Wellman, B. and Berkowitz, S.D. (eds) (1988) *Social Structures*. Cambridge: Cambridge University Press.

Werbner, P. (1990) *The Migration Process*. New York: Berg.

White, D. and Reitz, K.P. (1983) 'Group and Semi-group Homomorphisms on Networks of Relations', *Social Networks*, 5.

White. H.C. (1963) *An Anatomy of Kinship*. Englewood Cliffs, NJ: Prentice–Hall.

White, H.C. (1970) *Chains of Opportunity*. Cambridge, MA: Harvard University Press.

White, H.C. (1992a) *Identity and Control: A Structural Theory of Social Action*. Princeton, NJ: Princeton University Press.

White, H.C. (1992b) 'Social Grammar for Culture: Reply to Steven Brint', *Sociological Theory*, 10.

White, H.C. (1993) *Careers and Creativity: Social Forces in the Arts*. Boulder, CO: Westview Press.

White, H.C., Boorman, S.A. and Breiger, R.L. (1976) 'Social Structure from Multiple Networks, I', *American Journal of Sociology*, 81.

Whitten, N.E. and Wolfe, A.W. (1973) 'Network Analysis', in Honigmann (ed.), 1973.

Willmott, P. (1986) *Social Networks, Informal Care and Public Policy*. London: Policy Studies Institute.

Willmott, P. (1987) *Friendship Networks and Social Support*. London: Policy Studies Institute.

Winship, C. and Mandel, M. (1984) 'Roles and Positions: A Critique and Extension of the Blockmodelling Approach', in Leinhardt (ed.), 1984.

Wu, L. (1984) 'Local Blockmodel Algebra for Analysing Social Networks', in Leinhardt (ed.), 1984.

Yablonsky, L. (1962) *The Violent Gang*. Harmondsworth: Penguin.

Zegers, F. and ten Berghe, J. (1985) 'A Family of Association Coefficients for Metric Scales', *Psychometrika*, 50.

Index

Page references which contain a formal definition of a term are shown in **bold** type